Poverty: the facts

6th edition

**Alan Marsh, with Karen Barker, Carla Ayrton,
Morag Treanor and Moussa Haddad**

CPAG • 30 Micawber Street • London N1 7TB

Child Poverty Action Group works on behalf of the nearly one in three
children in the UK growing up in poverty. It does not have to be like this.
We use our understanding of what causes poverty and the impact it has
on children's lives to campaign for policies that will prevent and solve
poverty – for good. We provide training, advice and information to make
sure hard-up families get the financial support they need. We also carry
out high-profile legal work to establish and protect families' rights. If you
are not already supporting us, please consider making a donation, or ask
for details of our membership schemes, training courses and publications.

Published by the Child Poverty Action Group
30 Micawber Street
London N1 7TB
Tel: 020 7837 7979
staff@cpag.org.uk
www.cpag.org.uk

The views expressed are those of the authors and do not necessarily
represent the views of the Child Poverty Action Group.

© Child Poverty Action Group 2017. Contains public sector information
licensed under the Open Government Licence v3.0. Crown Copyright 2014

A CIP record for this book is available from the British Library
ISBN: 978 1 910715 21 5

Child Poverty Action Group is a charity registered in England and Wales
(registration number 294841) and in Scotland (registration number
SC039339), and is a company limited by guarantee, registered in England
(registration number 1993854). VAT number: 690 808117

Cover design by Colorido Studios
Typeset by Devious Designs
Printed in the UK by CPI Group (UK) Ltd, Croydon CR40 4YY

About the authors

Alan Marsh is Emeritus Professor of Social Policy, and previously Deputy Director, at the Policy Studies Institute, University of Westminster. From 1990, he led the Social Security Research Team, carrying out national surveys of low-income families, low-paid workers and disabled people, studying the effects of tax credits on families' opportunities to work, their health and welfare, contributing to the evidence base for the government's anti-poverty programme. Previously he worked in social research, both in government and universities, including a stint as Director of Research for the Economic and Social Research Council, and later worked on the National Child Development Study. Publications include *Families, Work and Benefits* and two projects involving CPAG.

Karen Barker is a research analyst at the New Policy Institute. Her recent research has focused on poverty, regional inequalities and local government services. Karen previously worked as a research consultant for charities, and in frontline homelessness services. She has an MSc in Social Policy and Planning from the London School of Economics and a BA in Anthropology from Haverford College in the USA.

Carla Ayrton is a research analyst at the New Policy Institute. Her recent research has focused on the social security system, council tax support, work and low pay. Carla was previously an analyst at SafeLives, a national charity dedicated to ending domestic abuse. Carla has a BSc in Geography from The University of Manchester and an MSc in Globalisation from University College London.

Dr Morag Treanor is an academic, social researcher and quantitative data analyst with over 15 years' experience of working across the private, voluntary and public sectors. The primary focus of her work is child poverty – its measurement, causes, consequences, mitigation and prevention. Her work spans academic research and publications, applied social research for public and voluntary bodies and statistical analysis of large-scale datasets.

Moussa Haddad is a senior policy and research officer at CPAG. He has conducted research across a range of issues relating to social policy, at CPAG and at Oxfam, the Social Market Foundation, Royal Statistical Society and Equality Challenge Unit, focusing particularly on poverty, inequality and social security.

Acknowledgements

The authors are indebted to Fran Bennett and Jonathan Bradshaw for their detailed and patient comments on earlier drafts. At CPAG, Alison Garnham, Alison Key, Imran Hussain, Josephine Tucker, Lizzie Flew and Alice Woudhuysen all made valuable contributions to the completion of this book. We would particularly like to thank the New Policy Institute, especially Adam Tinson, for all their help.

A wider debt is owed to the community of social and economic researchers in UK universities and research institutes, and researchers in government departments, the NHS and the Office for National Statistics, whose work provided the data and analysis reported in this book.

Contents

Foreword   vii
Gordon Brown, Prime Minister of the UK 2007 to 2010

1 **Introduction**   1

2 **Understanding poverty**   14

3 **Measuring poverty: income**   32

4 **Measuring poverty: hardship**   49

5 **Poverty and costs**   80

6 **Who is at risk of poverty?**   110

7 **Child poverty in the UK**   131

8 **The dynamics of poverty**   139

9 **Poverty in the UK and other countries**   151

10 **The causes of poverty**   167

11 **The effects of poverty on children**   190

12 **What is it like to experience poverty?**   212

13 **Conclusions: the new poverty**   228

To the memory of Peter Townsend, 1928–2009.

Foreword

Gordon Brown, Prime Minister of the UK
2007 to 2010

It is a remarkable fact that today child poverty is higher than when the Child Poverty Action Group was formed in 1965. But it is even more shameful that child poverty is already higher than at any point in the last 50 years. According to the respected Institute for Fiscal Studies, there will be more than five million children in poverty by the end of this Parliament. So, with a child poverty crisis today and with the prospect of it worsening in the future, this book appears at a critical time.

Poverty means lost income, opportunities and often lost health and lost childhoods. But it can be different. The theme that cuts right through every chapter of this important book is that the level of child poverty is not an accident, but a choice – and one that can be made differently. We can see that from other countries and from our own recent history.

The Institute for Fiscal Studies suggests that between 1997 and 2010, changes to benefits and tax credits increased the average income of lone-parent families by over £2,500 a year, some 20 per cent higher in real terms. A lone parent with one child and working part time was 36 per cent better off, even after inflation is taken into account over the same period. By 2010 we had in place the Child Poverty Act, subsequently abandoned, that required all governments to eradicate child poverty.

Today, the majority of the poor are in working families – the biggest section of the 'new poor' are 'traditional' families with stay-at-home mothers who now cannot make ends meet on one wage. The fastest rising new poor are millennials – couples in their twenties who, no matter how much 'get up and go' they have or how hard they work, cannot get ahead. Child benefit will have gone up only 2 per cent between 2010 and 2020, while prices will have gone up 35 per cent.

No child should grow up ill-clad and undernourished, with their needs neglected and under-provided – condemned to poverty throughout their school years.

I believe in a Britain where we do not talk passively about equal opportunity, but work ceaselessly so that there is a fair start and a fair shot for all: doors opened, barriers removed, ladders up.

It is not poverty, but a fair chance in life that should be every boy's and every girl's birthright, and it is not poverty but decent opportunity that should be every single child's destiny. Every single child should be brought up in a world where they can dream dreams, nurture ambitions and have hope for the future.

This book should be a call to arms: there is so much we can do. Protect children's benefits; invest in housing and childcare to reduce costs and help parents work; tackle low wages and insecure work and boost productivity. Above all, we need to treat child poverty as a national priority and produce a proper strategy to overcome it.

One
Introduction

What is poverty?

The UK remains one of the richest countries in the world. Yet substantial numbers of UK citizens live in poverty. Their household resources, particularly their cash incomes, are too small to allow them the standard of living that most people in the UK consider an acceptable minimum.[1]

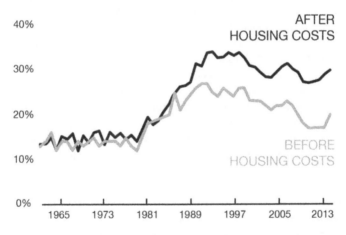

% CHILDREN LIVING IN POVERTY

That is what it means to be poor in a rich country. It is not just a simple matter of inequality – having less money than most other people. A persistently low income degrades your standard of life and cuts you off from the common ways of your community. All your household resources are diminished. It leaves you in the poorest housing. You eat a poor diet and stay cold in winter. Worn clothes, shoes and broken household goods are not replaced. You cannot afford to travel much, entertain at home or participate in the social and leisure activities that are the essential aspects of other people's lives. Any savings you may have had will soon vanish. If you borrow to try to keep up standards, you can fall into unmanageable debt. Crucially nowadays, you can lose access to the streams of communication that fill other people's lives.

Living in poverty in a rich country, where standards of consumption and lifestyle choices all serve, even define, better-off households, quickly isolates you and your family. As standards and expectations rise, we invent new ways of 'going without'. Deprivation and isolation extends beyond having restricted access to the goods, lifestyle and the social participation enjoyed by others; it exposes you to the narrative promoted by so much of the media in this country that your condition is somehow shameful. People living in poverty in the UK are told by many newspapers and television programmes that they are unlikely to be genuinely entitled to the help they receive, that they are 'scroungers', unwilling to work and to support themselves and their children. But being 'on benefits' is not a definition of poverty. As we will show in what follows, the majority of families living in poverty have at least one adult in paid work, sometimes two.

This basic definition of poverty, of persistent low incomes leading to hardship and isolation, has not gone unchallenged. Who, for example, decides what are necessities and what people on small incomes can be expected to do without? Is *relative income* poverty important anymore? Does only *absolute* poverty matter – when people's basic safety and wellbeing are threatened by lack of food, water or shelter? Might poverty be better defined by people's social location, by their access to education and work, and by a better understanding of their 'life chances'?

These ideas are explored in **Chapter 2**, where we examine the ideas associated with poverty such as inequality, social exclusion, unmet needs, values, powerlessness and degraded life chances. While people living in poverty are unequal compared to others who are better off, it may matter *how* unequal they are, how stretched the gap between rich and poor has become. Poverty seen as social exclusion helps us understand that human agency is involved in poverty – it is not a blind economic process. Poverty is something that is done to people and it is affected by political decisions. Exclusion also affects the amount of access people living in poverty can have to the means to redress their position – are they powerless or can they hope to influence these decisions in their favour?

Ideas about 'life chances', particularly as they have recently been applied to addressing child poverty,[2] are more ambiguous. Governments have always striven, to a greater or lesser degree, to improve people's life chances. They would do so if no one was in poverty. CPAG has always urged greater investment in child health, education, better housing and so on, that might help children overcome the effects of living in poverty. But the recent emphasis of government policy has tended to focus solely on behavioural aspects of people's life chances. They tend to deny the importance of current income and immediate, everyday wellbeing. They stress instead the need for long-term solutions to worklessness, family instability and low educational achievement. They stress too the need to 'level playing fields' and to tackle alcoholism, drug addiction and poor mental health among families in poverty. In this view of poverty, poor parenting is held particularly culpable.

To concentrate on people's behaviour, rather than the real structural and political causes of poverty, takes us beyond the point where the effects of poverty begin to be mistaken for its causes. As we show in **Chapters 11** and **12**, the effects of poverty and hardship upon children are so large and so immediate, determined even by their mothers' diet before they were born, that it is impossible to discount the basic importance of present income and the need to improve children's wellbeing by greater public investment now. We show how higher family incomes can reduce family hardship and improve outcomes. The policy that will most improve the 'life chances' of children living in poverty is that their parents' incomes should increase sufficiently to provide the standard of living most people agree they should have. One lesson, though, is clear: how you define poverty has a lot to do with what you think ought to be done about it.

Measuring poverty

In **Chapters 3** and **4** we explore ways of measuring poverty, respectively, in terms of relative incomes and the incidence of hardship.

Income

In terms of relative incomes, the annual publication by the Department for Work and Pensions (DWP) of *Households Below Average Income (HBAI)*, provides an income threshold for measuring relative income poverty, though the DWP does not call it that.

HBAI publishes the proportion of households found below 60 per cent of the national equivalised median[3] both before each household has met its housing costs and after. **Chapter 3** weighs the arguments as to which is the better measure of relative income poverty. Overall, 16 per cent of the UK population live in households whose income falls below this relative income poverty threshold in 2015/16 (in about 4.3 million households) before housing costs, 22 per cent (in about 6 million households) after.

As Table 1.1 illustrates, higher levels of income poverty are found in households with children and disabled people, lower levels among pensioners. Poverty rates among pensioners in the 1960s were appalling; typically more than four in 10 were below 60 per cent of median incomes. In recent years their state pensions have risen faster than inflation, protected by a 'triple lock': they received annual uprating of their state retirement pension by price or wage inflation, or by 2.5 per cent each year, whichever is the better figure for them. Increasing numbers of pensioners now bring into their retirement valuable private pensions (whose contributions were made tax free) from their years of employment. It is a valuable illustration of how policy changes can reduce poverty.

Table 1.1:
Poverty rates, 2015/16

	Percentage of individuals living in households below 60% of median income	
	Before housing costs %	After housing costs %
Children	20	30
Pensioners	17	16
Disabled people	20	26
Working-age adults without dependent children	14	18
All	16	22

Source: Department for Work and Pensions, *Households Below Average Income: an analysis of the income distribution, 1994/95–2015/16*, 2017

It is important to remember that households in poverty are not a fixed population. It is true that substantial numbers remain in income poverty for a long time, but others move in and out of poverty at different times and at different stages in their lives. These transitions are explored in **Chapter 8**. Thus, the population of the UK that is at risk of poverty and will experience poverty at one time or another, is much larger than the population found in poverty at any one point. Almost everyone will claim a social security benefit at some point in their lives.

It is also important to recognise that income poverty is experienced differently in different kinds of households, who face differing kinds and levels of costs. In **Chapter 5** we explore how these costs differ for families with children, for disabled people, and how inflationary pressures can increase poverty by falling more severely on low-income households.

Costs can also fall unfairly on families with the smallest budgets, who pay disproportionately more for many goods and services, who are unable to obtain cheap credit, and who face instead high charges to access money needed to replace essential household goods, for example.

Hardship

In terms of hardship, **Chapter 4** explores perhaps the most challenging, but informative, aspect of measuring poverty: the extent to which people interviewed in nationally representative surveys say they are living in impoverished conditions and going without essential goods and services – a good basic diet, adequate clothing and footwear, heating in winter, social activity, and so on. These measures of hardship have evolved over the years. The question of who decides what are and are not necessities was addressed by asking random samples of the population what they thought families ought not to go without. People were then asked to say which of these agreed 'consensual' items they had and, if they lacked any item, such as more than one pair of waterproof shoes, they were asked whether they went without it by choice or whether they '... cannot afford it'. Items have been added over the years as some consumer goods stopped being luxuries and became in the popular view 'essentials', such as telephones, refrigerators and televisions.

Some of the results are startling, especially where children's wellbeing is examined. Unacceptably large minorities of families are unable to provide adequately for their children, who are ill-fed and go without warm clothes and good shoes. The 2012 Poverty and Social Exclusion survey said: 'Almost 12 million people are too poor to engage in common social activities considered necessary by the majority of the population.'

On the other hand, results over time from the Families and Children Study show that the increases in family incomes through child benefit and tax credits provided by the Labour government between 1999 and 2001 significantly reduced reports of hardship among the lowest income families. Among out-of-work families, reports of hardship halved in two years. This is the clearest proof possible that poverty responds to policy, quickly and effectively.

The hardship that relative income poverty imposes on a family is not just a matter of counting what they can and cannot afford. As we explore in **Chapter 12**, it is an 'overwhelmingly negative experience' that adversely affects all areas of your life 'psychologically, physically, relationally and practically' and has particularly damaging personal and social effects.[4]

The special problem of child poverty

Supplementing wages

Wages are not paid according to whether or not you have children, or how many you have. So it has long been recognised that parents require extra help with the costs of bringing up children. Not only have children to be fed, clothed and housed, they increase the need to maintain a home in ways that people living in poverty, but without children, need not. For a while, at least, adults living alone can 'do without', if they must; children should not. State payments to parents are also thought fair because people without children ought to help out with the costs of raising the next generation, whose work will sustain everyone, including the childless, in their old age. Family allowances, now child benefit, were introduced in 1946, transferring funds to times in people's lives when they needed assistance: when they have small children and, typically, a reduced income.

During times of post-war full employment, few paid much attention to the position of unemployed families, but as benefit rates rose during the 1960s and then unemployment grew in the later 1970s and 80s, it became clear that many families, especially large families, would be at least a little better off on benefits than they would be in low-paid work. No one was very comfortable with the idea that benefits given to meet need might discourage parents from working. So, in 1971, family income supplement was introduced (later called family credit), giving extra money to low-income families in full-time work, helping parents on low wages to remain a little better off in work than they would be claiming out-of-work benefits. This was later developed into the modern system of tax credits, helping working families with children, later extended to all low-paid workers, including many working part time, and will be incorporated into universal credit for all claimants when it is finally fully implemented in 2022.

This policy of wage supplementation has not been without its critics. Not everyone entitled to payments applies for them. As low-paid workers increase their hours or get pay rises, much of their in-work payments are reduced and then ended, making it harder to raise standards of living by working longer hours or getting promoted. Some believe it reduces wages,[5] which made it more urgent to introduce a national minimum wage in 1999.[6] Nevertheless, there was strong evidence[7] that it helped lone parents get jobs with shorter hours that fitted around childcare and helped low-paid couples stay in work.

Blair's pledge

After 30 years of this kind of assistance to parents, too many families remained in relative income poverty, including many of the lowest paid working parents with larger families. In March 1999, the then Prime Minister, Tony Blair, spoke at Toynbee Hall in East London to celebrate the memory of Sir William Beveridge and his legacy: our modern social security system. He took his audience by surprise by making a commitment to end child poverty within 20 years. Poverty having ended, it was never to return. He said:

> 'I will set out our historic aim that ours is the first generation to end child poverty for ever, and it will take a generation. It is a 20-year mission, but I believe it can be done.'

Later, as the details of the policy unfolded, some waymarkers were added. Child poverty would fall by a quarter by 2005; by half by 2010. By 2020, child poverty would at least fall to the best European standard: typically no more than between 4 per cent and 7 per cent, certainly less than 10 per cent of all children (before housing costs). And in 2010, this commitment was passed into law with the support of all parties.

Child poverty rates

Having seen child poverty rates more than double between the 1970s and 1990s, we began the new millennium with 33 per cent of British children living in relative income poverty after housing costs – more than four million of them living in families whose incomes fell below 60 per cent of the median after housing costs (Figure 1.1), while 23 per cent were in poverty before housing costs. From 1999, the national minimum wage had come into full effect, family benefits and tax credits were substantially increased, together with increased support for childcare. New Deal programmes gave support and advice to families in poverty who were trying to establish themselves in work. Child poverty rates fell substantially: by 1.1 million, to 27 per cent (after housing costs) and 18 per cent (before housing costs) by 2010.[8] This was actually halfway towards the 10 per cent before housing costs target by 2020: on target, but ironically, not halfway to zero – the task the government had set itself.

The latest figures, in 2015/16, show a return to 30 per cent of children living in poverty after housing costs (20 per cent before housing

costs): so far off target that the Welfare Reform and Work Act 2016 officially abandoned it. Since the UK population has increased over the past
20 years, still four million UK children remain in poverty. We are essentially
back where we started in 1997, when the incoming government faced
unacceptably high levels of child poverty, levels that were set to continue
to rise.

That growth of child poverty in the 1980s and 1990s in Britain was
the most rapid among OECD countries. The subsequent fall was also the
most rapid, illustrating how effective a change of policy can be that is
aimed to reduce child poverty rates. Rates rose during the last quarter of
the twentieth century because the value of benefits rose only with price
inflation, not by wage inflation. This denied claimants any participation in
increases in our national wealth, expressed by the gap between wage and
price inflation. In this way, benefit incomes fell further behind the value of
the median. At the same time, demand for traditional manual labour and
routine work fell and its rewards shrank, so the real incomes of low-paid
workers rose only little. Waves of unemployment grew larger and more fre-

Figure 1.1:

Child poverty rates, after housing costs, 1961 to 2015/16

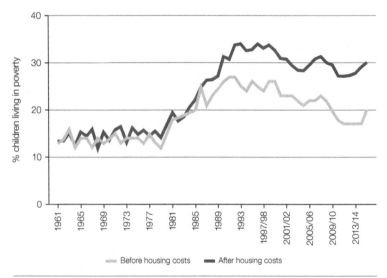

Source: Department for Work and Pensions, *Households Below Average Income: an analysis of the income distribution, 1994/95–2015/16,* 2017

quent. This 'low-pay, no-pay' cycle degraded families' incomes over time, particularly so during the 1990s. Housing costs rose disproportionately. Finally, the growth of a 'flexible' labour market promoted the spread of low-paid temporary, part-time and self-employed work.

Even work itself did not guarantee freedom from poverty: there was always a substantial proportion of working families found below the 60 per cent line. This is true even with help from tax credits and other in-work benefits. This last point is important: tax credits will not always get you out of poverty if the family's income is too low. And as we show in **Chapter 2**, families living in poverty are not just below 60 per cent of the median, many are a long way below.

The future

The Institute for Fiscal Studies has estimated that the proportion of children in poverty can now only increase:[9]

> The targets were always extremely ambitious, but given the latest data available and the likely upwards trajectory of child poverty in the years ahead, it looks inconceivable that the targets could be achieved (or even got close to).

Its latest estimates indicate that by 2022 the rate of child poverty will rise to 36 per cent, leaving more than five million UK children in poverty.[10]

Families with children living in poverty have suffered most since the post-2008 recession and will suffer more as universal credit completes its roll-out.[11] The failure to uprate working-age benefits with inflation, the restriction of in-work benefits to only two children per family, the benefit cap, the massive cuts to universal credit and other measures will reduce the incomes of families in the lower part of the income range.[12] It will most affect single-earner families, large families and lone parents, who will lose, on average, more than £40 a week by 2020. Interestingly, the Institute for Fiscal Studies also forecasts that poverty rates among pensioners will not rise and may continue to fall, protected by the 'triple lock'.[13] *Whose* lives become more austere during austerity is a political choice made by politicians.

The causes of poverty

In **Chapter 10**, we look in detail at the causes of poverty: unemployment, low wages and inadequate benefits. Meanwhile, it is important not to mistake outcomes for causes. For example, since the 1970s, the rate of lone parenthood in the UK increased from 5 per cent to 26 per cent. Children of lone parents are more likely to be in poverty compared with those of two-parent families. This is because lone parents' access to the labour market is limited, partly by the difficulties of bringing up children alone while maintaining a home, by the persisting low rate of child support paid by non-resident parents, by new reductions in the value of benefits that are penalising lone parents more than other families, by persisting lower wages for women, and by their increased need for childcare. Like child poverty, this situation is not inevitable.

The effects of poverty

If poverty is essentially a relative idea, does it matter all that much when living standards throughout society are rising? Families living in poverty in modern Britain, while they may be relatively poor, still have a basic standard of living that in previous centuries and in many other parts of the world today would be thought acceptable. Yet, as the basic definition of poverty predicts, it is the relative deprivation of people living in poverty that does the damage.

The evidence, reviewed throughout this book, and particularly in **Chapters 4 and 11**, is that poverty and inequality still matter a great deal. We show that hardship still exists for families in poverty, living in inferior and overcrowded homes, denied essentials that nearly everyone agrees they should not go without. More than daily deprivation, though, their opportunities are reduced or actually denied. They get ill more often and die younger. Those most likely to be in poverty are those least able to resist its effects: the youngest, the oldest, sick and disabled people, and those living in areas least favoured economically.

Poverty affects their health, educational achievement and housing opportunities. In particular, income poverty in childhood is associated with poor educational attainment and this throws a long shadow into adulthood. Children from families in poverty see that other children at school do not 'go without' and they become discouraged.[14] They discover that 'social exclusion' is not just a term invented by sociologists in universities. It is what is starting to happen to them and its cause is having parents who do not have enough money, nor enough resources to live as others live. The impact of these effects of poverty is immediate and unforgiving. In the UK, those with a low level of educational attainment are almost five times as likely to be in poverty now as those with a high level of education.[15]

The cost to the economy

If protecting children from this process of disadvantage, deprivation and exclusion were not itself reason enough to be concerned about the impact of poverty, the economy suffers from the waste of talent and potential that it causes. Donald Hirsch calculates that child poverty costs the country £29 billion a year, which he insists is a cautious estimate.[16] About half this cost arises from lower productivity among adults who grew up in poverty and the higher risk of unemployment they typically face. The other half is the additional public spending required to deal with social problems resulting from high levels of child poverty.

It does not have to be like this

In **Chapter 13**, we discuss some of the realistic policy options that will first reduce and then eliminate poverty in the UK.

A first step will be to restore to universal credit the higher benefit rates and universal entitlements that it was originally designed to provide and to end the present freeze on benefits for working-age claimants. We especially need to protect families from rising living costs by restoring the value of benefits against inflation, particularly protecting children's incomes with the same 'triple lock' long since awarded to their grandparents.

We need to prevent hardship and reduce the demand for food banks by ending costly delays and poor decision making in the benefits system.

Children in poverty need to be protected from their exclusion from many school activities that parents now have to pay for.

We must end the growing impermanence of paid work, especially zero-hour contracts and temporary jobs that evade employment protection laws, helping those who leave the out-of-work benefits system not merely to enter work but to stay in work and advance their earnings over time.

We must build on the progress made in supporting childcare. There is a clear principle that supports extending the provision of free state education down to the youngest age ranges, as well as extended schools and holiday childcare for older children, developing an ambitious childcare strategy.

More than anything, as a nation we need to commit to ending poverty, as a national priority. We especially need to end the narrative that has demonised people in poverty and instead see more clearly that we all have the same positive interest in bringing people out of persistent poverty and into full participation in society and the economy. Our investment will, in the long run, be rewarded by greater productivity, higher tax receipts and lower social costs, enriching everyone financially, socially and morally.

Notes

1 This definition of poverty was first formulated by the British sociologist Peter Townsend, who wrote in 1979: 'Individuals, families and groups in the population can be said to be in poverty when they lack resources to obtain the type of diet, participate in the activities and have the living conditions and amenities which are customary, or at least widely encouraged and approved, in the societies in which they belong.' P Townsend, *Poverty in the United Kingdom: a survey of household resources and standards of living*, Allen Lane and Penguin Books, 1979

2 See the then Prime Minister David Cameron's speech on life chances and poverty, 11 January 2016. However, an approach based specifically on 'life chances' has been officially abandoned against the promise of one based on 'social justice'.

3 These figures are derived from the Office for National Statistics annual survey of 20,000 randomly-elected households: the Family Resources Survey. The total disposable income for each household is added up and, in order to make a fair comparison between households of different sizes, their incomes are 'equivalised'. These equivalised incomes are then ranked and the median value found: that is, the '50 per cent household'. Half of all other households will have more income than the median household, half have less. Households 'below average' or, in our terms, in relative income poverty, are those with incomes below 60 per cent of the national equivalised median. These incomes are equivalised by adjusting incomes to the size and composition of each households, discounting them by the number of adults and children they have to support.

4 T Ridge, *Living with Poverty: a review of the literature on children and families*, Department for Work and Pensions Research Report No.594, 2009, p62

5 It is thought by some economists that workers entitled to a wage supplement would be willing to accept a job at lower wages, or be less willing to press for pay rises, than they would without one.

6 Thus, it is possible to see the national minimum wage (now called the national 'living wage') as a kind of stealth tax on employers, as it reduces the total tax credits paid by the Exchequer.

7 See A Marsh and S McKay, *Families, Work and Benefits*, Policy Studies Institute, 1993

8 For its June 2016 release, the Department for Work and Pensions revised down its estimate of the number (but not the percentage) of children in poverty in 1998/99, meaning that in this and the latest March 2017 release the drop in poverty to 2010/11 is measured at 1 million.

9 R Joyce, *Child Poverty in Britain: recent trends and future prospects*, Working Paper W15/07, Institute for Fiscal Studies, 2014

10 A Hood and T Waters, *Living Standards, Poverty and Inequality in the UK: 2016–17 to 2021–22*, Institute for Fiscal Studies, 2017

11 See especially CPAG's briefing paper, *Broken Promises: what has happened to support for low-income working families under universal credit?*, March 2017

12 Families with children in the bottom fifth of the income range received 61 per cent of their disposable income from benefits, tax credits and other cash transfers in 2014/15, so are especially vulnerable to 'reforms' that reduce this source. See C Belfield and others, *Living Standards, Poverty and Inequality in the UK: 2016*, Report No.R117, Institute for Fiscal Studies, 2016, available at www.ifs.org.uk/publications/8371

13 It is true, however, that pensioners' contribution to reducing the deficit has been to grow a little older before they receive their pensions. In addition, the fate of the 'triple lock' in future is under consideration.

14 See especially T Ridge, *Childhood Poverty and Social Exclusion: from a child's perspective,* Policy Press, 2002 and T Ridge, 'Benefiting children? The challenge of childhood poverty', in J Millar (ed), *Understanding Social Security: issues for policy and practice*, Policy Press, 2009, pp151–69

15 Office for National Statistics, *How Do Childhood Circumstances Affect Poverty and Deprivation as an Adult?, 2014*

16 D Hirsch, *An Estimate of the Cost of Child Poverty in 2013,* Centre for Research in Social Policy, Loughborough University, 2013. Hirsch predicted that these costs would rise to £35 billion if child poverty rose by one million. It will, and more.

Two
Understanding poverty

Summary

- Poverty is going without the necessities of life; inequality is some people having less than others.
- Living in poverty means having a low 'trend' income – having insufficient money or other resources to meet your basic needs month on month, year on year.

DESTITUTION	**POVERTY**	**INEQUALITY**
LACKING FOOD LACKING FUEL LACKING CLOTHING LACKING SHELTER	STRUGGLE TO PAY FOR ESSENTIALS AND TO PARTICIPATE IN SOCIETY	SOME HAVING A LOT LESS THAN OTHERS

- Peter Townsend defined poverty as lacking the resources to meet those basic needs (including social participation) which others take for granted. As well as income, savings and property, a person's resources also include public services, like education, housing and healthcare.
- More elaborated concepts of poverty seek to describe and explain how people are captured in poverty: how their labour market position is weakened by social and economic exclusion, spatial isolation, degraded opportunity and diminished political authority.
- Most people believe the government should act to reduce the hardship caused by low income, but the nature of that intervention divides public opinion. How you define poverty is shaped by what you think should be done about it.

Introduction

This chapter is about some definitions of poverty and the concepts from which they arise.[1] It is less about *measures* of poverty, which occupy much of the remainder of this book. But it is important to look carefully at definitions. When fair-minded people are asked to consider questions about poverty, they almost always begin by saying, 'It depends what you mean by poverty'. Often what they mean is that people living in poverty do not have enough money.

Poverty or inequality?

To be clear: poverty is going without the necessities of life; inequality is some having less than others.

It is possible for whole populations to be poor but equal. Other populations might be unequal but have no one in poverty. Neither is likely, but poverty and inequality are not the same thing. True, in the real world they are linked together: people living in poverty are usually the minority of people who are denied access to enough money or other resources to buy enough food, fuel or clothing, or to have adequate shelter, or to be able to participate in the expected ways of their communities. These expectations are, in part, determined by the better-provided majority, who can afford them. Though linked, they are different things and have different solutions.

Poverty, especially poverty that reduces people's basic health and wellbeing, may be challenged on the basis of both a moral and a practical determination: it is wrong that some people should suffer and, by their suffering, load a great deal of strain onto other services while being prevented from making their full contribution to the common good. The solution is to increase their resources through cash transfers or better access to well-paid work, or in many other ways improve their circumstances and opportunities. There is no case in favour of poverty.

Inequality is a different problem. It is possible to say that, provided perhaps no one is really going without basic necessities – that there is no 'real' poverty – inequality is acceptable, even desirable in an economy requiring strong incentives for people to work hard. On the other hand, inequality too may be challenged on both ideological and practical grounds – that it is simply not fair that some should have so much more than others, especially if their entitlement to their advantage is unclear.

And it has been shown that very unequal nations are less healthy compared with nations that are similarly rich (or similarly poor) but are much more equal.[2] This challenge may extend to much more than inequalities of income and wealth. The working of social and political institutions may be biased towards defending and increasing the advantage of those at the top, denying those below proper access to power and influence that might be used to lessen inequality.

The problem of *poverty* is that people suffer physically, psychologically and socially in ways that they should not. The problem of *inequality* is that, even in the absence of poverty, it can still cause unsustainable social and political tensions. People can come to resent it enough to do something about it.

Poverty and income

In Chapter 1, we spoke of poverty as a process leading to low income and having too few resources to maintain an acceptable standard of living. Children living in poverty – currently three out of 10 children in the UK – will find it harder as adults to avoid poverty themselves. The poverty they experience as children already affects their education, health and expectations and, for many of them, will reduce their earnings as adults. Some will escape their disadvantage and attain middle or even higher income levels. Those who do not escape will be joined by others falling into disadvantage and income poverty through ill fortune – typically, unemployment, illness and disability, family break-up, or simply being in the lowest paid jobs or living in places where their work is no longer needed. The clearest expression of their impoverishment is their low position in the distribution of incomes from the poorest to the richest.

Families in the UK whose incomes dip below 60 per cent of the equivalised national median (the 'poverty line') are not instantly 'living in poverty' in the sense most people would recognise. But it does not take long. 'Living in poverty' is having a low *trend income* – having insufficient money or other resources to obtain enough basic necessities and to keep warm, month on month, year on year. Both income poverty and the deprivation it causes can be measured by social surveys, and the following chapters show the evidence. The 60 per cent of equivalised national median threshold is not entirely arbitrary: it is the point below which families living in income poverty will start to go without basic necessities and begin to lose the capacity to participate fully in their communities.[3] It also falls a long way below a 'minimum income standard', which is the level of income the public think is the basic acceptable level. The rise in deprivation below 60 per cent of median income is discussed in detail in Chapter 4.

A practical policy focus on low income has advantages. It is relatively easy to measure and with enough political consent it is easy to address, as the actions taken in the first decade of this century began to show. It emphasises the importance of cash transfers to low-income families and, currently, the need to shore up low-paid employment with cash supplements and the national minimum wage. It suggests other remedies, such as limiting the scale of unemployment and controlling the rise of housing, childcare, fuel and transport costs, which those on the lowest incomes struggle to afford, even if they are receiving the limited subsidies currently offered. We can also improve children's life chances by investing in, and honing, key family supports and public services to improve children's prospects. Provision such as investment in universal early childhood education and care, family support, education, skills and training, housing, health, mental health services and so on, are all vital. But having enough money to ensure a decent childhood in the here and now is still of paramount importance.

How you define poverty depends a lot on what you think ought to be done about it. This is the recurrent theme explored in the remainder of this chapter.

Meeting need

When we think about poverty, many of us recall television images from the developing world: of famine, of shanty towns, or of children dying from preventable diseases. Yet this is clearly not what we observe in the UK. So is there any poverty here?

Peter Townsend, the sociologist who did so much to advance our understanding of poverty and its relationship to wider society and who was also one of CPAG's founders, certainly thought so. In 1979, he defined poverty as follows:[4]

> Individuals, families and groups in the population can be said to be in poverty when they lack resources to obtain the type of diet, participate in the activities and have the living conditions and amenities which are customary, or at least widely encouraged and approved, in the societies in which they belong.

As this definition makes clear, in affluent societies such as the UK, poverty can only properly be understood in relation to the living standards typical in each one. Townsend's definition also highlights that poverty is about a lack of resources. Poor people lack capital (both income and wealth). But they can also be resource-poor in other ways: they may lack human capital (such as education or good health) or social capital (such as positive and trustful communities). They lack the power to influence social policy in ways that might help them. Yet it is money that, to a large extent, determines whether people in the UK are able to compensate for other shortfalls in their lives. That is why a lack of adequate financial resources, while it is not of itself a *definition* of poverty, is the decisive *characteristic* of poverty.

This was acknowledged recently by the Joseph Rowntree Foundation, which began a series of studies in modern poverty by stating that someone is in poverty:[5]

> ... when a person's resources (mainly their material resources) are not sufficient to meet their minimum needs (including social participation).

The Joseph Rowntree Foundation acknowledged, as others have done before, that there is no universal agreement defining human needs nor their relation to resources. Some needs are out of scope: people who lack affection, companionship and personal fulfilment may lead poor lives but they are not necessarily in poverty. Those who lack food, water, shelter and warmth certainly are in poverty, unless, very rarely, they somehow choose to lead poor lives while having the resources to avoid hardship. But a modern definition cannot end there. Modern societies require more of people than huddling at home eating a subsistence diet. As Townsend insisted, you have to participate, see people, receive them at home, buy them presents on their birthdays, watch TV, take the children out, appear presentable (especially if you ever want to get a decently paid job), keep your home clean, replace consumables, curtains and furniture, and, just occasionally, have fun. These are what Townsend called 'the ordinary patterns, customs and activities' of society and they cost more than just the rent, food and utility bills.

True, such minimum standards vary over time and can sometimes even be retrenched. Recent research indicates that public opinion since the 2008 financial crisis now expects greater thrift from everyone, including the poorest, in response to austerity.[6] This was certainly true in wartime, when everyone suddenly had to 'make do and mend'. But it has been recognised for a long while that even the most grudging provision of cash benefits should meet more than basic subsistence needs. In the 1930s, George Orwell railed against people who wrote to the newspapers explaining how the poor could feed a family of six for 5/9d a week if they lived on a diet including '... margarine and broken biscuits...',[7] although Orwell's understanding of non-basic necessities included aspirins and Woodbine cigarettes. Things change, and definitions must work hard to keep up with the reality of people's lives.

Finding resources

The Joseph Rowntree Foundation's cautious expansion of 'needs' is matched by its treatment of 'resources'. It is, it says, '... material resources that matter.' But more than simply money incomes, resources include valuable assets, like savings and property, and a household's current stock of consumer durables, transport and gadgets. And like all modern industrialised societies, the UK provides what Prime Minister Harold Wilson called a *social wage*: not just cash benefits and pensions but free education, free healthcare, housing and transport subsidies and discounts for families on benefits for charges for things like dental and eye care, school meals and so on. Farming subsidies reduce food prices. There are other social protections: some remaining legal aid, for example, and it is unlawful to cut off someone's water supply, irrespective of how much money they owe.[8] In times of high stress, children may be cared for by local authorities – currently, 70,440 of them in England alone.[9]

As well as state benefits and protections, families in advanced countries can access resources from private and commercial sources, using credit cards, bank overdrafts and payday loans, although such loans are expensive. Relatives and friends are usually a better option for loans and subsidies. Charities too provide cash transfers and help in kind. Some families, typically those with a self-employed worker as their sole breadwinner, have private insurance that provides cash benefits when earned income fails. Families and friends also supply assistance in kind when a family's income dips below the cost of their needs: they look after children, help with household repairs and replacement, provide holidays, and so on. Often, they are a family's most valuable additional resource, especially when income loss is short term.

In many ways, it is the social wage that distinguishes poverty in developed countries like Britain from poverty in the subsistence economies of many developing countries. People in the less developed countries of Africa, Asia and South America do subsist and, in favourable years, they can subsist adequately and meet basic needs from natural resources. Their costs are low and they too have access to supportive relatives and community groups. But they have little of the elaborate safety nets and subsidies provided in Europe and North America. Often, they have to pay for anything that is more than the most basic education and healthcare and, in unfavourable years, they can want for real basics like water. When all fails, as sometimes it does, they experience the poverty described in UN definitions, whose threshold of a 'dollar-or-two-a-day per person' determines its notion of 'extreme' or *absolute* poverty, rather than the *relative* poverty usually spoken of here.[10]

This, on the other hand, is not to give the impression that the UK's safety net always works, at least in terms of the benefit and tax credit system's capacity to keep people from hardship. As the evidence in this book will show, it does not always work, and it certainly does not always work for families with children. If you have children, you have to maintain a household in ways that you can avoid if you have none. For many families, especially large families, it is a safety net laid on the ground, and hitting it will have a profound effect on your standard of living and sharply raise your risk of hardship. Even many of those managing to stay just above the safety-net level, employed in low-paid work, find themselves in income poverty, even if they are receiving tax credits. In Britain, in 2016/17, The Trussell Trust issued more than a million three-day emergency ration packs from its 424 food banks, at least a third of them to help feed children. Failures in the benefits system were the main cause of referral.[11] The most recent report by the Joseph Rowntree Foundation found almost 700,000 British households, including 300,000 children, to be 'destitute', unable to afford some of the most basic necessities.[12] 'Absolute poverty' has not yet left our shores entirely.

Happily, we are no longer required to spend several pages debating the distinction between absolute and relative poverty, although it has preoccupied many in the past. There now seems to be general agreement that the distinction has little meaning and is actually unhelpful. There are degrees of poverty. Some are life-threatening and are no more or less so for being called 'absolute'; some are less than life-threatening but are painful and damaging, the more so the longer the condition continues. All such poverty leaves you a lot worse off than others among your fellow citizens, and so you are poor relative to them. One of the first people in Britain to take the measurement of poverty seriously, Charles Booth, understood this very well. He referred to poor people as:[13]

> … living under a struggle to obtain the necessaries of life and make both ends meet; while the 'very poor' live in a state of chronic want.

Some support remains for a separate category of biologically based 'absolute poverty' among those who think that support from better-off tax-payers should be limited to relieving only these most basic, life-threatening conditions. They believe that a lack of anything more, especially social participation, is simply inequality, which, to them at least, matters only little.[14] There is a great deal in what follows that shows it does matter, and we will examine carefully the relationship between people's perceptions of poverty and their wider social and political values.

Whether or not people's resources are sufficient for their needs also varies in ways that are not obvious at first. Those relying too much on informal resources from private provision or family and friends are the more vulnerable and insecure. Resources that appear adequate to an analyst may not always find their target to meet need. Power relations within families can be unequal, and those with more power, usually men, can divert resources away from essential expenditure.[15] Women in poor households often miss out on what little is available, while disabled people have enhanced needs that can only be met by greater resources.[16] There are others, too, who are outside the whole concept of a household income. We need to consider what resources need to be mobilised to keep from poverty those who have no regular home, those in prison, children in care and those in other forms of institutional care – none of whom appear in official measures of poverty.

So far, then, we understand poverty to be, essentially, this shortfall of material resources relative to the needs of maintaining a standard of life which any fair-minded person would recognise as the minimum a fellow citizen should be forced to accept. We need now to expand this basic idea of relative poverty in relation to other concepts and ideas that contribute to its wider understanding.

Poverty and related concepts

Among many who have tried to help us understand how all the ideas related to poverty fit together, Paul Spicker has done much, providing a map.[17] He insists that poverty as a concept has no single meaning, nor any that is solely 'right' or 'wrong'. He agrees that poverty includes concepts of material insufficiency and unmet needs, as we have discussed. He also includes ideas of poor standards of living, of inequality and of disadvantaged economic position, which are also familiar, so far. Interestingly, though, he places at the centre of his map – the core idea of poverty – the notion of 'unacceptable hardship', which of course is a value judgement.

Figure 2.1:

Family resemblances between different concepts of poverty

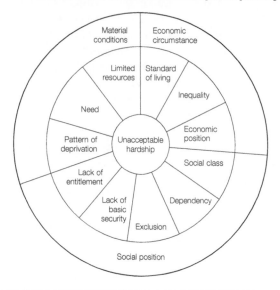

Source: P Spicker, 'Definitions of poverty: twelve clusters of meaning', in P Spicker and others (eds), *Poverty: an international glossary*, Zed Books, 2007, reproduced with permission from Zed Books.

Poverty and values

Spicker quotes David Piachaud, who said in 1981:[18]

> Poverty carries with it an implication and moral imperative that something should be done about it. Its definition is a value judgment and should be clearly seen to be so.

This remained a popular view, as Pete Alcock wrote:[19]

> ... poverty is a political concept – it does not just describe a state of affairs, it also implies that some action must be taken to remedy it.

Writing now, 35 years later, is it possible to pause and wonder if this is still so? Has this idea weakened?

Is it at least possible to wonder to whom hardship is unacceptable, in addition to those living in poverty? Few would offer a definition of *acceptable* hardship, but critics of social policies designed to reduce poverty by increased cash transfers did not hesitate to revive a distinction between the deserving poor, who merit help, and the undeserving poor, who are scroungers lost to dependency. And historically the deserving poor were always a fairly exclusive group, limited to widows, orphans and the most severely disabled. What they were thought to deserve was never very much.

Another way to blunt the force of 'poverty' as a condition that suggests its own cure is to characterise those in poverty as having made a 'lifestyle choice'.[20] This opinion may have its origins in a Victorian religious view that the poor were advantaged, almost unfairly so, in the quest for eternal salvation.[21] If this were so, or true on any scale that would matter, we would find among the poor many who would otherwise have an obvious capacity to improve their income but choose not to. As Mack and Lansley say:[22]

> The rich do not choose the lifestyles associated with the lack of resources.

Oddly, those most prone to accuse the poor of choosing their poverty are those most likely to cléave to a view of standard economic behaviour as one driven solely by self-interest.

Probably, we retain in the UK a national consensus that hardship caused by a low trend income is unacceptable and should attract official intervention. How much and what kind are questions that divide public opinion. Direct provision through a universal system of social security and socialised services is one emphasis; incentives (some positive, others coercive) to encourage people in poverty to improve their own earned resources is another. Few cleave solely to one approach. Those stressing universal benefits tend to see freedom from hardship as a right of citizenship. Those stressing incentives tend to focus on personal responsibility and freedom from dependence on the state.

Poverty and social exclusion

One of the few serious debates on the meaning of poverty conducted at high government levels occurred during the 1970s and 1980s in Brussels. Those in the senior administration of the then European Community (now the European Union) were people who could remember the 1930s. To them, poverty meant the masses of unemployed workers and their families during the Depression in Europe – a memory of real and widespread destitution, which in some places in Europe led to actual starvation. They began to feel uneasy about naming the benefit recipients and low-paid workers of the 1980s as people 'in poverty'. In the UK, the government was keen to deny that such people were living in poverty at all.[23] On the other hand, the number of such people was increasing quite rapidly, with a rise in long-term unemployment, ageing populations, more lone-parent families, benefit cuts and stagnating wage levels for people in routine jobs. Whatever poverty was to be called, it was demanding that action be taken to reduce it, or to contain its rise once more.

By the mid-80s they had managed to pass into statute a basic definition, whose debt to Peter Townsend was obvious:[24]

> The poor shall be taken as to mean persons, families and groups of persons whose resources (material, cultural and social) are so limited as to exclude them from the minimum acceptable way of life in the Member State in which they live.

Subsequently, this view grew to incorporate the risks of falling into poverty as part of the process. When named as social exclusion it became an active verb, something that is done to people. It promoted the idea of human agency in the process of poverty – that it is a social and political phenomenon and not just a blind economic process.

In the UK, since the 1970s, the impact of increasing social exclusion has seemed particularly harsh. Whereas the great British divide was once between manual working-class and non-manually employed middle-class families, with all the social, cultural and economic distance that that distinction implied, the growing prosperity of skilled workers left those in unskilled routine occupations adrift, located in areas prone to recurrent mass unemployment and seeing little wage progression when in work. The good life, enjoyed by what the Bishop of Liverpool called 'comfortable Britain', receded from their grasp.[25]

Since the 1980s, profound changes in the labour market have reduced the value of less-educated labour and, in some sectors, discarded it entirely. An economy comprised now of more than 70 per cent service activities demands from employees good social skills as well as cognitive skills. People short of such skills found themselves in increasingly marginal positions. The social effects of these changes have been dramatic. Yet the popular narrative about 'poverty' that emerged in the 1990s drew a false picture of an increasingly dispossessed 'underclass' dependent on state benefits in and out of work, living unstable and often disorganised lives in shrinking islands of social housing. Lone parents were held typical of underclass membership.

Talk of an underclass proved unhelpful, evoking as it did Aldous Huxley's dystopian class system in *Brave New World* and even the Nazi notion of *Untermenschen*. But something was going on that revived (as they are revived in different forms in every generation) ways to shift the blame for poverty back onto the poor. Yet the evidence strongly opposes such a view. Half the people living in income poverty in the UK live in households in which at least one adult is working. Two-thirds of children in poverty have at least one working parent. And 75 per cent of people who claim jobseeker's allowance find work within 12 months; the majority claim for just a few weeks. The problem is that increasingly the low-paid jobs they typically find prove to be temporary, throwing them back onto benefits rather than establishing them as full-time permanent workers.

Yet whole sections of the UK media continue to denigrate claimants and low-paid workers. Ruth Lister writes of the 'othering' of people living in poverty:[26]

> What people in poverty are reacting to is a process of what we might call 'othering' – ie, they are treated and talked about as people who are 'other' to the rest of us. It is a process of differentiation and demarcation, by which the line is drawn between 'us' and 'them' and through which social distance is established and maintained. The line is imbued with negative value judgements that construct 'the poor' variously as a source of moral contamination, a threat, an 'undeserving' economic burden, an object of pity or even as an exotic species.

However, just because unsympathetic elements use the marginalised position of low-income families to stigmatise them and so increase their exclusion, this does not mean that what is happening to them is not real. Families in poverty have become socially excluded, economically marginalised, and geographically isolated from better-provided neighbourhoods. A key moment in this process occurred in the 1970s when young people leaving school with no qualifications found their value in the labour market sharply reduced. By the early 1990s, Marsh and McKay's national surveys of low-income families described what they called a 'benefit fault-line'.[27] Families with children claiming benefits in and out of work were far more likely to be in social housing, to have only basic education, to be in the more routine low-paid jobs, and far more likely to be going without basic necessities. The differences were large: claimant families were strikingly more likely to be in what Spicker named as unacceptable hardship.

Poverty as powerlessness

A difficulty with the concept of social exclusion is that it can make its impact on income poverty rates look too intractable. While it is good to have, as part of a definition of poverty, a concept that points so clearly to its causes – one that describes the dynamic of how families are placed in poverty and discouraged from progress – it can also suggest that low-income families are somehow caught in the maw of social and market forces too powerful for them to resist or reverse. It can suggest that people who have been excluded cannot be readmitted, that they are powerless, individually and collectively, to redress their disadvantage.

Placing powerlessness at the centre of an understanding of poverty is an approach that tends to inform thinking about poverty worldwide, again mainly in the poorer developing countries. The World Bank (whose articles of incorporation, interestingly, proclaim its main purpose to be the abolition of poverty) drew together in the 1990s participatory studies of thousands of poor families in 47 countries called *Voices of the Poor*.[28] What poor people themselves had to say dwelt a great deal on their impotence and humiliation in the face of what seemed to them, probably rightly in many cases, to be the monopoly of decision making retained by the rich and their pliant governments. They contrasted the precarious nature of their daily lives in rural poverty with the insular privileges of an urban few, speaking often of their poverty as a debt-laden trap – as a kind of imprisonment – and of their exclusion from any means of advancement. While in many of the countries studied, though by no means all, poor people could count a vote among their few possessions, their comprehensive exclusion from real political efficacy was apparent. Put simply, grossly unequal societies are not democratic, vote or none.

The extent to which this view of poverty as powerlessness can be played back to rich countries is less clear. It can be as much a question of ideology as it is of social scientific judgements about the distribution of income and resources. In the third quarter of the twentieth century in the UK, for example, differences in income and wealth had narrowed markedly and many essential services were still socialised. In the 1980s, income equality grew rapidly, and has remained wide since. Much essential provision has been surrendered to the market, and the exclusion of families in poverty has become so much more pronounced as to call into question the extent to which families living in persistent poverty enjoy full citizenship. A more coercive administration of out-of-work benefits and the decline of trade union representation among low-paid workers have also increased a sense of powerlessness among them. On the other hand, social mobility remains fairly widespread and families do move in and out of poverty to an extent that is far less common in less developed countries (see Chapter 8).

Poverty as degraded life chances

Perhaps the best example of the way people define poverty by their preferred solutions is the present emphasis on the limited 'life chances' confronting children in poverty. Lately, in seeking to abandon the measurement of low income as the primary measure of poverty in the UK, the government proposed instead to monitor 'life chances'. Two statutory measures were put forward:

- children in workless households, and in long-term workless households; *and*
- educational attainment at key stage 4 (GCSE) for all children and for disadvantaged children.

The then Prime Minister, David Cameron, also identified four areas he saw as crucial:

- improving family life and the early years;
- education;
- levelling the playing field so that positive social connections and experiences are available to all;
- tackling alcoholism, drug addiction and poor mental health among families in poverty.

'Life chances' is usually a helpful concept, and it would be unreasonable to challenge any proposal that would improve the wellbeing of the children of families in poverty, or to deny that such improvements might, 20 years hence, leave them to some extent less vulnerable to falling into poverty themselves. However, the version of a life chances approach that the Cameron government sought to embed in its official understanding of poverty[29] left little doubt that poor parenting was seen as one of the main causes of later adult poverty: a poverty of opportunity, ambition and degraded life chances. Aside from the government interpretation, the usefulness of the life chances approach lies in its future-orientated approach to child outcomes. However, childhoods matter too – children are not just 'becomings'; they are ends in themselves. And it is hard to make sense of any life chances approach that ignores child poverty. It is income poverty itself that steals away children's life chances, beginning even in the womb by reducing their mothers' nutrition and continuing throughout their childhood.

The main criticisms of the government's proposed life chances approach, while not opposing policies to improve the wellbeing of children growing up in poverty, point out that much of the causality flows in the opposite direction – that income poverty itself causes the reduced wellbeing of children. And it is about more than simple matters of diet and environment. A systematic review with a very high evidentiary standard identified a distinct and significant effect of income on child cognitive and social developmental outcomes, beyond any effects of parental education or attitudes which might correlate with income.[30] This research suggests that the main mechanism is the stress and anxiety experienced by parents living in poverty which makes it hard to parent calmly and responsively, as well as reducing their spending on children. The authors cite a number of studies which saw improvements in maternal mental health as a result of increases in family income. Also, since two-thirds of poor children live with working parents, by focusing on worklessness the government indicators completely overlook the main issue facing families in poverty. We return to this evidence when we examine both the causes and the outcomes of poverty in Chapters 10 and 11.

The life chances strategy, however, was shelved in favour of a 'social justice strategy', but this has never emerged.

Conclusions

This chapter has emphasised CPAG's view that, as Peter Townsend foretold, poverty is still best understood as a persisting lack of material resources that denies people in poverty many of the basic necessities of life and proper participation in the expected ways of their communities. Families lacking resources, whose incomes rarely rise above the key measure of 60 per cent of equivalised median income, and who lack other resources of capital, gifts, loans and help in kind, will, more and more as time goes on, end up with a standard of living that is lower than most people would find acceptable. The extent of this acceptability is a relative judgement. But, however judged, such families will experience hardship that denies them basic necessities and a proper engagement in society.

More elaborated concepts of poverty seek to describe and explain how people are captured in poverty: how their labour market position is weakened by social and economic exclusion, spatial isolation, degraded opportunity and diminished political authority. The value of such concepts is that they are a template: they can help shape policy and anti-poverty strategies, such as higher benefits that are universally applied, higher educational attainment, more secure and better paid jobs, affordable childcare, better and more affordable housing, better access to services, and raised incentives, aspirations and job attainment. How you understand poverty – what template you choose – influences where you place the emphasis among such strategies. That choice in turn is guided by values and by politics. As Ruth Lister says:[31]

> ... definitions (of poverty) cannot be divorced from the political use to which they are put. Moreover, implicit in definitions are explanations of poverty and its distribution, which generally reflect individualistic or structural perspectives. The former attribute the main responsibility for poverty to the 'the poor' themselves; the latter point to how economic, social and political structures and processes – from the global to the local – create and perpetuate poverty. Together, explanations, definitions (and their translation into measurements) and broader conceputalisations combine to shape policy responses to the phenomenon called 'poverty'.

The next chapter takes us on to this translation into measurements of poverty and its incidence in the UK today.

Notes

1   See especially R Lister, *Poverty,* Polity Press, 2004
2   R Wilkinson and K Pickett, *The Spirit Level: why more equal societies almost always do better*, Allen Lane, 2009
3   Some scholars argue that the 60 per cent of equalised median threshold underestimates poverty among low-paid working parents because the calculation of disposable income does not include childcare costs. See for example D Hirsch and L Valadez, *How Much Does the Official Measure of Child Poverty Underestimate its Extent by Failing to Take Account of Childcare Costs?*, Centre for Research in Social Policy Loughborough University, June 2015
4   P Townsend, *Poverty in the United Kingdom: a survey of household resources and standards of living,* Allen Lane and Penguin Books, 1979
5   C Goulden and C D'Arcy, *A Definition of Poverty*, Joseph Rowntree Foundation, 2014
6   B Baumberg, 'Benefits and the cost of living: pressures on the cost of living and attitudes to benefit claiming', in A Park, C Bryson and J Curtice (eds), *British*

Social Attitudes: the 31st report, NatCen Social Research, 2014

7   G Orwell, *The Road to Wigan Pier,* Left Book Club, 1937, Chapter 6

8   You can still be taken to court for what you owe, of course.

9   Department for Education, *Children Looked After in England*, Statistical First Release 41/2016, September 2016

10 United Nations, *Report of the World Summit for Social Development,* 6–12 March 1995. More recently the UN adopted new sustainable development goals, including the target to 'by 2030, eradicate extreme poverty for all people everywhere, currently measured as people living on less than $1.25 a day.' In October 2015, the World Bank uprated this to $1.90 per day.

11 J Perry and others, *Emergency Use Only: understanding and reducing the use of food banks in the UK*, Child Poverty Action Group, Oxfam GB, Church of England and The Trussell Trust, 2014

12 S Fitzpatrick and others, *Destitution in the UK*, Joseph Rowntree Foundation, 2016

13 C Booth (1902), quoted in P Spicker, 'Definitions of poverty: twelve clusters of meaning', in P Spicker and others (eds), *Poverty: an international glossary*, Zed Books, 2007, p236

14 See for example, the Adam Smith Institute: '… what is our child poverty statistic really telling us? Britain has a certain amount of inequality, a little less than it had 8 years ago but rising again as we climb out of the effects of the recession. This may or may not worry you. It does not particularly worry us. T Worstall, *A Little Something About Those Child Poverty Figures*, Adam Smith Institute blog, 2017

15 See European Institute for Gender Equality, *Poverty, Gender and Intersecting Inequalities in the EU. Review of the Implementation of Area A: women and poverty of the Beijing Platform for Action*, 2016

16 This is no longer acknowledged for all disabled people. Those judged to be fit to work will, from April 2017, be given the same allowance as non-disabled job-seekers.

17 P Spicker, 'Definitions of poverty: twelve clusters of meaning', in P Spicker and others (eds), *Poverty: an international glossary*, Zed Books, 2007, pp229–43

18 D Piachaud, 'Peter Townsend and the Holy Grail', *New Society*, 10 September 1981, pp419–21

19 P Alcock, *Understanding Poverty,* Macmillan, 1993

20 David Cameron answering Prime Minister's questions on 2 February 2016 said: 'We want a benefit system that's there for people who can't find a job who need support. It shouldn't be a lifestyle choice and if people can work, they should work.'

21 Verse three of *All Things Bright and Beautiful* is: 'The rich man in his castle/The poor man at his gate/God made them high and lowly/And ordered their estate.' From Mrs Cecil Frances Alexander's *Hymns for Little Children*, 1848

22 J Mack and S Lansley, *Poor Britain,* George Allen and Unwin, 1985, p39

23 J Moore, *The End of the Line for Poverty*, Conservative Political Centre, 1989, lecture delivered by John Moore at the St Stephen's Club, 11 May 1989

24 European Community, 1985

25 D Sheppard, *The Other Britain*, Dimbleby Lecture, 1984

26 R Lister, *Poverty and Social Justice: recognition and respect*, Third Bevan Foundation Annual Lecture, 24 June 2004

27 A Marsh and S McKay, *Families, Work and Benefits,* Policy Studies Institute, 1993

28 D Narayan and others, *Can Anyone Hear Us? Voices from 47 countries*, World Bank, 1999

29 www.gov.uk/government/speeches/prime-ministers-speech-on-life-chances, 11 January 2016

30 See CPAG's response to the government's life chances proposals, citing K Cooper and K Stewart, *Does Money Affect Children's Outcomes? A systematic review*, Joseph Rowntree Foundation, 2013. Also see J Griggs with R Walker, *The Costs of Child Poverty for Individuals and Society: a literature review*, Joseph Rowntree Foundation, 2008

31 R Lister, *Poverty,* Polity Press, 2004

Three

Measuring poverty: income

Summary

- More than one in seven UK households (one in five after their housing costs are taken into account) have an 'equivalent' income below the poverty line.
- After housing costs are accounted for, 30 per cent of children live in households below the poverty line. This is almost double the poverty rate (16 per cent) for pensioners.

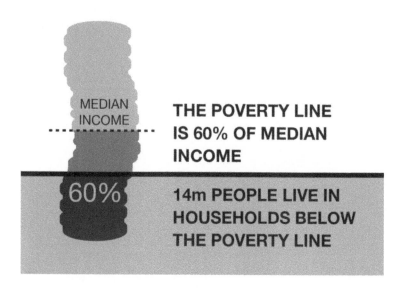

MEDIAN INCOME

THE POVERTY LINE IS 60% OF MEDIAN INCOME

60%

14m PEOPLE LIVE IN HOUSEHOLDS BELOW THE POVERTY LINE

- Poor families with children are typically a further £56 a week worse off than those already on the poverty line.
- In the 1970s and 1980s, income inequality in the UK widened rapidly and the gap has remained wide since. Nearly all the increases in our national income have gone to people in the upper half of our income distribution, leaving the top fifth between five and six times better off than the bottom fifth.

Income data in the UK

Since 1992, household income in the UK has been measured each year by the Family Resources Survey, carried out jointly by the Office for National Statistics and the National Centre for Social Research, funded by the Department for Work and Pensions.[1] The Family Resources Survey interviews a nationally representative sample of 20,000 private households every year.[2] The data have many uses, but our main focus here is on measures of income poverty and inequality.

Disposable income

The income of each household interviewed is added up. This total includes all reported sources of income for every individual in the household. For most households, these are wages and state benefits (including housing benefit), making up about 85 per cent of all national household income, and nearly all the income of working households. Private pensions make up an increasingly significant proportion of the income of retired people.[3] Total household income is reported after all taxes, including council tax (but not water charges) and national insurance contributions, have been deducted. This total is a household's disposable income. It does not take account of further tax paid through VAT and other indirect taxes.

Income before and after housing costs

Income for each household is reported both before and after their housing costs have been deducted.[4] Both have advantages.

Income before housing costs

Income before housing costs (BHC) is the simpler measure of disposable income. Households who have high housing costs are often those paying interest and repayments on large mortgages, or renting large properties in nice locations, which is, in one sense, a lifestyle choice – it is as much their consumer choice as their expenditure on other things. Over the past decades, investment in property has laid up wealth too. Income before housing costs is also preferred for international comparisons because no one can agree on how to deduct housing costs in the same way in each country. When the focus is on poverty, however, a real disadvantage of measuring income before housing costs among low-income households is that when their rent increases, more housing benefit may be received, which gives the false impression that income has increased.

Income after housing costs

Income after housing costs (AHC) recognises that housing costs, in particular for those on low incomes, are not like other expenditures – they are not discretionary, and so should be taken out of the reckoning. The money someone has left to spend each week is a better reflection of their day-to-day standard of living. This is especially true when assessing low incomes because some regions and some groups of people have very different housing costs. People in the South East and London can look well off before their huge rents and mortgages are deducted. People in Northern Ireland can look much poorer, but their housing costs are small by comparison and they can have much more income to cover their other daily living expenses. Poverty rates after housing costs have usually been higher than poverty rates before housing costs. But since housing costs have recently risen as a proportion of income in the UK, the gap has widened.

Comparing incomes: equivalisation

Before household incomes can be compared and used to estimate poverty and inequality, the Office for National Statistics has to equivalise them. Households are richer or poorer according to the total of their disposable income and according to the number of people that income has to support, whether those people are adults or children, and even the ages of the children.

Consider households made up of just two adults and no children receiving £300 a week. A single person getting £300 a week all to her/himself would be that much 'richer', so the Office for National Statistics records her/his equivalised income as £448 a week, thus reducing the chance of her/him showing up as 'poor' in the distribution of equivalised incomes. In the same way, a couple with two children (one 14 years old, one younger) getting £300 a week are 'poorer', so their equivalent income is reduced to £214 a week, plunging them down the income distribution towards the poor end.[5] It is worth adding that there is no great consensus on how to calculate equivalent incomes. There is evidence from the minimum income standards research[6] that this method gives insufficient weight to the needs of children.[7]

If the UK population was comprised solely of households containing two adults, the numbers in Figure 3.1 would also be actual cash incomes. After equivalisation, though, they become a kind of *cash-equivalent index of relative standards of living* between households of different sizes and composition. As such, they tell us more accurately than unadjusted incomes who is in income poverty and who is not.

The columns in Figure 3.1 show the number of individuals found in each ascending £10 per week band, from the lowest (£10 a week) to the highest (£1,500 a week). These columns are also grouped into 10 bands representing 'income deciles' from the poorest 10 per cent of people up to the richest. These bands are narrow and tall in the middle of the distribution, where a lot of people have quite similar incomes, and are much wider and shallower among the rich, whose incomes stretch to very high amounts. The tall column on the far right of the graph shows the nearly 1.8 million people living in households receiving *more* than £1,500 a week. The smaller column on the far left shows the almost half a million people who, when interviewed, reported no household income at all and are not included in calculating incomes and poverty rates. (In fact, the Department for Work and Pensions' calculations for its annual *Households Below Average Income* publication omit the first three percentiles of the income distribution.)

The national median equivalised household income is £481 a week before housing costs are paid (£413 a week after): half the population have higher incomes than £481 a week; half have less. Those in income poverty are the 16 per cent of the population (about 13.5 million people) living in households receiving less than 60 per cent of this equivalised median (£288 per week).

In the past, we measured relative income poverty as 50 per cent of the *average* income (the total of national income divided by the number of households receiving it, or the 'arithmetic mean'). But this average was being dragged upwards, year by year, by the increasingly vast incomes of the richest households. Between 1961 and 2009, the share of our national income received by the top 1 per cent of the population tripled, from 3 per cent to 9 per cent – to say nothing of their corresponding accumulation of wealth. In 2015/16, more than five million people lived in households receiving more than £1,000 a week. People on 'average' incomes are quite well off: only 35 per cent of households got more than the 'average' (mean) equivalised income of £593 per week.

In terms of *actual* net incomes, our reference household – a couple with no children – would need to receive the same £481 a week to occupy that median household position. A single person without children would

Figure 3.1:

Distribution of equivalised incomes, before housing costs, 2015/16

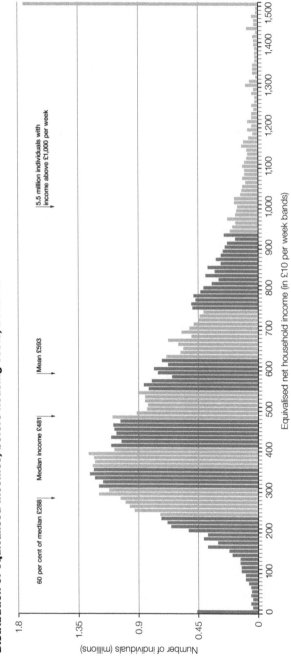

60 per cent of median £288

Median income £481

Mean £593

5.5 million individuals with income above £1,000 per week

Number of individuals (millions)

Equivalised net household income (in £10 per week bands)

Source: A Norris Keiller, 'Living standards', in J Cribb and others, *Living Standards, Poverty and Inequality in the UK: 2017*, Institute for Fiscal Studies, July 2017 (Author's calculation using the Family Resources Survey, 2015/16.)

need just £322, while a couple with two young children under 14 would need £674 a week. To be on average incomes, the same households would need £593, £397 and £831 a week.

Income below the poverty line

Estimates of the incidence of income poverty in the UK are published each year in the Department for Work and Pensions' *Households Below Average Income* series. For the purpose of measuring who was living in income poverty, the poverty line was established (originally, though no longer, by the UK government) to include all UK private households whose disposable incomes, once equivalised, fall below 60 per cent of the contemporary median income. This measure is open to the criticism that it is an arbitrary line – although it does appear to mark the point at which people's standards of living start to deteriorate disproportionately compared with those above the line (see Figure 4.3 in Chapter 4). It is also open to criticisms that it is only one of several 'symptoms' of poverty and ignores causes such as family breakdown, alcoholism, and so on, as argued by the proponents of the government's 'social justice' approach. For the moment, however, we will concentrate on the numbers – the debate on the causes of poverty is addressed in Chapter 10.

BOX 3.1:
Households and individuals

Official statistics, and the numbers used in this chapter, sometimes refer to **households** – as in '... x per cent of households have an income of £y per week – which is straightforward, and sometimes to **individuals** – as in '... x per cent of children are in income poverty' – which is not. Reference to 'individual incomes' means 'individuals living in households which have that income', not the income received by that individual alone.

Also, analysis of benefit incomes relate to 'benefit units'. Households can be made up of more than one 'benefit unit', typically single people sharing accommodation and cooking facilities. They comprise a single household, but are different benefit units.

The equivalised value of the 60 per cent below median income poverty line in 2015/16 was £288 a week (BHC) or £248 (AHC). The proportion of the UK population living in households below these thresholds was 16 per cent (BHC) and 22 per cent (AHC). The difference reflects the greater proportion of income spent on housing costs among low-income families, particularly among those lower paid working families who do not qualify for continuing housing benefit in work. So, depending on your preferred measure – and naturally the government prefers the smaller figure – between one in seven and one in five of the population of the UK live in households below the poverty line.

Table 3.1 summarises the headline poverty rates, before and after housing costs, for the three main groups traditionally viewed by governments as 'at risk' – children, pensioners and disabled people – in the financial year 2015/16. Pensioners have clearly felt the benefit of the 'triple-lock' defence of their state pensions, the pension guarantee and the increase in private pensions to the extent that they now have headline poverty rates that are actually below the national average. Forty years ago, pensioners were outstandingly the group most at risk, with more than four in 10 below the poverty line. Now, after housing costs, they are significantly less likely to be in poverty than working-age households. It is families with children and households with disabled adults that have the higher poverty rates.

Table 3.1:

Poverty rates, 2015/16

	Percentage of individuals living in households below 60% of median income	
	Before housing costs %	After housing costs %
Children	20	30
Pensioners	17	16
Disabled people	20	26
Working-age adults without dependent children	14	18
All	16	22

Source: Department for Work and Pensions, *Households Below Average Income: an analysis of the income distribution, 1994/95–2015/16*, 2017. See also F McGuinness, *Poverty in the UK: statistics*, House of Commons Library Briefing Paper, No.7096, June 2017

Changes in incomes and poverty rates

Equivalised incomes can also tell us how things have changed over recent years. The 2015/16 weekly median figure of £481 (BHC) is £8 a week higher than the previous year in real terms. This rose above the median national income of £468 a week found in 2009/10 (adjusted for inflation). This 2009/10 figure was followed by a *fall* in median incomes since the post-credit crunch period of fiscal austerity began, falling to a low of £458 a week in 2011/12.

As has been typical of the story of wage and reward in the UK over recent years, this recovery of incomes has not been evenly shared. Among the other inequalities (discussed in more detail below) an age gap is opening up. The Institute for Fiscal Studies reports that by 2014/15 the median income for those aged 60 and over rose 11 per cent higher than its 2007/08 level, while for people aged 31 to 59 it returned to its 2007/08 level. But for 22–30-year-olds, it was still 7 per cent.[8]

Although the UK has avoided the mass youth unemployment typical of southern European countries since 2008, this loss of income share among the youngest workers in the UK is especially significant because they tend to be the parents of the youngest children, or soon will be.

This dip in national median income during austerity is important to bear in mind when considering the trends in the proportions found in poverty. Between 2009 and 2015, households below 60 per cent of the median saw falls in their incomes, but, on average, *so did everyone else*. So, as the value of the median income fell under the impact of wage freezes and benefit cuts, so the proportion found below 60 per cent of the median also fell a little, giving a false impression that, somehow, in the middle of a recession, we had made progress in raising the living standards of households living in poverty. The Labour government deliberately increased child tax credit to protect families from the effects of the recession. The coalition continued this after 2010 for a year before the then Chancellor George Osborne reversed it. Also, benefits continued to be uprated in line with inflation for two years. As it turned out, the dip in the proportion below median income (BHC) was quite small, returning to its 2009/10 figure of 16 per cent in 2014/15. After housing costs it rose to 22 per cent in 2015/16.

Figure 3.2:

Changes in headline poverty rates: percentage below 60 per cent of UK contemporary median income, before housing costs, 2003/04 to 2015/16

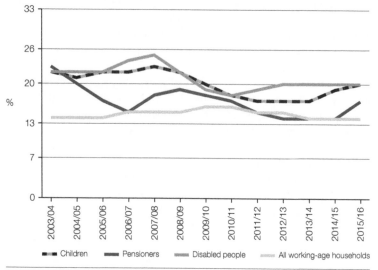

Source: Department for Work and Pensions, *Households Below Average Income: an analysis of the income distribution, 1994/95–2015/16*, 2017

Figure 3.2 shows how the poverty rates of children, pensioners and disabled people have moved over the last dozen years.

The fate of Tony Blair's millennial promise to end child poverty is shown by the dotted line. Even after switching to the far more favourable figures of income before housing costs, the progress surrendered is clear and in 2014/15 the line begins what will be an inexorable climb back towards its pre-millennial peak, unless cuts to benefits and tax credits are urgently reversed.

How poor is poor: the poverty gap

In Figure 3.1, the 16 per cent of the population found below 60 per cent of the national median income of £481 a week before housing costs do not all cluster together just below the poverty line. This raises the question of how compressed low incomes are. What is the 'poverty gap'? By how much do the equivalised incomes of households living in poverty fall short of the actual poverty line?

This is an increasingly important question because low incomes have been under so much pressure in these last few years. Bradshaw and Keung point out that the UK has tended in the past to have comparatively high poverty rates – among families with children they have been the highest in Western Europe – but quite small poverty gaps.[9] This was because the UK minimum income support system worked quite well to keep low-income families out of the direst poverty, even if it failed often to give them a standard of living the whole population thought acceptable. Now this minimum system is being eroded by benefit caps, the 'bedroom tax', local rent limits for housing benefit, cuts in benefit rates, frozen tax credit and child benefit rates, the two-child limit in universal credit and child tax credit, and soon by the slide into the lower benefit rates offered by universal credit.

Already these restrictions have particularly affected households with dependent children: lone parents in the lowest 20 per cent of the income distribution have lost 8 per cent of real income since 2010, couples with children about 11 per cent. Table 3.2 shows the extent of the poverty gaps affecting children in households on incomes below 60 per cent of the median.

Just as average incomes are dragged upwards by the richest, so the average poverty gaps are exaggerated by families who report very low

---

Table 3.2:

Poverty gaps of families with children with incomes below 60 per cent of the equivalised national median, 2013/14

	Lone parents £ per week	Couples with dependent children £ per week	All families below 60% of median income £ per week
Poverty gap before housing costs			
Average gap	£54	£69	£65
Median gap	£34	£51	£47
Poverty gap after housing costs			
Average gap	£63	£82	£75
Median gap	£47	£63	£56

Source: J Bradshaw and A Keung, *UK Child Poverty Gaps Increasing*, University of York, Department of Social Policy and Social Work, 2016. See also K Gardiner and M Evans, *Exploring Poverty Gaps Among Children in the UK*, Department for Work and Pensions Working Paper No.103, 2011, which explains the methodology in detail.

incomes, or even none. Many of these are families interviewed by the Family Resources Survey when they were between jobs and not claiming benefits, often because they had more savings than benefit claimants are allowed. But the median values are still large: after housing costs are paid, half of poor couples with children were £63 a week short of the poverty line, and lone parents were £47 a week short. This means that half of them fell further short of this value. These figures represent potentially a very significant surrender of living standards for families with children, *even compared with families who are themselves a long way short of the national median income*. And these gaps are growing larger in real terms, up by £4 a week from the previous year for all poor families with children.

Income inequality

As well as identifying who is in income poverty (below 60 per cent of the median), it is helpful to understand the extent of inequality in incomes across the whole range. Those in poverty do not need merely to ease over an arbitrary poverty line; they are looking upwards at a long, steep slope of income inequality. There is a sense in which the shape of the income distribution dictates the political climate of policy towards poverty. Rapid increases in the rewards to the upper half of the income range have fuelled the need of the rich to defend and justify their position, since to lessen inequality and/or reduce income poverty might require higher levels of taxation. The greater the degree of inequality, the more likely those living in poverty will be blamed for their own misfortune. It changes the position of those living in poverty, left behind as everyone else moves on. And what is thought by the majority to be an acceptable standard of living also changes, placing greater pressure on low-income households to conform to standards they increasingly cannot reach. This in turn emphasises their social isolation and estrangement from what Peter Townsend referred to as the normal ways of their communities.

The Gini coefficient

The distribution of UK incomes illustrated by Figure 3.1 is, obviously, an unequal one. If the distribution were a lot 'peakier' – more households in the middle, fewer at the poorest and richest ends – then as a nation we would be less unequal. A flatter distribution would signal greater inequality.

However, though visually simple to look at, income inequality can be quite difficult to capture in a single measure. The most commonly used is the 'Gini coefficient', which is a number varying between zero and one. In an unlikely population where everyone has exactly the same income, the coefficient would be zero; in an (equally unlikely) place where a single person (or household, or family) has all the income and everyone else has none, the coefficient would be one.

In the UK in 2015/16 the Gini coefficient summarising Figure 3.1 was 0.32. This is lower – less unequal – than in developing countries, where coefficients between 0.5 and 0.6 are common. It is higher than in Scandinavian countries and, interestingly, higher than in some of the former European Soviet Union countries where coefficients between 0.2 and 0.3 persist – although in the Russian Federation itself, it has risen to 0.4. As well as being useful for international comparisons, the Gini coefficient can give a clear picture of trends over time. The Office for National Statistics shows how income inequality in the UK has changed since 1977 (Figure 3.3).

Figure 3.3:

Gini coefficients for disposable income by household type, 1977 to 2015/16

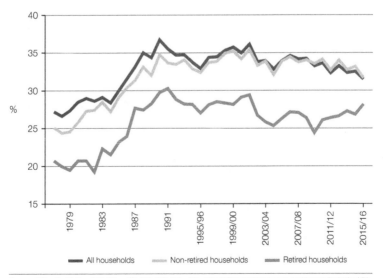

Source: Office for National Statistics, Statistical Bulletin, *Household Disposable Income and Inequality in the UK: financial year ending 2016*, January 2017

There were four distinct phases. Prior to 1984, inequality in the UK was much narrower than it is now, more closely resembling present-day Scandinavian countries. Indeed, in terms of wages alone, the narrowest gap between the least and best paid workers in the UK was recorded in 1973. Between 1984 and 1990 – in just six years – it rose steeply and the Gini coefficient then remained at around 0.35 until 2000. Then, under the impact of greater redistribution, mainly by increases in tax credits for low-paid workers and then by the brake on wage growth among the better paid during the post-2008 recession, it fell back a little. But the story is clear: at the end of the 1970s, the post-war settlement in the UK – the welfare state and supported by progressive taxation – broke down. We became, and remained, a far more unequal nation.

Income on the breakpoints

Though useful as a single indicator, the Gini coefficient gives us little indication of the scale of inequality in real terms. It is helpful therefore to look at the equivalised value of the incomes of those households sitting on some of the significant 'breakpoints' in the income distribution. Table 3.3 sets out the equivalised incomes of the households occupying the 10th,

Table 3.3:

Equivalised income at the 10th, 50th, 90th and 99th percentiles, 2014/15

	Single households	Couples without children	Couples with two children under 14
Poor (10 per cent poorer, 90 per cent richer)	£8,500	£12,700	£17,800
Median income (50 per cent poorer, 50 per cent richer)	£16,500	£24,600	£34,500
Rich (90 per cent poorer, 10 per cent richer)	£33,000	£49,200	£68,900
Richest (99 per cent poorer, 1 per cent richer)	£82,100	£122,500	£171,500

Source: C Belfield and others, *Living Standards, Poverty and Inequality in the UK: 2016*, Institute for Fiscal Studies, 2016

50th, 90th and the 99th percentile to illustrate what a Gini coefficient of 0.34 (in 2014/15) actually means in relative standards of living. Those in the middle of the income distribution have a cash equivalent standard of living twice that of households found down at the 10th percentile; the rich, at the 90th percentile, are four times better off. The richest households, found as we enter the top 1 per cent, are 10 times better off. This is broadly true for all types of households, except retired people, whose incomes are more compressed (see Figure 3.3).

The '20/80 gap'

A third way of looking at income inequality (and there are, of course, many more) is to take a broader view and ask: what is the real difference in the standard of living enjoyed by the top fifth of households found in the income distribution compared with the living standards of the bottom fifth? Figure 3.4 shows this comparison, again for each year since 1977. The trend, naturally, is the same pattern shown for the Gini coefficient: lower

Figure 3.4:

Ratio of equivalised incomes comparing the top fifth of households with the bottom fifth, 1977 to 2014/15

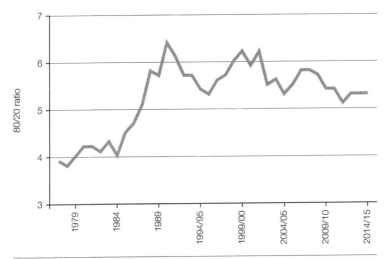

Source: Office for National Statistics, Statistical Bulletin, *Household Disposable Income and Inequality in the UK: financial year ending 2015*, February 2016

differences in living standards before 1984, higher since. But the scale of these differences is startling. In 1984, the top fifth were four times better off than the bottom fifth. Just seven years later they were more than six times better off and have remained at least five times better off ever since. The top fifth have more than 40 per cent of all national income, the bottom fifth just 8 per cent (Figure 3.5).

Figure 3.5:

How is income shared in the UK?

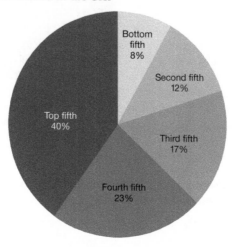

Source: The Equality Trust, *The Scale of Economic Inequality in the UK*, April 2017, using figures sourced from Office for National Statistics, Statistical Bulletin, *The Effects of Taxes and Benefits on UK Household Income: financial year ending 2015*, May 2016

Conclusions

This chapter has emphasised CPAG's widely supported view that income remains central to the process of poverty. More than one in seven UK households have an equivalised income below the poverty line. After meeting their housing costs, which after all denotes people's real weekly disposable incomes, this rises to one in five. Among UK households bringing up children, it rises to nearly one-third. Lone parents are most at risk of income poverty but, confounding the view of successive governments that work is the surest way out of poverty, even the 'traditional' family –

single-earner couples with children – now have poverty rates higher than average. Because of this, two-thirds of poor children living in poverty in 2015 have a working parent.

Poor families with children also have the greater shortfalls in income. Compared even with those already at the poverty line, their standard of living is typically a further £50 a week less. In each of recent years, benefit cuts have increased this shortfall, causing the proportion of children living in income poverty to rise once more.

In the 1970s and 80s, income inequality in the UK widened rapidly and the gap has remained wide since. Nearly all the increases in our national income have gone to people in the upper half of our income distribution, leaving the top fifth between five and six times better off than the bottom fifth.

Notes

1 Before that, all the way back to 1961, it was measured by the Family Expenditure Survey, whose data differs in a number of respects.

2 People in institutions are not included in the Family Resources Survey sample, nor are homeless people. A 'household' is defined as: 'one person living alone, or a group of people (not necessarily related) living at the same address who share cooking facilities and a living room, sitting room, or dining area'. This is not the same thing as a 'family or benefit unit', which is the family grouping used for assessing benefit entitlement. It is defined as: 'a single adult or couple living as married and any dependent children'. For example, adult children still living at home with their parents form their own benefit unit (for the purposes of the Department for Work and Pensions' definition), but will probably remain part of their parents' household, unless they have their own separate living arrangements. In multi-household dwellings, one household is randomly selected.

3 The latest Office for National Statistics figures show that the proportion of income from private pensions (44 per cent) now exceeds that provided by state pensions (37 per cent) – see Office for National Statistics, Statistical Bulletin, *Household Disposable Income and Inequality: financial year ending 2016*, January 2017

4 Housing costs include rent, water charges, mortgage interest, structural insurance premiums, ground rent and service charges, but not local taxes.

5 This example is the one given each year in *HBAI*. The multipliers used by the Office for National Statistics count a single person at 0.67, an additional adult at 0.33 (hence together they are the standard household weight at 1.00), a child aged 14 and older at 0.33 and a younger child at 0.20. This is the OECD (revised) standard method.

6   For example, see J Bradshaw and others, *A Minimum Income Standard for Britain: what people think*, Joseph Rowntree Foundation, 2008

7   J Bradshaw and others, *A Minimum Income Standard for Britain: what people think*, Joseph Rowntree Foundation, 2008

8   C Belfield and others, *Living Standards, Poverty and Inequality in the UK: 2016,* Institute for Fiscal Studies, 2016

9   J Bradshaw and A Keung, *UK Child Poverty Gaps Increasing,* University of York, 2016

Four

Measuring poverty: hardship

Summary

- Peter Townsend's *Poverty in the United Kingdom* (published in 1979) showed how persistent low income reduced people's ability to buy necessities and led to their being socially isolated.
- The Policy and Social Exclusion surveys (1983–2011) established the public view of essential expenditure and how many households are going without these essentials.

100,000
CHILDREN

LACK THREE
MEALS A DAY
OR A WARM
WINTER COAT

400,000
CHILDREN

GO WITHOUT
FRESH FRUIT OR
VEG AT LEAST
ONCE A DAY

3.2m
CHILDREN

DON'T HAVE
A ONE-WEEK
HOLIDAY ONCE
A YEAR

- The Policy Studies Institute's surveys of low-income families show that severe hardship is rare for families with incomes over the 60 per cent of median income poverty line.
- Modest increases in income reduce hardship swiftly and effectively. In 2001, child poverty was 400,000 lower than in 1999 and severe hardship among out-of-work families almost halved – from four in 10 to less than one-quarter in just two years, 28 per cent among lone parents and 22 per cent among couples.

- Eighty-five per cent of families in severe hardship have incomes below the poverty line.
- In 1969, more than half of those over 60 said they could not heat their homes adequately – in 2014/15, just 4 per cent of pensioners complained of inadequate heating.
- The Department for Work and Pensions' hardship index classes 8 per cent of pensioners as in hardship, but overall figures mask the fact that 23 per cent of pensioners who rent their homes from their local authority and 19 per cent relying solely on the state pension are in hardship.

The Townsend tradition

There are two parallel paths taken by quantitative research in the study of poverty in the UK. One is the measurement of household incomes falling below a poverty threshold, as we have seen in Chapter 3. The second is the measure of deprivation or hardship – the extent to which income-poor households 'go without', lacking goods and services that everyone thinks they should not go without, living in material circumstances and accommodation few of their fellow citizens would find acceptable. This second approach measures poverty as the lack of 'socially perceived necessities'.

In modern times, both these traditions of measurement owe their origins to Peter Townsend. He seized on the first Family Expenditure Survey in 1962 and, with Brian Abel-Smith, published *The Poor and the Poorest*.[1] This work, as well as being the inspiration to found the Child Poverty Action Group in 1965, began the stream of survey-based evidence of poverty in the UK, sweeping away contemporary complacency that poverty was a pre-war memory abolished by full employment and the welfare state. Then, as now, low wages blighted the British economy and affected families with children more acutely. Meagre pensions affected old people. But as early as 1952, Townsend was also wondering why, just 10 years after the *Beveridge Report*, we had '… nothing that matched the accounts of Charles Booth and Seebohm Rowntree of social conditions in Britain at the turn of the century.' In 1964, he began his monumental study, *Poverty in the United Kingdom*, published in 1979.[2]

Townsend's enquiry was extraordinarily detailed. In 1969/70, his team interviewed nearly 3,000 (very patient) people who, as well as reporting all their financial and social circumstances, were asked to say a lot about their consumption and lifestyles. They answered questions about their diet: 19 per cent went without fresh meat '… on most days…'; about their home: four out of 10 households in 1969 still had no fridge and 8 per cent no TV; and about their social lives: 5 per cent had no money to go out in the evening.

However distantly quaint some of the measures now seem – only 'housewives' were asked whether they had had a new winter coat in the past three years (one-third had not) – Townsend established the value of an audit of hardship. The great importance of this new approach was that persistent low incomes not only reduced people's ability to buy household necessities and stay warm, it showed the effects of income poverty in reducing people's social participation, leading to the identification and social isolation of 'the poor'. Think, if you will, of people who enjoy middle or higher incomes but who fail to go out, receive visitors, exchange gifts, and so on. Their friends and family worry about them.

Townsend added other indicators of deprivation: at work (paid holidays, pension entitlements...), housing (overcrowding, defects...) and environmental factors (no garden, pollution...), building up a rounded picture of material deprivation and hardship. Average scores on Townsend's deprivation index were predictably about two to three times higher among low-income households compared with the better off, but the highest scores were found among pensioner households, among whom, of course, the most income poverty was then concentrated.

Subsequently, this method of enquiry was taken up by three major research projects in the UK:[3]

- the Poverty and Social Exclusion surveys, 1983 to 2011;
- the Policy Studies Institute's series on low-income families 1991 to 2008;
- the Family Resources Surveys, 2004/05 to 2014/15.

Before looking at this evidence, it is fair to note that not everyone agrees that 'going without' is, of itself, a *measure* of poverty, which, as we said in Chapter 2, is essentially a lack of resources to meet (socially determined) needs and to be able to participate in society. There is a view that deprivation measures are really no more than indicators that income poverty results in low living standards.[4] They are subject to variations and uncertainties: the cost of essentials, for example, can differ regionally. Deprivation is as much a relative measure as income itself and can confuse preferences and constraints. And as we shall see, not everyone agrees on what deprivation and hardship means. Yet, in the end, hardship is the experience of poverty. If a low income provided everything a poor person could reasonably need, then it would matter less.

The Poverty and Social Exclusion surveys

Consensus about need

There is a sense in which every generation has to discover poverty for itself. As Townsend and Abel-Smith dented the optimism of the 1960s, so in 1985 the publication of Mack and Lansley's *Breadline Britain* survey discomforted the Thatcher generation, or some of them at least.[5] Mack and Lansley had responded to a number of criticisms of Townsend's 1969 survey, including those asking by whose authority certain items of consumption, including durables like a washing machine or going out in the evening, were deemed 'essentials' other than the fact that other people had them.[6]

Mack and Lansley sought their authority from a representative sample of the population, asking them whether or not they thought that each item in a list of common goods and services was essential or merely desirable. Items that at least a majority of people felt were essential were included in the list to be used to test who could afford them and who were going without. Their approach, what they now call their 'consensual method', was further developed in subsequent surveys in 1990, 1999 and 2012, where separate surveys were employed first to establish the public view of essential or inessential expenditure and then applied to detailed national surveys of households. The content of these surveys was first established by qualitative methods and focus groups, which discussed what goods and services are nowadays thought to be essential or merely desirable.[7]

Over the 30 years of surveys, the public had consistently endorsed the basic essentials and, by 2012, most people agreed on the necessity for adults of:

- heating to warm living areas of the home (96 per cent);
- a damp-free home (94 per cent);
- two meals a day (91 per cent).

And for children of:

- a warm winter coat (97 per cent);
- fresh fruit and vegetables once a day (96 per cent);
- new, properly fitting shoes (93 per cent).

Support for other consumer items grew, together with greater recognition that social participation for adults was important:

- visiting friends/family in hospital (90 per cent);
- celebrations on special occasions (80 per cent);
- a hobby or leisure activity (70 per cent).

And also for children:

- a garden or outdoor space in which to play safely (92 per cent);
- children's clubs or activities (74 per cent);
- going on a school trip at least once a term (55 per cent).

Over the years, beyond these fairly constant items, attitudes changed in response to taste and technology. A roast joint on Sunday and 'a weekly family meal' were thought essential both in Townsend's and Mack and Lansley's surveys, but not in 2012. Videos were introduced in 1990 and vanished again by 2012.

The modernised list in 2012 found that more than three-quarters also agreed that adults should be able to repair broken electrical goods promptly, eat meat or fish (or a vegetarian equivalent) and have a telephone, attend weddings and family events, and that children should have construction toys, and access to their own space to play or do homework.

More than half also thought adults should be able to insure their homes, pursue a hobby, and be able to meet £500 of unexpected expenses. Children, they said, should have a computer with internet access, pocket money and a day out with the family at least once a month. The need for a car did not make the 50 per cent cut off (ie, had not attracted a bare majority support), but support for it had grown from just 22 per cent in 1983 to 44 per cent in 2012. The need for a mobile phone (41 per cent) had also risen towards the 50 per cent mark. A television finally won majority approval as a necessity, though only just (51 per cent). While 66 per cent thought children should have access to the internet, only 42 per cent thought adults should.

The extent of deprivation

Another objection to Townsend's survey was that it was wrong to assume that people who lacked various items went without them solely because they could not afford them. While few would imagine people willingly going without enough heat in winter, not everyone may have wanted a Sunday joint, for example, even if a majority of people thought they ought to have one.

Mack and Lansley introduced the refinement of asking their respondents who said they lacked any item (among those items thought 'essential' by a majority of the public) whether they went without because they 'did not want it' or because they 'could not afford it'. This provided a much more stringent test of deprivation. It is possible to argue that some respondents were unwilling to admit they could not, for example, afford to feed their children adequately – or at least to a standard set by a national consensus about an adequate diet for a child – or were quick to say they had no need to insure their home or pursue a hobby, even though they clearly had no spare income to be able to do so. In the survey itself, 22 per cent of adults said they had been embarrassed by their low income, but those who agreed their income poverty was the cause of their deprivation were very clear about it.

Adult deprivation

About a third of adults in the UK in 2012 said they could not save money or contribute to a pension plan; a quarter could not afford to repair broken electrical goods nor to take a proper holiday away from home that they would have to pay for; a fifth despaired of keeping their home decorated to a decent standard (Table 4.1). Substantial minorities could not afford dental charges (17 per cent), to replace worn clothes with new (15 per cent) or to entertain friends (11 per cent). Smaller minorities lacked other items in the list but they were the items attracting the greater endorsement from the public that no one should do without. Eight per cent had no second pair of serviceable shoes nor any clothes they might wear to a job interview; 7 per cent could not afford annual presents for friends or relatives. And while 5 per cent is never a large proportion of anything, it is still surprising that 5 per cent of adults had no table or chairs to use for a family meal and 4 per cent had no coat: this is two million people. Diets suffered too: 7 per cent could not afford fruit or vegetables on most days; 3 per cent could afford no more than a single meal a day.

Table 4.1:

The Poverty and Social Exclusion surveys 1999 and 2012: adult deprivation

	% lacking each item because they 'could not afford it' 1999	% lacking each item because they 'could not afford it' 2012	Change since 1999 %
Adult necessities			
Heating to keep home adequately adequately warm	3	9	+6
Damp-free home	7	10	+3
Two meals a day	1	3	+2
Visit friends or family in hospital or other institutions	3	3	0
Replace or repair broken electrical goods	12	26	+14
Fresh fruit and vegetables every day	5	7	+2
Washing machine	2	1	-1
All recommended dental treatment	n/a	17	–
Celebrations on special occasions	2	4	+2
Warm waterproof coat	4	4	0
Attend weddings, funerals and other such occasions	3	3	0
Telephone	2	2	0
Meat, fish or vegetarian equivalent every other day	2	5	+3
Enough bedrooms for every child aged 10+ of a different sex to have her/his own room	3	9	+6
Curtains or window blinds	n/a	1	–
Hobby or leisure activity	7	8	+1

	% lacking each item because they 'could not afford it' 1999	% lacking each item because they 'could not afford it' 2012	Change since 1999 %
Enough money to keep the home in a decent state of decoration	15	20	+5
Household contents insurance	10	12	+2
Appropriate clothes for job interviews	4	8	+4
Table (and chairs) at which all the family can eat	n/a	5	–
Taking part in sport/exercise the family can eat	n/a	10	–
Two pairs of all-weather shoes	7	8	+1
Regular savings (of at least £20 a month) for rainy days	27	33	+6
Television	0	0	0
Regular payments to an occupational or private pension	n/a	30	–
Replace worn-out clothes with new, not second-hand, clothes	6	15	+9
Presents for family or friends once a year	4	7	+3
Friends or family around for a meal or drink at least once a month	6	11	+5
Holiday away from home, not staying with relatives	18	25	+7

Source: S Lansley and J Mack, *Breadline Britain: the rise of mass poverty*, Oneworld, 2015

There were also worryingly high levels of basic housing deficiencies: 10 per cent of adults lived in damp homes and the same percentage could not provide older children of different genders separate bedrooms nor afford sufficient fuel to heat their homes adequately. This means that 2.3 million households in the UK, housing 1.5 million children, cannot afford to heat their living areas; 600,000 children live in homes that are *both* damp and poorly heated.[8]

Although not named as a necessity in 1983, everyone can now afford a television and almost everyone has a phone.

Child deprivation

Some of the evidence for deprivation among children echoes deprivation among adults in predictable ways (Table 4.2). About a third cannot save money, about a quarter miss out on holidays and day trips, and 16 per cent have no pocket money of their own. Between one in 10 and one in 20 children lack the things most children take for granted: construction toys, school trips, sports equipment, computers, inviting friends around. Between 3 per cent and 5 per cent of children also lack basic items such as a good diet, good shoes and new clothes.

There are an estimated 100,000 children in the UK who are said to lack three meals a day or a warm winter coat because their parents cannot afford to feed or clothe them properly. Taking the food items together, 4 per cent of parents, caring for half a million children, cannot afford to feed them properly. These parents are keenly aware of the link between their income poverty and their inability to provide for their children: parents who say they feel 'poor all the time' and are aware they have an income 'well below the poverty line' are 21 times more likely to say they cannot afford to give their children three meals a day.

Table 4.2:

Poverty and Social Exclusion surveys 1999 and 2012: child deprivation

	% lacking each item because they 'could not afford it' 1999	% lacking each item because they 'could not afford it' 2012	Number of children in 2012 (round 1,000s)	Change since 1999 %	Which children did the question apply to?
Child necessities					
Warm winter coat	2	1	100	-1	0-18 years
Fresh fruit or vegetables at least once a day	2	3	400	+1	0-18
New properly fitting shoes	2	4	500	+2	0-18
Three meals a day	1	1	100	0	0-18
Garden or outdoor space to play in safely	4	5	600	+1	0-18
Child celebration or special occasions	4	1	100	-3	0-18
Books at home suitable for age	0	2	200	+2	>2-18
Meat, fish or vegetarian equivalent at least once a day	4	3	400	-1	0-18
Suitable place at home to study or do homework	n/a	5	500	–	>5-18
Child hobby or leisure activity	3	6	500	+3	>5-18
Toddler group or nursery or play group at least once a week for pre-school-aged children	n/a	4	100	–	<5
Indoor games suitable for age	n/a	1	200	–	0-18
Enough bedrooms for every child aged 10+ of a different sex to have her/his own room	3	11	600	+8	>10

	% lacking each item because they 'could not afford it' 1999	% lacking each item because they 'could not afford it' 2012	Number of children in 2012 (round 1,000s)	Change since 1999 %	Which children did the question apply to?
Children's clubs or activities, such as drama or football training	n/a	9	1,000	–	>2–18
Computer and internet for homework (not a necessity in 1999)	36	6	500	-30	>5–18
Some new, not second-hand, clothes	3	4	500	+1	0–18
Day trips with family once a month	n/a	21	2,500	–	0–18
Outdoor leisure equipment, such as roller skates, skateboard and footballs	3	6	700	+3	0–18
At least four pairs of trousers, leggings, jeans or jogging bottoms	3	5	600	+2	0–18
Going away on a school trip at least once a term	2	8	600	+6	>5–18
Money to save	n/a	32	2,800	–	>5–18
Pocket money	n/a	16	1,300	–	>5–18
Child holiday away from home for at least one week a year	22	26	3,200	+4	0–18
Construction toys (like Lego and Duplo)	3	5	500	+2	0–18
Child has friends round for tea or a snack once a fortnight	4	8	1,000	+4	0–18

Source: S Lansley and J Mack, *Breadline Britain: the rise of mass poverty*, Oneworld, 2015

Better or worse?

Many of the results of the 2012 Poverty and Social Exclusion survey were broadly consistent with the 1999 survey and many of the smaller differences are likely to be attributable to sampling variations. Interestingly though, there were more changes in the direction of more deprivation than of less, especially concerning housing conditions. The proportion unable to afford adequate heating rose from 3 per cent to 9 per cent; the same change indicated that more older children of the opposite sex were denied separate bedrooms, and more could not keep up with decoration needs. Social participation also suffered significantly for adults and children alike.

Looking further back to the 1990 and 1983 surveys, there was a clear trend that housing deprivation had increased, especially with respect to overcrowding, and the higher cost of fuel was reducing people's ability to afford adequate heating. The provision of other items, particularly food and clothing, appeared to improve between 1983 and 1999 but then to fall back again by 2012. However, the most surprising trend over the nearly 30 years covered by the Poverty and Social Exclusion surveys is that the proportion of adults lacking three or more essential items, judged by the standards of the time, more than doubled from 14 per cent to 33 per cent. Among children, the numbers in the UK lacking two or more essential items rose from two to four million in the most recent period between 1999 and 2012.

On first encounter, these findings make no sense at all. The UK was in recession in 1983 with record levels of post-war unemployment.[9] Since then, real incomes have more than doubled and many of the things thought of as luxuries in 1983 have become relatively easier to afford. So why are people still going without? Much of the answer was seen in the previous chapter, charting the growth of inequality, as the authors explain:[10]

> Many consumer goods have become relatively cheaper over the thirty years and more people can afford them. These items become embedded in our lives until the point where to go without them is to miss out. Some items not chosen as necessities in 1983, such as a telephone, have come to be seen as essential. And some which are now central to our lives, such as a computer with internet access for children, were not even a part of them in 1983. Those who can't afford these items today are now included in the PSE [Poverty and Social Exclusion survey] count of poverty numbers, though they would not have been in the past. These changing patterns of necessities and expectations add to the overall pressures on the budgets of the poorest households.

Deprivation of many of the food, clothing and housing items also increased, particularly recently, with more people going without these basics in 2012 than in the earlier surveys. This can only be due to much greater wage inequality, the rise of zero-hour contracts and wage freezes, which have combined to make income-poor households relatively poorer and consequently more deprived. Lower real incomes from benefits, due to cuts and freezes in rates after 2010, will continue to make this worse.

There are other pressures too: greater inequality exposes poor families to keener public notice. Sending your children to school ill-dressed and ill-fed attracts official attention. Modern sensitivities to apparent child neglect, increasingly weighted by sad news headlines, place real pressure on poor parents to meet standards their incomes do not support. Parents, however poor, have always made sacrifices for their children, but now many parents say they go without, and even skip meals, to try to keep up standards for them. On the basis of a national survey of 2,000 households, The Trussell Trust in 2015 made the startling claims that:[11]

> ... more than twenty per cent of parents have skipped meals, gone without food to feed their children or relied on family members or friends for food in the last twelve months... Nearly a third of parents with incomes less than £25,000 have said they have skipped a meal to ensure their children do not go hungry.

Main and Bradshaw's analysis of the 2011 Poverty and Social Exclusion data showed:[12]

> Strong evidence was found suggesting that where resources are limited, adults prioritise children's needs – children were less likely to go without than adults, and where children were in poverty, adults were much more likely both to be poor themselves and to engage in economising behaviours. Some such behaviours were specifically aimed at protecting others in their households – such as skimping on food so that others could have enough.

The numbers are striking: a quarter of poor adults with children say they have '... skimped on food so that others would have enough', a third postponed their visits to the dentist, half stopped going out.[13]

On the other hand, Monica Magadi and Sue Middleton's analysis of the 2004/05 Family Resources Survey showed that no amount of parental sacrifice could protect children in large workless families from 'severe poverty'.[14]

The Policy Studies Institute surveys

Severe hardship

In 1990, the Policy Studies Institute began a 20-year programme of research for the then Department of Social Security (now the Department for Work and Pensions). It began as a study of the effects of means-tested benefits on the incentives and welfare of low-income families with children and after 1999 grew to become the Families and Children Study, sampling (after 2001) all families in Great Britain, and continuing until 2008.[15]

The first (1991) survey had two interesting advantages: it included an elaborated set of measures of hardship and it had a large sample of 2,300 *low-income* families with children, including nearly 1,000 lone parents. In this way, it placed a magnifying glass over the distribution of material hardship among children in Great Britain and their families. The subsequent surveys included both new cross-section surveys of low-income families and, later, all-income families, together with follow-up surveys of the same families over time.

The Policy Studies Institute hardship index used the list of items familiar from the Townsend and Policy and Social Exclusion surveys, but added measures of savings and debt, because some low-income families will first use up savings and then go into debt to maintain their material wellbeing. Respondents were also asked to say whether there were other things *they* felt were essential, but that at the moment they could not afford for themselves and for their children.

The index was then constructed in two stages, adding a point for families who could not afford:

- two or more food items;
- three or more clothing and leisure items;
- four or more consumer durables;
- to repay two or more problem debts or to afford any savings;[16]

and who had:

- other spontaneously mentioned unmet needs for adults *and* children; *and*
- the highest levels of financial anxiety.

The advantage of a large sample of low-income families enabled the Policy Studies Institute measures to distinguish between the poor and the poorest. Much of the research was aimed at testing the effectiveness of benefits, both in terms of incentives and wellbeing, so keeping families with children out of the worst poverty was thought to be the essential focus. Consequently, this was a very conservative measure of poverty: only those scoring three or more out of these six hardship scores were said to be in 'severe hardship'.

In 1991, only 5 per cent of families with 'modest' incomes (just above qualifying for in-work benefits) were in severe hardship, rising to 24 per cent among out-of-work couples with children and to 30 per cent among lone parents.

Throughout the programme, this measure was updated in ways similar to the Poverty and Social Exclusion surveys. By 1999, the index had been further developed, creating a nine-point scale:[17]

- reports two or more problems with accommodation and cannot afford to repair (if owner);
- lives in overcrowded accommodation;
- cannot afford to keep home warm;
- worries about money almost all the time and runs out of money most weeks;
- has no bank account and has two or more problem debts;
- has a relative material deprivation score on food items in the highest 7.5 per cent;
- has a relative material deprivation score on clothing items in the highest 7.5 per cent;
- has a relative material deprivation score on consumer durables in the highest 7.5 per cent;
- has a relative material deprivation score on leisure activities in the highest 7.5 per cent.

When, after 2001, all families were sampled in the Families and Children Study, about 5 per cent to 8 per cent of families in Great Britain were found to be in severe hardship at any one time, about 20 per cent registered some hardship and about 70 per cent none. As you would expect, nearly all cases of severe hardship were found among low-income families, but the Policy Studies Institute surveys throughout the 1990s also showed that the experience of hardship was socially structured too.

- Among those families above the 60 per cent of median income poverty line, even among those only just over the line, severe hardship was rare.
- Low-income families below the poverty line who nevertheless had some of the characteristics of better-off families – owner-occupiers, non-manual jobs, better education, married rather than cohabiting couples, and so on – were much less likely to experience severe hardship compared with others whose incomes were similarly poor.
- Low-income families living in social rented accommodation, in manual or routine work, or with few qualifications, were far more likely to be in severe hardship.
- Lone parents were *six times* more likely to be in severe hardship than other families (Figure 4.1).

This pattern of socially structured hardship continued to be found consistently throughout the following two decades. Trend income over several years, rather than income at any one point in time, was the problem. A recurring lack of regular wages left typically about a third of out-of-work families with children in severe hardship. But even about a quarter of those working and receiving tax credits[18] also remained in severe hardship.

Figure 4.1:

Hardship among couples and lone parents

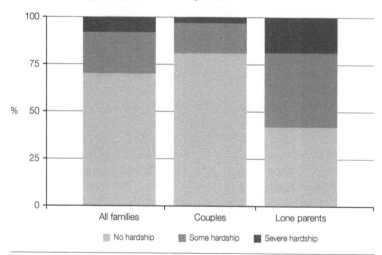

Source: S Vegeris and J Perry, *Families and Children 2001: living standards and the children*, Department for Work and Pensions Research Report No.190, June 2003

Many had moved into work from periods of unemployment and their living standards were yet to catch up – especially so since, in the early 1990s, the net gain from moving into work was, on average, about £10 a week.

More money, less hardship

In October 1999 the Labour government raised both universal and means-tested out-of-work benefits, crucially increasing child benefit for the first child by 26 per cent over two years. The allowance for the youngest children (aged under 11) for families on income support rose by 83 per cent. Out-of-work families got an extra £40 a week. For those in paid work, to realign their incentives, family credit was replaced by working families' tax credit, paying higher rates and imposing a shallower rate of withdrawal against new income (50 per cent as opposed to 70 per cent). In-work families were guaranteed £214 a week in wages and benefits, and childcare support, based on a proportion of actual costs, began to approach realistic levels too.[19] Overall, the incomes of the bottom 10 per cent of all households rose by about a fifth; among those with children and pensioner households, it rose by a quarter.[20]

The extra money began to move families above the poverty line: about 400,000 fewer families were below the poverty line in 2001 compared with 1999, a fall of about 10 per cent. But it affected hardship too. Before 1999, severe hardship among the poorest families had got worse: four out of 10 out-of-work families were in severe hardship in 1999, but so were a quarter of those in work and relying on family credit[21] to raise their wage incomes beyond out-of-work benefit levels. Just two years later, the proportion of these families on working families' tax credit in severe hardship almost vanished, falling from almost a quarter to 8 per cent. Among the out-of-work families, it almost halved, from four in 10 down to less than a quarter: 28 per cent among lone parents, 22 per cent among couples.[22]

The Policy Studies Institute had the good fortune of beginning the Families and Children Study in 1999, just before this pulse of new money reached low-income families. If reassurance were needed, this new money was not spent on marginal luxuries, but went instead to buy children's shoes, clothes, an improved diet and, often it seems, relieving families of petty debt. Among lone parents, for example, the proportion unable to afford 'good quality, new, brand-name clothes/shoes for children' fell from 45 per cent to 32 per cent in two years. A modest rise in income does lift low-income families out of the worst poverty.

Confirmation of this welcome finding was provided by Paul Gregg and colleagues, who examined changes in the expenditure patterns of low-income households using the Family Expenditure Surveys, comparing 1995/97 with 2000/03.[23] They found:

> ... children in low-income families catching up in terms of their families' spending in the overall areas of housing and utilities, food, clothing, leisure goods and services, and motoring and travel.

> The evidence also suggests reduced spending on alcohol and tobacco, perhaps because of an increase in other opportunities for leisure or because of a decrease in stress or depression. Moreover, when we look in detail within these broad spending categories, we find gains for low-income children in spending on specific items such as children's clothing and footwear, fruit and vegetables, and books. Low-income families with children are also catching up in terms of ownership of durable goods, in particular, a car or van, and a telephone, both items that are increasingly essential for employment and for social relations.

We will return to the question of movements in and out of poverty in Chapter 8.

By 2005, the Families and Children Study had adopted a different approach again and calculated a score for each family according to the number of items the family could not afford, weighted by the number of other families who actually had each of the 34 items.[24] While the progress made earlier had been broadly maintained, the familiar inequalities remained. For example, while only 2 per cent of owner-occupiers lacked two or more of the essential clothing items, 18 per cent of social tenants went without them. The weighted overall deprivation score for couples with children was 3.3, but for lone parents it was 12. The families in the richest fifth of incomes hardly registered at all on this deprivation index, but the poorest fifth scored 14. The score for Black families was twice that for White families.[25]

Figure 4.2:

The effects of additional income on levels of hardship

Percentage of families receiving family credit/working families' tax credit in severe hardship

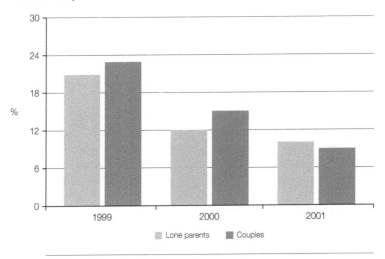

Percentage of out-of-work familes in severe hardship

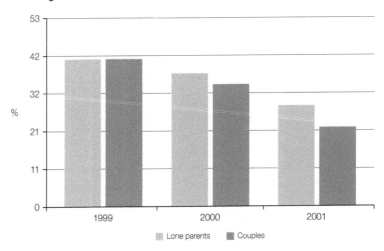

Source: S Vegeris and J Perry, *Families and Children 2001: living standards and the children*, Department for Work and Pensions Research Report No.190, June 2003

The Family Resources Survey

By 2003 it became clear that we ought to be monitoring deprivation and hardship on an annual basis. This job was given to the Family Resources Survey, on behalf of the Department for Work and Pensions. A review[26] decided on a few key items to track and the most recent results are shown for 2015/16 in Table 4.3.

Many of the 2015/16 results align well with the Poverty and Social Exclusion survey in 2012. Nine per cent say they cannot afford to heat their homes properly, a third had no savings and took no holiday, and 7 per cent were falling behind with bills.

The results for families with dependent children are particularly striking – almost half lived in households which took no holiday. More than one in four children lived in families who could not save – rising to two-thirds among the poorest fifth of families. One in ten lived in inadequately heated homes and had parents who were getting behind with bills, again rising to 20 per cent among the poorest fifth. Among the child-related items, 16 per cent of parents could not provide older children of different sexes with separate rooms, a substantially higher figure than the 9 per cent in the Poverty and Social Exclusion study. These are clear indicators that austerity measures and low wage growth are placing pressure on low-income families' ability to maintain their households. Minorities similar to the numbers in the 2012 Poverty and Social Exclusion study reported that they could not provide children with social activities and a proper diet. Among the poorest fifth of families, for example, 8 per cent of children were denied fresh fruit or vegetables each day, 13 per cent could not entertain friends or go on trips, and 3 per cent had no winter coat.

Hardship or income?

As measures of poverty, both income and deprivation have their supporters and critics. We began this chapter warning that no amount of qualification of the questions asked can quite remove the subjectivity in the answers that survey respondents give. Older people, for example, are noticeably more likely to deny they need things that the majority of people think they ought to need. And the extent to which hardship items themselves are seen as necessities can change rapidly. But income too can be a less precise measure than most would expect. Income can vary week by week and many benefits in kind are not measured as income. And sur-

Table 4.3:

Family Resources Survey: adult and child deprivation, 2015/16

Adult items	Percentage of children living in households that 'cannot afford' each item	Percentage of all working-age adults who say they 'cannot afford' each item	Child items	Percentage of children living in households that 'cannot afford' each item for their children
Money to decorate home	19	13	Outdoor space/facilities to play safely	7
Holiday away from home one week a year, not with relatives	43	32	Enough bedrooms for every child aged 10+ of a different sex to have her/his own bedroom	14
Home contents insurance	22	14	Celebrations on special occasions	2
Make savings of £10 or more a month	41	31	Leisure equipment, such as sports equipment or a bicycle	6
Replace worn-out furniture	32	22	At least one week's holiday away from home with family	34
Replace broken electrical goods	23	15	Hobby or leisure activity	6
Money to spend on self each week	36	21	Have friends round for tea or a snack once a fortnight	7
Keep house warm	11	9	Go on school trip at least once a term	4
Keep up to date with bills	9	7	Go to a playgroup at least once a week	4
			Attend organised activity once a week	8
			Eat fresh fruit and/or vegetables every day	3
			Have a warm winter coat	1

Source: Department for Work and Pensions, *Households Below Average Income: an analysis of the income distribution, 1994/95–2015/16*, 2017, Tables 4.7b and 4.8b from the Family Resources Survey, 2014/15. See also House of Commons Library Briefing Paper No. 7096, May 2017, p34.

vey respondents simply mis-report their income – many self-employed respondents (whose numbers have recently increased) notoriously report low, or even negative, incomes at the time of asking, but seem to have living standards as good as those of most other people.

It is not surprising, therefore, that the relationship between income and hardship, measured in the same survey, can show up some puzzling patterns. Looking at the Families and Children Study, for example, Vegeris and Perry noted that 40 per cent of families with dependent children whose incomes were below the 60 per cent of the median poverty line said that they were not in any real hardship, even when the self-employed were left out.[27] On the other hand, 22 per cent of those below the poverty line were in severe hardship compared with only 4 per cent of families above. So, essentially, 85 per cent of families in severe hardship have incomes below the poverty line, though some reports of hardship are also found among the better off. Even a few of the richer households might say they are unable adequately to heat their large homes, for example. Many of those above the poverty line who are still in some hardship tend to be those who have only recently returned to work after a spell of unemploy-

Figure 4.3:
Living standards and income

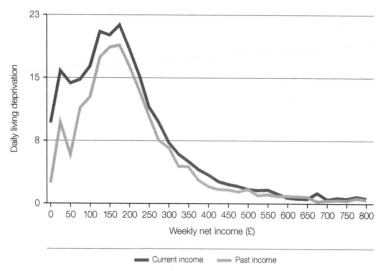

Source: M Brewer and others, *The Living Standards of Familes With Children Reporting Low Incomes*, Institute for Fiscal Studies, 2009

ment. Also, having your children grow up can raise your position in the equivalised income range above the poverty line, but it will not instantly furnish your home with all the goods and services that the general public agrees you need. This especially applies to consumer durables and debt clearance. However, ignoring those reporting both unrealistically low incomes (below £100 a week) and a lack of hardship, the relationship between income and the measures of daily living standards (food, clothes, and so on) is pretty convincing, as shown in Figure 4.3.

It follows therefore that a more secure measure of poverty might be found in combining income and deprivation. So from 2004/05 onwards, part of the purpose of including annual measures of hardship in the Family Resources Survey was to gauge progress towards a new child poverty target: to eliminate severe poverty. Two such combined measures were chosen for the analysis of *Households Below Average Income* series:

• children in households that were below 70 per cent of the contemporary median income and in material hardship;[28] *and*

Figure 4.4:

Proportion of children falling below severe poverty thresholds, 2014/15

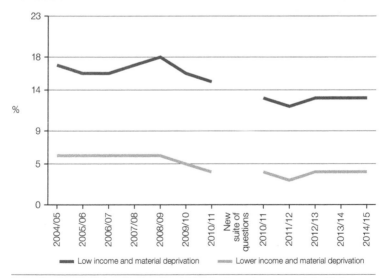

Source: Department for Work and Pensions, *Households Below Average Income: an analysis of the income distribution, 1994/95–2015/16*, 2017

- children in households that were below 50 per cent of contemporary median income and in material hardship.

Figure 4.4 shows what progress has been made up to 2014/15.

It is important to note that the first measure (below 70 per cent and in hardship) rose ominously as the UK fell into recession after 2008, but fell back again to about 15 per cent of children by 2010/11. Interestingly, in common with the Families and Children and the Poverty and Social Exclusion surveys, the Family Resources Survey too has had to modernise its range of deprivation items from 2010 onwards. These changes reduced the percentage below the threshold down to 13 per cent, where it has remained since. Meanwhile, the severe hardship measure (below 50 per cent and in hardship) followed a similar pattern over 10 years, placing just 6 per cent below this severe threshold and 4 per cent following the revisions in the material deprivation items. This means that, according to the government's own criterion and using the more favourable measure of income before deduction of housing costs, half a million UK children are in intolerable degrees of poverty.[29]

Figure 4.5:

Percentage of families experiencing child material deprivation in 2014/15, by income poverty status

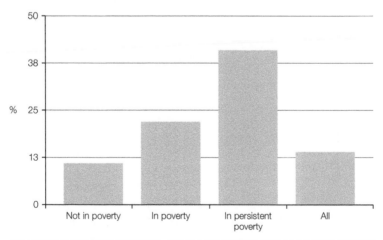

Source: J Cribb, A Hood, R Joyce and A Norris Keiller, *Living Standards, Poverty and Inequality in the UK: 2017*, Institute for Fiscal Studies, 2017

A theme of this book is that persistent poverty does the greatest damage, especially to children's wellbeing. Important new research by the Institute for Fiscal Studies analysed five years of longitudinal data in the Understanding Society survey, between 2010 and 2015.[30] It showed that while living in poverty at one point in time (which it calls 'snapshot poverty') doubles a family's risk of experiencing child deprivation, being in persistent poverty (at least three years out of four) almost doubles their risk again (Figure 4.5).

The authors say:

> ... having a low household income, even on a temporary basis, is associated with a markedly higher probability that a child is materially deprived. Whereas 14% of all children are materially deprived, the rate is 11% among children who are not in snapshot poverty and 22% among children in snapshot poverty but not in persistent poverty. The risk of being materially deprived increases even more dramatically for children who are in poverty on a persistent basis, with over 40% of children in this group being materially deprived. More formal statistical analysis finds that, looking at households with below average income, their income in the three years prior to the current period is predictive of current material deprivation, even when comparing people with the same current income.

Pensioners and hardship

We saw in the previous chapter that income poverty among UK pensioners has fallen. The annual 'triple-locked' improvement in their state pensions[31] and the growth of private pensions among them has reduced the proportion below the poverty line to less than one-seventh by 2015/16 (Table 3.1). Is this improvement reflected in their experience of hardship?

It has proved quite difficult over recent years to get pensioners to admit to experiencing hardship. Their frame of reference tends to be their memories of how poor many of their own grandparents and parents were in old age.[32] Their expectations and needs are different from those of younger people, or they are differently felt and expressed, or perhaps both. The approach now adopted by the Family Resources Survey is to ask pensioner households[33] whether or not they have each item in a list of goods and services, including items important to older people, like getting a taxi if they need one and getting their hair done. For each item they do not have, they are asked more widely why they go without.

Table 4.4:

Hardship among pensioner households, 2014/15

	Percentage of all pensioners who do not have each item %	Percentage of pensioners in bottom fifth of incomes who do not have each item %	Most common reason given for going without (all pensioners)
At least one filling meal a day	1	1	n/a
Go out socially at least once a month	22	29	Poor health (36%)
See friends or family at least once a month	4	5	Other reason (28%)
Take a holiday away from home	37	50	Poor health (35%)
Able to replace cooker if it broke down	9	12	No money for this (87%)
Home kept in a good state of repair	3	5	No money for this (57%)
Heating, electrics, plumbing and drains working	2	2	No money for this (48%)
Have a damp-free home	7	9	Other reason (55%)
Home kept adequately warm	4	6	No money for this (71%)
Able to pay regular bills	3	4	No money for this (79%)
Have a telephone to use, whenever needed	4	5	Not something I want (41%)
Have access to a car or taxi, whenever needed	11	20	No money for this (30%)
Have hair done or cut regularly	10	12	No money for this (26%)
Have a warm waterproof coat	1	2	Not something I want (35%)
			Most common reason given for saying 'yes'
Able to pay an unexpected expense of £200	10	14	Use savings (45%)

Source: Department for Work and Pensions, *Households Below Average income: analysis of the income distribution, 1994/95–2014/15*, 2016

The picture in Table 4.4 might have surprised, and would probably have pleased, Peter Townsend. In 1969, more than half of his respondents over 60 said that they could not heat their homes adequately.[34] In 2014/15, just 4 per cent of pensioners complained of inadequate heating, rising to 6 per cent among the poorest fifth among them – and not all of these said that a lack of money was the problem. This is currently better than the general population (9 per cent), perhaps in part due to the £200 winter fuel allowance received by each pensioner household each year.[35] Most of the constraints now faced by pensioners are, predictably, to do with social participation and mobility. A third took no holiday, rising to half among the poorest pensioners, but again relatively few blamed a lack of money for staying at home: a third said their health would not allow them to go away. Ten per cent could not get their hair done, but only a quarter of these said that money was the reason why. Most pensioners now have a telephone, even among the poorest, and almost half those without said they did not want one.

Despite this relatively benign picture, there is evidence that the inequalities that widened during the past three decades are being exported into old age, despite the levelling effect of people moving from paid work and relying on a pension instead. The Department for Work and Pensions calculates a deprivation index[36] for pensioners, which shows that in 2014/15 just 8 per cent of pensioners exceed the deprivation threshold and were in hardship. But 23 per cent of pensioners who rent their homes from their local authority were in hardship, as were 16 per cent of British Asian pensioners and, remarkably, 33 per cent of Black pensioners. The effect of the growth of private (occupational and personal) pensions is also evident: just 5 per cent of those with such pensions were in hardship on the index, compared with 19 per cent of those relying solely on the state pension.

Conclusions

Regular monitoring of the UK population from several sources has shown that low-income households continue to go without many of the goods and services that the majority, usually a large majority of people, believe no one should go without. Some of these unmet needs are acute: unacceptably large minorities of families are unable to provide adequately for their children, who are ill-fed and go without warm clothes and good shoes. It is possible, in some cases, that such shortcomings are made up by charitable or wider family intervention; but it remains a fact that their parents say they *cannot afford* to look after them properly.

The increased costs of accommodation and fuel, unmatched by corresponding increases in income, have reduced household living conditions over the past two decades, strikingly so for those in the bottom fifth of the income range. This is not just a matter of rising standards and expectations, though these do play a role. Still far too many UK households go without the basics too.

There is encouraging evidence that when more money is available to them, low-income families immediately improve their basic standards of living.

Peter Townsend's great insight, that poverty was about the inability of people on low incomes to participate properly in the common ways of their communities, remains true 40 years later. The 2012 Poverty and Social Exclusion survey provided the simplest summary:

> Almost 12 million people are too poor to engage in common social activities considered necessary by the majority of the population.

The implications for policy are clear: low trend incomes do result in what Paul Spicker called unacceptable hardship. Modest increases in income reduce hardship swiftly and effectively.

Notes

1   B Abel-Smith and P Townsend, *The Poor and the Poorest: a new analysis of the Ministry of Labour's Family Expenditure Surveys of 1953–54 and 1960*, G Bell & Sons, 1965

2   P Townsend, *Poverty in the United Kingdom: a survey of household resources and standards of living*, Allen Lane and Penguin Books, 1979

3   There is a fourth: the British Household Panel Survey, later the Living in Britain survey, now the Understanding Society survey.

4   See, for example, Richard Berthoud's view that 'deprivation scores make an enormous contribution to our understanding of poverty. But they are just indicators, and it is unhelpful to treat them too literally as direct measures of people's experience', R Berthoud and M Bryan, 'Deprivation indicators' in R Berthoud and F Zantomio (eds), *Measuring Poverty: seven key issues*, Institute for Social and Economic Research, University of Essex, 2008, p15

5   J Mack and S Lansley, *Poor Britain*, George Allen & Unwin, 1985

6   See, for example, D Piachaud, 'Peter Townsend and the Holy Grail', *New Society*, 10 September 1981, and J Veit-Wilson, 'Consensual approaches to

poverty lines and social security', *Journal of Social Policy*, 16(2), 1987, pp183–211

7   The Poverty and Social Exclusion team at the University of Bristol has a website that allows visitors to explore the data. See D Gordon and others, *The Impoverishment of the UK*, Poverty and Social Exclusion in the UK, 2013, available at www.poverty.ac.uk

8   During the eight years prior to the 2012 Poverty and Social Exclusion survey, the combined cost of domestic heating fuels and lighting costs doubled in real terms, having fallen throughout the preceding decade. See N Dempsey, C Barton and D Hough, *Energy Prices,* House of Commons Briefing Paper No.04153, 7 March 2016, p3

9   The proportion of the workforce unemployed and seeking work peaked in December 1983 at over 13 per cent, levels unmatched since the Great Depression of the 1930s.

10 'Going backwards: 1983–2012', Poverty and Social Exclusion at http://poverty.ac.uk/pse-research/going-backwards-1983-2012

11 Caroline Mortimer in *The Independent*, 17 July 2015

12 G Main and J Bradshaw, 'Child poverty in the UK: measures, prevalence and intra-household sharing', *Critical Social Policy*, 36(1), 2016, pp38–61. See also T Ridge, *Child Poverty and Social Exclusion: from a child's perspective*, Policy Press, 2002

13 G Main and J Bradshaw, *Child Poverty and Social Exclusion: final report of 2012 PSE study*, Poverty and Social Exclusion in the UK, 2014

14 M Magadi and S Middleton, *Severe Child Poverty in the UK*, Save the Children, 2007

15 But not Northern Irish families.

16 By including debt and savings, the Policy Studies Institute researchers hoped to identify families who had, for a while at least, maintained living standards their incomes alone could not support by drawing on savings and then by borrowing, but whose strategy had now left them in unmanageable debt.

17 A Marsh and others, *Low-income Families in Britain: work, welfare and social security in 1999,* Department of Social Security Research Report No.138, 2001

18 Tax credits were preceded by equivalent benefits, known as family credit, since only families with children qualified for in-work wage supplementation. See A Marsh and S McKay, *Families, Work and Benefits,* Policy Studies Institute, 1993

19 HM Treasury, *Tackling Poverty and Making Work Pay: tax credits for the 21st century,* The Modernisation of Britain's Tax and Benefit System No.6, March 2000

20 T Sefton and H Sutherland, 'Inequality and poverty under New Labour', in J Hills and K Stewart (eds), *A More Equal Society? New Labour, poverty, inequality and exclusion*, Policy Press, 2005

21 Family credit was replaced by working families' tax credit during 1999. However, families on family credit in 1999 were not allowed to transfer directly on to working families' tax credit and there was a low rate of new take-up of working families' tax credit. So the majority of qualifying families remained on family credit until 2000.

22 S Vegeris and J Perry, *Families and Children 2001: living standards and the children*, Department for Work and Pensions Research Report No.190, 2003

23 P Gregg, J Waldfogel and E Washbrook, *Expenditure Patterns Post-Welfare Reform in the UK: are low-income families starting to catch up?* Centre for Analysis of Social Exclusion, London School of Economics, 2005

24 2005 was the last year that the Families and Children Study carried a full list of deprivation items.

25 L Hoxhallari, A Conolly and N Lyon, *Families with Children in Britain: findings from the 2005 Families and Children Survey (FACS)*, Department for Work and Pensions Research Report No.424, 2007, Table 10.7

26 See S McKay and S Collard, *Developing Deprivation Questions for the Family Resources Survey*, Working Paper No.13, Personal Finance Research Centre, University of Bristol, 2003, and for subsequent revisions see S McKay, *Review of the Child Material Deprivation Items in the Family Resources Survey*, Department for Work and Pensions Research Report No.746, 2011

27 S Vegeris and J Perry, *Families and Children 2001: living standards and the children*, Department for Work and Pensions Research Report No.190, 2003

28 A family is in low income and material deprivation if it has a material deprivation score of 25 or more and a household income below 70 per cent (50 per cent) of contemporary median income, before housing costs. See Department for Work and Pensions, *Households Below Average Income (HBAI): Quality and Methodology Information Report 2013/14*, 2015

29 See Department for Work and Pensions, *Households Below Average Income: analysis of the income distribution 1994/95 to 2014/15*, 2016, Table 4.5tr

30 J Cribb, A Hood, R Joyce and A Norris Keiller, *Living Standards, Poverty and Inequality in the UK: 2017*, Institute for Fiscal Studies, 2017

31 The basic state pension is increased each April by the higher of: the growth in average earnings, the Consumer Price Index (CPI), or 2.5 per cent.

32 A follow-up survey by the Department for Work and Pensions on Family Resources Survey respondents from pensioner households concluded that 'expectations for living standards in retirement and comparisons with other people or with their pre-retirement life influenced the extent to which respondents felt "deprived" in terms of their material circumstances.' See M Kotecha, S Arthur and S Coutinho, *Understanding the Relationship Between Pensioner Poverty and Material Deprivation,* Department for Work and Pensions Research Report No.827, 2013

33 It is important to remember that the Family Resources Survey is a household survey that excludes everyone living in institutional care. So the data for pensioners is solely for those remaining in their own homes or living with others.

34 P Townsend, *Poverty in the United Kingdom: a survey of household resources and standards of living*, Allen Lane and Penguin Books, 1979, Table 13.3

35 Pensioners (and anyone else) receiving additional means-tested state benefits get an extra £25 for each full week the temperature falls below freezing.

36 A weighted score ranging between 0 and 100 was calculated for each pensioner, and anyone with a score of 20 or more is said to be experiencing material deprivation. See M Kotecha, S Arthur and S Coutinho, *Understanding the Relationship Between Pensioner Poverty and Material Deprivation,* Department for Work and Pensions Research Report No.827, 2013, p57

Five

Poverty and costs

Summary

- In 2017, the additional basic cost of a child, from birth to age 18, was £75,436 for a couple family, and £102,627 for a lone-parent family. The full cost, incorporating housing-related and childcare costs, in the same year was £155,142 and £187,120 respectively.
- A couple family with two children, with each parent working full time on the minimum wage, only has 87 per cent of the income it requires to meet the costs of its minimum needs.
- One recent estimate suggests that, using a poverty line adjusted for the costs of disability, the poverty rate for individuals with at least one family member with a disability could be 32 per cent, compared to 25 per cent using an unadjusted poverty line.
- Childcare costs can vary greatly – from £154 a week in Inner London to £101 a week in the West Midlands for 25 hours of care at a nursery for a child under two.
- In London, the poverty rate almost doubles when housing costs are taken into account (from 14 per cent to 27 per cent).

% IN POVERTY

BEFORE HOUSING COSTS   AFTER HOUSING COSTS

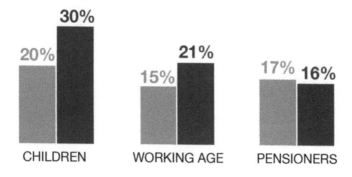

20% / 30%	15% / 21%	17% / 16%
CHILDREN	WORKING AGE	PENSIONERS

- Between 2000 and 2010, richer households saw prices increase by 33 per cent in a decade, compared with 41 per cent for the second poorest decile.

Introduction

In our definition of poverty (see Chapter 2), we described the situation in which people lack the financial resources to have the living conditions and participate in the activities that are mainstream in their society. Moreover, we discussed the view that poverty is a moral, as well as a descriptive, term: that it carries with it the implication and the moral imperative that something should be done about it. At its most fundamental, this must involve bridging the gap between the incomes people have, and the goods and services they need to buy to live and participate in the society in which they find themselves. It is about the incomes and resources people have; but it is also about what things cost.

Policy responses to poverty often focus largely on incomes. But there are occasions when policymakers may have good reasons to try to tackle costs as part of their strategy for reducing poverty. This may be because it is more efficient, because a market failure in a certain area means that costs for low-income households are disproportionately high. More commonly, in the UK, the government may choose to make payments on the basis of particular costs that may vary widely by household locality or circumstances, such as those associated with housing, having a disability, or with children.

Costs or income?

Costs and incomes can be seen as two sides of the same coin: in order not to be poor, a household must have sufficient income (or other resources) to pay for, or otherwise obtain, the living conditions and lifestyle of the mainstream population. (In developed societies, as we discuss below, many things are provided free of charge – for example, education and healthcare.) For a household, it matters little whether a decrease in income or an increase in the cost of this basket of goods is what pushes them below this standard. The difficulties remain the same (although the way they are reflected in measures of poverty may be different).

One attempt to quantify what a sufficient income would be in relation to contemporary costs in the UK is the Joseph Rowntree Foundation's 'minimum income standard'.[1] This is based on research with members of the public, informed by experts where needed, seeking to identify a 'low cost but acceptable' set of goods and services that different types of household need (though it is not explicitly a poverty measure). The actual cost of these items can then be calculated, producing detailed budgets for 107 household types. These budgets are updated annually to take account of inflation and changes in the tax and benefit systems, and a biennial 'rebasing' reconsiders the basket of goods to take into account changing social expectations. In recent years, for example, certain social expectations have been revised downwards, in light of the austerity agenda and falling real incomes.

In general, when economists and politicians talk about incomes, they talk about 'real incomes', meaning incomes which have been adjusted for general price inflation. Assuming that all households are affected in broadly the same way by price changes (an assumption we discuss below), this means that we have already factored in changes in costs when we compare incomes across years. This approach also helps us to understand the impact of changes made to taxes and benefits – for example, recent freezes in benefit rates – which allows us to quantify the 'real-terms' cuts that these entail. For example, as a result of these freezes, child benefit would need to be 20.6 per cent higher in 2017/18 than it is in order to account for inflation since 2010/11.[2]

But this assumption – that all households are affected in broadly the same way – is not necessarily a fair one. Lower income households do not spend their incomes in the same proportions as those on average or high incomes. With less money to go round, they tend to spend a higher proportion of their income on what might be termed 'essentials' – things like food, energy and housing. In recent years, there have been times when the cost of food and energy in particular has risen rapidly, while average inflation has been relatively low, due to lower price increases for goods and services more likely to be bought by those on higher incomes. Uprating of benefits and pensions (the process by which their levels are increased year by year) and wage settlements that are based on, or informed by, the general inflation rate can hide differential inflation rates faced by different groups, particularly at times when the costs of essentials are rising fastest.

Beyond these caveats around inflation, there are some costs that are so significant for different reasons that we may want to consider them separately. Housing is the cost that varies most across the country, and one over which people on low incomes, in particular, often have very little control. So – as Beveridge acknowledged[3] – it needs to be treated as a distinct issue by public policy. Childcare poses analogous challenges for policymakers. In each case, for an individual low-income household, the cost can represent a very high proportion of household income; but these costs can vary widely according to individual circumstances, so there are limits to the extent to which a policy focus on incomes can relieve or reduce poverty.

Governments may choose to regulate or otherwise intervene in markets for essential goods and services. In the UK, there are some markets in which there are universal service obligations, where providers are required to provide a basic level of service to everyone, regardless of geography and cost. Regulators exist in a number of these markets, notably those for utilities such as water and energy, and are obliged to pay careful attention to particular categories of consumer, including those with low incomes, usually as part of their customer protection role. Regulation can be a strong tool in tackling the 'poverty premium' in goods and essential services. Nationalisation, in which markets are not merely regulated, but provision is taken on by the public sector, is another form of government intervention that can help with the costs of essentials. Water and sewerage services were privatised in England and Wales in 1989, but not in Scotland. Since then, bills have increased by more than 40 per cent in real terms in England and Wales, but are £40 a year lower, on average, in Scotland.[4]

There are also additional costs specific to certain circumstances. CPAG estimates annually the additional cost that children create for a family. This leads to powerful arguments for policies tailored to the needs of families with children, particularly with regard to social security. And there are also additional costs associated with having a disability, and for which there is a strong case for making specific provision. In each case, the factor that creates additional costs may also act to reduce earning potential (for example, being able to work fewer hours), which creates further complications, this time on the income side.

Meanwhile, being in poverty can result in paying more for certain goods and services. Often known as a 'poverty premium', this situation can lead to calls for governments to take action to try to ensure that the markets in question better serve low-income customers. Policymakers should also be sensitive to such disparities when assessing the incomes people need to live on.

Finally, we are used in the UK to certain needs being met as standard by public provision. Universal healthcare and universal education relieve people of what would otherwise be substantial costs, or a dangerous or undesirable lack of access to what we think of as essential basic services. The 'social wage' offered by such provision is substantial in the UK, and fulfils needs that would otherwise have to be met from private incomes. Yet the parameters for which costs are met and which are not met are not fixed. This is true both within publicly funded services (for example, who pays for prescriptions or for school meals) and with regard to the question of which costs are a public, and which are a private, responsibility.

The cost of children

One of the main reasons that families with children are at particular risk of poverty is that children bring additional costs (but no expectation that they should earn money to cover them). There is a long history in social policy, both in the UK and abroad, of the state playing a role in helping to meet these costs.[5] The additional costs associated with children not only increase the poverty risk, they also affect all parents across the income spectrum.

CPAG's annual *Cost of a Child* looks at quantifying the specific costs of children. Based on the Joseph Rowntree Foundation's 'minimum income standard' and its benchmark of a low-cost but acceptable standard of living, the calculation tells us the minimum additional cost to a household of raising a child (which varies according to the characteristics of that household – whether it is headed by a single adult or two adults, and how many children are already in the household). This provides us with an estimate of how much – at a minimum – parents *should* have available to spend on the additional cost of children, and thus provides a method of assessing the adequacy of government support for meeting those costs.

This research splits costs into 'basic' and 'full' costs – with the latter also including estimates of the additional costs children bring in the form of housing (extra bedrooms), council tax and childcare, assuming no government support – costs which, as we will discuss, can vary enormously. The additional cost of a child is expressed separately for couple and lone-parent families, on the basis that there is a social expectation that parents will forgo some spending on themselves when they have children, and that couples have two sets of discretionary spending to squeeze, where lone parents have only one (although for those parents whose incomes fall below the basic minimum, such discretionary spending will be limited). In 2017, the additional basic cost of a child, from birth to age 18, was

Figure 5.1:

The basic cost of a child, from birth to age 18

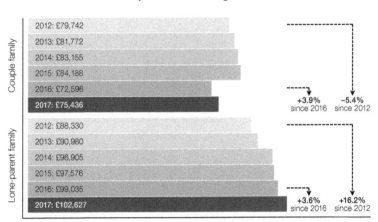

Note: This figure shows the basic additional cost of a child. Since housing, childcare and council tax can vary and are sometimes wholly or partly covered by state support, this basic calculation excludes those costs.

Source: D Hirsch, *The Cost of a Child in 2017*, Child Poverty Action Group, 2017

£75,436 for a couple family, and £102,627 for a lone-parent family. The full cost in the same year was £155,142 and £187,120 respectively.

At present in the UK, there are two main types of government support to meet the general costs of children (as opposed to specific support for childcare, housing or disability). Child benefit was until 2013 a universal benefit, available for the mothers (or designated other main carers) of all children, at a higher rate for the first child. From 2013, it has been near universal, with only those on high incomes (above £50,000 a year) having effectively to repay some or all of the benefit, on a sliding scale, through an additional 'high income child benefit charge' (unless they choose to give up their entitlement). The universal nature of child benefit means that it reaches many poor children that specific targeted benefits may not: the most recent government estimates suggest a 96 per cent take-up rate (among those eligible), against 86 per cent for child tax credit and 91 per cent for working tax credit, among families with children.[6]

The second type of support is through child tax credit, which is a means-tested payment. Tax credits can be seen as acting both to help with the costs of a child and as a form of earnings replacement and/or supplement. The distinction between child tax credit and working tax

Figure 5.2:

The full cost of a child, from birth to age 18

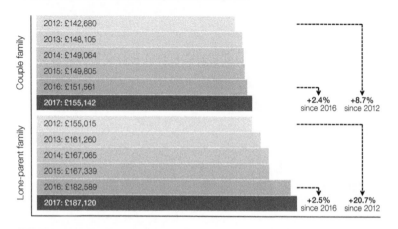

Note: This figure shows the basic additional cost of a child including estimates of housing, council tax and childcare (assuming parents work), not taking account of government help such as housing benefit and childcare support in tax credits.

Source: D Hirsch, *The Cost of a Child in 2017*, Child Poverty Action Group, 2017

credit can be seen to mirror the blurred boundary between income replacement and meeting costs, though even that distinction will disappear under universal credit, which is in the process of being rolled out to replace the functions of tax credits.

We can consider the relationship between policy and the cost of a child by looking at the adequacy of the financial support designed to contribute towards the cost of children. In addition, we can look beyond social security to labour market policy, and compare the cost of a child with the income of a parent working full time at the national minimum wage. Finally, we can consider how well typical incomes, when combined with available support, allow families with children to attain an acceptable standard of living, by considering the relationship between costs and median incomes.

Table 5.1:

The cost of a child against benefits and wages

A. How much extra a child adds to family costs, and how much benefits contribute towards this cost	Minimum additional cost of a child (averaged for first and second child)	
	Couple	Lone parent
1. Basic cost over 18 years	£75,436	£102,627
2. Full cost over 18 years	£155,142	£187,120
3. Percentage of basic cost covered by child benefit	21%	16%
4. Percentage of basic cost covered by child benefit plus maximum child tax credit	94%	69%
B. The extent to which families have enough to cover the minimum cost of living	Net income as a percentage of minimum family costs (family with two children, aged 3 and 7)	
	Couple	Lone parent
5. Not working	58%	60%
6. Each parent working full time on the minimum wage for people aged 25 and over	87%	82%
7. Each parent working full time on the median wage	108%	86%

Note: 'Basic cost' does not include rent, childcare or council tax. 'Net income' refers to disposable income, after subtracting rent, childcare and council tax.

Source: D Hirsch, *The Cost of a Child in 2017*, Child Poverty Action Group, 2017

Section A in Table 5.1 allows us to see what a small proportion of costs child benefit currently covers, and how significant the contribution made by child tax credit is – for those who receive it. It is important to note, however, that, with adult benefit levels so low, this will still leave a family as a whole far short of what it needs for an adequate standard of living (as defined by the 'minimum income standard') – as we can see in section B. This section also shows how all this taken together leaves a family with each parent working full time on the minimum wage short of meeting their basic needs. Finally, we can see how even working full time on the median wage is not sufficient for a lone parent with two children to meet all their costs.

We have described the financial support on offer to families with children as being about taxpayers playing a role in meeting the costs of children. And, certainly, there is some logic for this: with the need to raise the future workers and taxpayers of tomorrow, and with what we know about the importance of household income for life chances, the state has a strong and legitimate interest in ensuring that children are adequately provided for.

There is, however, an additional way of conceptualising such support. Lifecycle redistribution describes the idea that a major function of social security is to help individuals and households smooth the balance of income and costs over their lifetime.[7] So, for example, a working-age adult without children to support may have relatively low costs and a high amount of time available to work, while a parent faces the additional costs of children and has fewer free hours in which to work. The working-age adult without children may therefore pay relatively high taxes (for any given level of hourly earnings, given that s/he is likely to be working longer hours), while the parent may work fewer hours, while receiving state support in the form of children's benefits. At any point in time, one could say that there is a redistribution of income from the adult without children to the parent. But, at different points in time, the childless adult and the parent may be the *same person*, redistributing to themselves across their lifetime.[8] In 2015, the Institute for Fiscal Studies estimated that 56.6 per cent to 59.4 per cent of redistribution is 'intrapersonal': more than half of redistribution through the tax and benefit systems is effectively redistribution across individuals' lifetimes, rather than between individuals.[9]

Given that children indisputably bring additional costs – which can be quantified – there is a particularly strong case for supporting families with children on the basis of additional costs. This case is strengthened when one considers that most parents will spend time in the labour market, paying taxes, before and after they are parents in need of assistance. As well as the general costs associated with children, however, there remain several costs faced by parents (and in some cases others) which need to be dealt with separately.

The cost of disability

Many disabilities lead to direct costs associated with those disabilities, which disabled people have little choice but to bear. Meanwhile, in the current UK labour market, having a disability tends to have a negative impact on employment prospects and outcomes. The employment rate for disabled people stands at 49.2 per cent,[10] which, while gradually improving (for example, from 44.9 per cent three years previously), remains well below the general UK employment rate of 75.1 per cent (a gap of 25.9 per cent, compared with 27.9 per cent three years previously).[11] Disabled people who are in work are paid less well: the Papworth Trust reports an average hourly wage of £12.48 for disabled people in 2015, compared with £13.73 for non-disabled people.[12]

There is a strong case for supporting disabled people in meeting the costs of their disability, which the Papworth Trust estimates amount to an average of £550 a month, but which can vary widely. And, indeed, the social security system provides for this. Disability living allowance and its replacement for working-age adults, personal independence payment (in the process of being phased in since 2013), and their equivalent for people aged 65 or over, attendance allowance, all offer regular payments for those assessed as having costs related to their disability. While the maximum possible payments (£141.10 a week in 2017/18 for disability living allowance/personal independence payment and £83.10 a week for attendance allowance) fall short of the estimated average costs, they can make a substantial contribution towards them.

As we will see in Chapter 6, people with disabilities have a heightened risk of poverty, though disability benefits do play a role in reducing those rates. The poverty rate for disabled people does not, however, take account of the costs of disability. The New Policy Institute attempted in 2014 to adjust the poverty rate to take these into account, based on an adjusted poverty line (increased by 24 per cent or 35 per cent, depending on household composition).[13] It found that including a measure of the extra costs added 2–3 per cent to the overall working-age adult poverty rate, rising to an increase of 4–6 per cent if only those working-age adults with a disabled family member were included. Including children and pensioners in families with disabled working-age adults facing additional costs caused a 3–5 per cent increase in poverty. Where additional costs increased the poverty line by 24 per cent, there would be an additional 380,000 working-age adults and 960,000 individuals overall in poverty. At the 35 per cent increase in the poverty line, these figures would be 510,000 and 1.3 million respectively.

Direct financial support for the extra costs associated with disability is clearly one possible policy response, and it is one that exists in the UK, even if only at inadequate levels. Another possible approach would be to conceptualise a 'disability premium' analogous to the poverty premium discussed below, and seek to reduce some of those extra costs directly. A Demos report proposed doing this through: greater levels of suitable housing; improved provision for disabled people in both mainstream and specialist transport; and intervention in markets for specialist equipment, clothing, food and non-prescription medicines.[14]

Table 5.2:

The poverty rates for working-age adults, adjusted for the extra costs of disability

	Regular poverty line	Cost-adjusted poverty line (24%)	Cost-adjusted poverty line (35%)
	%	%	%
All working adults	22	24	25
Working-age adults with at least one disabled family member	29	33	35
Population	22	25	27
Individuals with at least one disabled family member	25	30	32

Source: T MacInnes and others, *Disability, Long-term Conditions and Poverty*, New Policy Institute, 2014

Childcare

As well as the additional costs associated with children, a second major reason why families with children are particularly vulnerable to poverty is that their earning potential is reduced as their caring responsibilities increase. For many families, formal childcare is an essential tool in helping them to mitigate this impact, and to find the balance of paid work and time with children that suits their family.

But childcare can create substantial costs. The Family and Childcare Trust has, since 2002, conducted an annual survey of childcare costs in Great Britain. Its most recent results, published in March 2017, show how costs are particularly high for the youngest children, at an average of £116.25 a week for under-two-year-olds for 25 hours' care in a nursery.[15] Of course, some families will need more, and some less, care than others, depending on their specific circumstances, including their levels of employment and their access to cheap or free informal childcare. Full-time care is, unsurprisingly, far costlier: defined as 50 hours' care per week, this costs on average £222.36 in a nursery, and only slightly less for older children or for those with a childminder. Cost is not the only consideration: the survey finds that a majority of local authorities in England report that there is not enough care available in their area for two-year-olds entitled to free childcare, for after-school care, for disabled children, and for children whose parents work non-typical hours, such as shift workers. Sufficiency gaps also exist in Scotland and Wales.

Table 5.3:

Average weekly childcare costs, 2017

	25 hours of care in a nursery		25 hours of care from a childminder		Care after school for a child aged 5–11	
	For under-two-year-olds	For two-year-olds	For under-two year-olds	For two+-year-olds	Childminder	After-school club
Scotland	£111.37	£106.16	£105.25	£104.53	£62.22	£55.71
Wales	£101.42	£102.30	£101.03	£101.03	£55.43	£45.13
England	£117.43	£113.43	£110.68	£110.11	£68.12	£52.80
Britain	£116.25	£112.38	£109.84	£109.29	£67.11	£52.58

Source: C Harding, B Wheaton and A Butler, *Childcare Survey 2017*, Family and Childcare Trust, 2017

As ever, broad averages hide a great deal of variation. Much of this is at a very local level, but even the regional variations picked up by the Family and Childcare Trust survey are striking. For example, the cost of 25 hours' care with a childminder for an under-two-year-old is 80 per cent higher in Inner London than in the North West.

Table 5.4:

Regional childcare costs for under-two-year-olds (weighted)

	Nursery for under-two-year-olds for 25 hours	Childminder for under-two-year-olds for 25 hours
Inner London	£154.08	£156.67
Outer London	£142.24	£137.38
South East	£136.35	£119.86
South West	£113.29	£103.92
East Midlands	£108.74	£96.98
East of England	£105.58	£116.45
North East	£104.98	£96.93
Yorkshire and the Humber	£101.50	£100.02
North West	£101.00	£86.98
West Midlands	£100.95	£93.44
Scotland	**£111.37**	**£105.25**
Wales	**£101.42**	**£101.03**
England	**£117.43**	**£110.68**
Britain	**£116.25**	**£109.84**

Source: C Harding, B Wheaton and A Butler, *Childcare Survey 2017*, Family and Childcare Trust, 2017

The high cost of childcare can have a substantial impact on family finances, potentially pushing households into poverty. Research conducted at Loughborough University for CPAG and Gingerbread in 2015 estimated this impact through developing a measure of poverty after housing and childcare costs.[16] The headline figure shows a relatively modest increase in the poverty rate – a difference of 0.6 per cent in 2012/13 – pushing an extra 80,663 children into poverty.

Table 5.5:

Number of children living in poverty, after housing and childcare costs, 2008/09 to 2012/13

	Percentage of children			Number of children			Breakdown of difference	
	AHC	AHCC	Difference	AHC	AHCC	Difference	In poverty AHCC not AHC	In poverty AHC not AHCC
2012/13	27.3	27.9	0.6	3,650,273	3,730,936	80,663	132,919	52,256
2010/11	27.3	28.1	0.8	3,609,428	3,713,758	104,330	151,701	47,371
2008/09	30.3	31.0	0.7	3,932,180	4,023,109	90,929	142,211	51,282

Note: AHC = After housing costs. AHCC = After housing and childcare costs

Source: D Hirsch and L Valadez, *How Much Does the Official Measure of Child Poverty Under-estimate its Extent by Failing to Take Account of Childcare Costs?*, Centre for Research in Social Policy, Loughborough University, 2015

These calculations cannot, of course, take into account families with parents who cannot work as much as they would like because of prohibitive childcare costs, in many cases remaining in poverty when affordable childcare might see them lifted out of it. This is reinforced when looking in greater detail at which families are pushed into poverty by childcare costs, as the authors do. The Family Resources Survey of 2012/13 found that the majority of children (58.5 per cent) lived in families that used only informal/free childcare, with only one-fifth (19.5 per cent) paying for all the childcare they used (and the remaining 22 per cent using a mix of paid-for and informal/free childcare). For the group paying for all their childcare costs, the poverty rate after housing and childcare costs increased by a third (from 18.9 per cent to 25.3 per cent), while for those paying more than £50 a week in childcare costs, their poverty risk was not far off trebling (from 8.6 per cent to 23.2 per cent). This level of increased risk would be a powerful disincentive against taking work if it entailed paying for childcare. The report concludes that this is 'almost certainly a much bigger impact' than the direct one on poverty levels.

There is therefore a strong argument for supporting families with childcare costs – to help reduce direct costs and to help parents earn money, reducing poverty directly and increasing parental employment. This support can be offered by either providing families with help with childcare costs or through the government supplying childcare places. In the UK, investment in childcare is largely focused on the demand side (ie, helping families with costs), though this is beginning to shift a little with the introduction and extension of free entitlement.

A patchwork of support is available, in three broad categories: free provision, tax relief schemes, and support through the social security system. England, Scotland and Wales all have universal free entitlement to early education and childcare for three- and four-year-olds. In England, this is currently 15 hours a week during school term times, due to rise to 30 hours a week for working parents (apart from those earning under the equivalent of 16 hours' work at the national 'living wage' or if either parent has an annual income of over £100,000) later this year. Scotland offers 600 hours a year, equivalent to 12.5 hours a week over 48 weeks. Wales offers 10 hours a week for 38 hours a year, with more in some local authorities. Similar support is available for two-year-olds, but with restrictions to entitlement based on income or locality.

Tax-free childcare is being rolled out from April 2017 to replace employer-provided childcare vouchers over time. The two are broadly similar schemes, the main differences being that the new scheme is also available to self-employed parents, and that, where childcare vouchers are only delivered through employers who choose to take part, tax-free childcare is available to all who meet its criteria. Tax-free childcare offers up to £2,000 a year for each child for parents not receiving universal credit or tax credits, provided no parent earns more than £100,000 a year. Childcare vouchers meet up to £55 of childcare costs per parent per week.[17]

Support through the social security system is more generous, but means tested and, in effect, limited to two children. Universal credit now funds 85 per cent of childcare costs, up to a ceiling of £175 a week for one child or £300 a week for two or more children. This is gradually replacing support through working tax credit, which funds up to 70 per cent of childcare costs – with the same ceilings as under universal credit – and additional support for households claiming housing benefit or council tax benefit. The major limitation to this support is the weekly cap on payments, which has remained unchanged since 2005. CPAG's *The Cost of a Child in 2014* found that the cost of childcare outside London had risen by 60 per cent since then, and that average fees for someone working full

Figure 5.3:

Childcare costs and the eligible working tax credit limit, 2005 to 2018

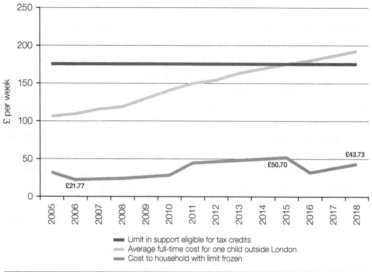

Note: It is assumed that costs continue to increase at the same rate (3.3%) as the latest year.

Source: D Hirsch, *The Cost of a Child in 2014*, Child Poverty Action Group, 2014

time were only just below the limit.[18] As we have seen, costs are highly variable, meaning that the limit will be exceeded in many cases. Figure 5.3 demonstrates both this effect and how consistent and substantial the inflation in childcare costs has been over recent years.

We have discussed elsewhere (Chapter 2, and above) the idea of a 'social wage', a set of essential services that is, by and large, offered to all citizens (or residents). Childcare seems to meet the criteria we might wish to set for inclusion in such a set of services: it is beneficial both to individuals and to the wider economy; lack of take-up limits the earnings of parents and the life chances of children; and it may well be most efficient if delivered as an essential service rather than through financial support to users, since costs and need vary so widely. Crucially, evidence shows that provision of childcare in the maintained sector and in children's centres is on average of higher quality, and thus better for young children and their development, than that provided through the market.[19] In some ways, policy on childcare in the UK is moving in this direction, with the extension of free entitlement, but it is clear that much of the potential of childcare to reduce poverty remains untapped.[20]

Housing

Housing is an essential good that is provided via a number of different markets in the UK, the cost of which varies widely between regions and localities. People on low incomes, in particular, do not usually have a great deal of choice as to how much they pay for housing, and typically pay a higher proportion of their income on housing than do those higher up the income scale. Meeting housing costs represents a particular challenge for policymakers that has long been recognised, with the *Beveridge Report* of 1942 unable to resolve 'the problem of rent'. That is, Beveridge could not see how to provide for the differential costs of housing with a standard level of benefit for all in the social insurance scheme he proposed.

Figure 5.4:

Percentage of children and pensioners living in households below 60% of median income, before and after housing costs

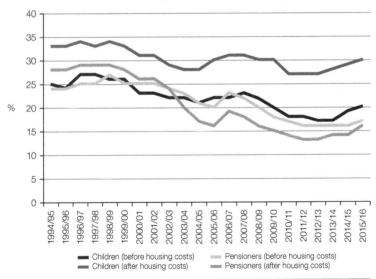

Source: Department for Work and Pensions, *Households Below Average Income: an analysis of the income distribution, 1994/95–2015/16*, 2017

The impact of this specific cost is borne out in the difference between the before housing costs and after housing costs poverty figures. Particularly for children and working-age adults, there is a big gap between the two, while for pensioners, poverty is actually slightly lower after housing costs than before. The gap has opened up over time for children, even as it has closed and then reversed for pensioners (Figure 5.4). Family type matters too: for example, the poverty risk for children in lone-parent families increases from 27 per cent to 47 per cent once housing costs are considered, whereas the increase for children in couple families with children is smaller, from 18 per cent to 24 per cent.[21]

There are also strong regional variations in the impact of housing costs on poverty. Between 2013/14 and 2015/16, 16 per cent of the UK population were in poverty before housing costs were considered. That figure rises to 21 per cent when housing costs are taken into account. But in London, the poverty rate almost doubles – from 14 per cent to 27 per cent – when housing costs are taken into account, whereas the rate in Northern Ireland remains unchanged, at 20 per cent.

Table 5.6:

Percentage of population below 60% of median income, before and after housing costs, 2013/14 to 2015/16

Region/country (three-year average)	Before housing costs %	After housing costs %
England	16	22
North East	18	22
North West	18	22
Yorkshire and the Humber	18	22
East Midlands	18	21
West Midlands	19	24
East of England	14	19
London	14	27
South East	12	18
South West	14	19
Wales	20	23
Scotland	15	19
Northern Ireland	20	20
UK	**16**	**21**

Source: Department for Work and Pensions, *Households Below Average Income: an analysis of the income distribution, 1994/95–2015/16*, 2017

Poverty in the UK is often identified with social housing and, indeed, living in social housing continues to be associated with a high poverty risk. But the private rental sector has increasingly significant associations with poverty as well. Indeed, we can see that the story of the last decade has been of poverty staying relatively stable in the social rented sector and for those owning their homes outright, falling among those buying with a mortgage, and rising among those renting privately. The Institute for Fiscal Studies has recently concluded that it is preferable to measure poverty on an after housing costs basis, at least at the present time, for three reasons: because the extent to which housing cost is a choice is limited for some relatively poor groups; because of the way housing benefit is counted as income for the before housing costs measure; and because recent housing cost trends have been very different for low- and high-income groups.[22]

Table 5.7:

Numbers in poverty according to housing tenure, millions, after housing costs

	2006/07	2011/12	2015/16
Owned outright	2.5	2.0	2.3
Buying with a mortgage	3.2	2.9	2.3
Social rented	4.7	4.2	4.8
Private rented	2.8	3.9	4.7

Source: Department for Work and Pensions, *Households Below Average Income: an analysis of the income distribution, 1994/95–2015/16*, 2017

It is important to note that most of these changes come from changes in the population living in the different tenures, particularly the private rental sector. The risk of being in poverty in any given tenure has in fact remained rather stable, as can be seen in Table 5.8.

Notably, the risk of poverty in the private rented sector nearly doubles (from 19 per cent to 37 per cent) when housing costs are considered, while it also rises substantially for those in the social rented sector (from 28 per cent to 44 per cent), whereas the poverty risk drops slightly after housing costs for those who own their homes outright, and rises only slightly for those who are buying with a mortgage. This too is suggestive of housing costs – but only certain types of housing costs – being a significant driver of poverty.

Table 5.8:

Risk of poverty according to housing tenure, after housing costs

	2006/07 %	2011/12 %	2015/16 %
Owned outright	16	12	13
Buying with a mortgage	12	12	10
Social rented	48	43	44
Private rented	41	37	37

Source: Department for Work and Pensions, *Households Below Average Income: an analysis of the income distribution, 1994/95–2015/16*, 2017

Support for housing costs is generally dealt with separately from other forms of financial assistance to households. As with childcare, this can be through supporting families with the cost of their housing ('demand side') or through the public sector and/or social enterprises providing housing at below market rates ('supply side'). The balance has shifted in the UK towards the former over recent decades, with one estimate suggesting that 81.9 per cent of housing subsidy was on the supply side in 1975/76, but that this had fallen, as part of a general trend, to 33.5 per cent by 2003/04.[23] The government is also ultimately responsible for the structure of the private housing market, and private rents in Great Britain increased by 14.3 per cent in the six years to January 2017. This national average masks substantial regional variations. For example, in August 2015, rents grew at an annual rate of 4.3 per cent in London, but only 0.6 per cent in the North East.[24]

In principle, the government covers the entirety of private rents through housing benefit, on a means-tested basis – ie, all the rent for those on the lowest incomes, reduced on a sliding scale as incomes increase. In reality, changes to entitlement and uprating policy since 2010 mean that, increasingly, households in the private rental sector who are, in theory, entitled to full housing benefit must contribute towards their rent from income intended to meet their living costs. The maximum local housing allowance paid under the housing benefit scheme is based on the 30th percentile of rents in a local area, reduced from the 50th percentile in 2011. At the same time, a decision was made to uprate the level of the local housing allowance in subsequent years by general consumer price index inflation – ie, with reference to general price inflation rather than actual housing market conditions specifically, despite the large regional and local variations in rental inflation. In addition, since 2013, a 'benefit cap' means that housing benefit can be reduced if the value of the benefits a household receives are above a certain level – a level since reduced in February 2017[25] – thus further increasing the gap between housing need and housing support. Under universal credit, the entire award, not just the housing element, may be reduced.

The contribution of housing to poverty is not inevitable: the gap between before and after housing costs poverty has increased in recent years and could equally change in the other direction, while regional variations in the gap show that the ratio between the two is not fixed. Similarly, the changing housing tenure profile of those living in poverty shows that the relationship between housing and poverty is not immutable. It is clear that solving 'the problem of housing' – finding the right mix of supply-side investment, housing subsidy and housing market structure – is an important part of tackling poverty.

The poverty premium

Having a low income can mean paying more for the same basic goods and services, like utilities and banking. This means that a given level of income may not go as far.

No official figures are collected on this 'poverty premium', but attempts have been made to quantify its effect. The most recent attempt was made in January 2017 by the End Child Poverty coalition, using methodology previously developed by Save the Children.[26] It cites a literature review conducted in 2016 at the University of Bristol, which found that the poverty premium arose from actions by individuals and by providers.[27] For low-income households, a poverty premium can arise from a need for tight budgeting control and avoiding behaviour that could upset this: this may entail, for example, preferring to make small, frequent payments. A poverty premium can arise from providers as a result of: pricing structures that penalise low usage; a focus on online service delivery; price offers that target new customers; and a failure to supply products or services that match the needs of low-income households. The premium may also reflect higher costs for providers, such as insuring people who live in high-risk areas, issuing paper bills or receiving payments by cheque.

Table 5.9:
The poverty premium in 2016

	Typical cost	Cost to low-income family	Difference
Loan for £500	£500.00	£944.84	**£444.84**
Basic household item: cooker	£237.33	£780.00	**£542.67**
Cost to cash three £200 cheques	£0	£49.50	**£49.50**
Annual electricity and gas bill combined	£1,249.55	£1,320.95	**£71.40**
Home contents insurance	£45.87	£53.11	**£7.24**
Car insurance	£470.04	£1,010.63	**£540.59**
Total	**£2,502.79**	**£4,159.03**	**£1,656.24**

Source: End Child Poverty, *Feeling the Pinch*, 2017 (all figures sourced in October 2016)

End Child Poverty estimates a potential poverty premium of up to £1,656.24 a year on six goods and services, or 66.2 per cent above the typical cost. This ranges from a relatively modest 15.8 per cent mark-up for home contents insurance, to a huge 228.7 per cent premium on a cooker. Premiums operate in difference ways: for example, those on insurance tend to be due to people in poverty living in higher risk areas, whereas the premium on a basic household item stems from the difference between buying outright from a high street or online retailer and purchasing from a rent-to-own retailer.

The 2016 research at Bristol University estimated a lower average annual poverty premium of £490, based on an estimate of the proportion of households actually incurring the premium. It found the largest factor to be not being on the best fuel tariff (£233 a year), followed by area-based premiums (£84 a year), largely accounted for by premiums related to car insurance and difficulties accessing good value shops.

The End Child Poverty research also identifies, but is unable to quantify, premiums in food costs, travel-to-work costs and cash machine charges. The causes are similar: lack of access to private transport; an inability to buy in advance or in bulk; and living in areas that are poorly served by cheaper shops and services.

Tackling this premium could effectively help reduce poverty, in the sense of reducing the number of people unable to afford a certain lifestyle, without any redistribution of income being required. Such approaches may not, however, register a reduction in poverty on purely income-based measures. This suggests that, where a poverty premium exists, this may mean that such measures understate levels of poverty and hardship.

Differential inflation

Income tends to be described in real terms – that is, adjusted for inflation. For much of the history of the social security system in the UK, payments have been adjusted in line with inflation, and wage settlements usually make reference to it. So when those on low incomes face higher rates of inflation than the average, this can cause hardship and increase poverty, unless policy responds accordingly.

There are a number of possible ways in which to quantify differential inflation and its impact on different income groups, particularly those living in, or close to, poverty. These include: considering how the 'minimum income standard' varies compared with average inflation; how the linked *Cost of a Child*, published annually by CPAG, varies; and efforts to break down official measures of inflation by income decile.

We can look at changes in the minimum income standard over time, from when it was first introduced in 2008, to consider three interlinked questions: how minimum budgets have changed over time for various households; how these changes compare to average inflation; and how much of the changes are attributable to price variation, and how much to altered social expectations.

We can see immediately that, for all family types listed, minimum budgets have increased faster than general inflation – in some cases substantially so – which suggests that differential inflation negatively affects those on low incomes (who are likely to be consuming something closer to the minimum budget than those on higher incomes). Moreover, these differences persist even after changes to social expectations of what the minimum should be are discounted. Indeed, in many cases – quite possibly linked to prevailing economic and political circumstances – expectations have been revised downwards, reducing the impact of the inflation differential on the minimum standard. As a measurement tool, therefore, the minimum income standard sends a strong signal to policymakers about the needs of those on low incomes, and how the cost of meeting those needs is changing.

CPAG's annual *Cost of a Child* report provides an estimate of the minimum additional cost of children to a household, based on the minimum income standard. We are able to see how these costs change from year to year, and compare this with general inflation. This allows us not only to assess the adequacy of government support for meeting those costs in the present, but also to see, year on year, what increase is needed to maintain that level.

Table 5.10:

Minimum income standard: changes in family budgets over time, and how much of this can be attributed to price increases

	April 2008	April 2012	Increase 2008–2012	April 2016	Increase 2012–2016	Overall increase 2008–2016	Attributable to price increases (broken down by components of RPI)	Residual attributable to change in baskets
Consumer Prices Index (2015 = 100)	84	96	14%	100.2	4%	19%		
Actual MIS budgets:								
Lone parent, one child	£210.31	£275.59	31%	£297.59	8%	42%	27%	12%
Lone parent, two children	£282.69	£361.99	28%	£372.21	3%	32%	27%	4%
Lone parent, three children	£379.94	£457.66	20%	£480.57	5%	26%	27%	0%
Couple, one child	£286.64	£374.17	31%	£381.67	2%	33%	29%	3%
Couple, two children	£370.05	£454.52	23%	£455.90	0%	23%	29%	−4%
Couple, three children	£465.71	£557.55	20%	£574.12	3%	23%	29%	−4%
Couple, four children	£504.69	£605.80	20%	£622.58	3%	23%	29%	−4%

Note: Change in baskets calculated such that, compunded with price increases, they explain the overall increase – eg, for lone parent with one child, (1 + 0.12) x (1 + 0.27) = (1 + 0.42).

Source: A Davis and others, *A Minimum Income Standard for the UK in 2016*, Joseph Rowntree Foundation, 2016, Table 6

Figure 5.5:

Percentage of the basic cost of a child covered by child benefit

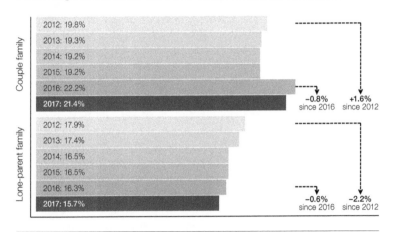

Source: D Hirsch, *The Cost of a Child in 2017*, Child Poverty Action Group, 2017

Figure 5.6:

Percentage of the basic cost of a child covered by child benefit plus maximum child tax credit

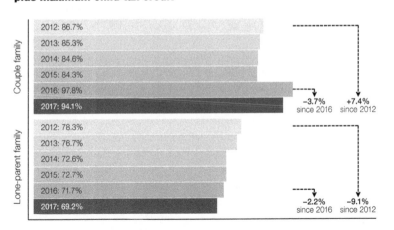

Source: D Hirsch, *The Cost of a Child in 2017*, Child Poverty Action Group, 2017

As we can see, 2016 was the exception in a general downward trend in the adequacy of child benefit and child tax credit for couple families (consistent with the loss in value in real terms). Meanwhile, the trend continued for lone parents. The difference is largely attributable to changing expectations – in this case, that longer travel distances to work may be necessary. This in turn means that families with children say they need a car, whereas working-age people without children say they can manage without. As having a car is a fixed cost, couple parents, being able to split that between the two of them, are better able to absorb it than are lone parents. While this could seem an obscure detail, it reminds us of the social dimension of poverty, changes in which are in this instance better picked up through the costs side of the equation than the income side – though, of course, we need both to make sense of the impact.

Looking more broadly, there have been various attempts to consider how inflation at any given point in time affects different income groups. The theory behind this is rather simple: general price inflation is based on how prices in a basket of goods, selected for their representativeness of the spending of the general population, vary month by month and year by year. Such an average, however, disguises different spending habits among different income groups. (Indeed, in reality, every individual household will have its own unique basket of goods that it purchases.) Measures of differential inflation involve measuring the spending habits of different segments of the population, and then calculating the rate of change of prices for each of these baskets of goods separately.

In 2011, the Institute for Fiscal Studies estimated how inflation had varied by income decile over the 11 years from 2000 to 2010. It found that there had been a strong association between low income and high inflation, with households in the second income decile experiencing average annual inflation of 3.5 per cent, compared with 2.9 per cent in the richest decile. Over the period, these seemingly small differences accumulated: the richer households saw prices increase by 33 per cent in a decade, compared with 41 per cent for the second poorest decile.

The Institute for Fiscal Studies also found that benefit-dependent households had faced a higher inflation rate than those who did not depend on benefits, which is unsurprising given that they tend to be more concentrated in lower income deciles, but is significant given that most benefits were uprated by average inflation during this period, suggesting that the purchasing power of benefit-dependent households went down.

More recently, the Office for National Statistics performed similar calculations against expenditure deciles, as well as income deciles. It found that, between 2003 and 2013, there was a relationship in all deciles

Figure 5.7:

Average annual inflation rates by income decile, 2000 to 2010

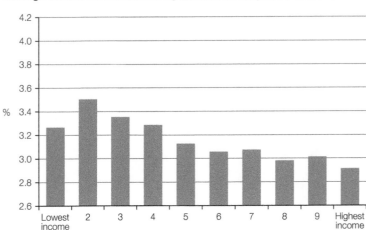

Source: P Levell and Z Oldfield, *The Spending Patterns and Inflation Experience of Low-income Households Over the Past Decade*, Institute for Fiscal Studies, 2011, p31

between expenditure level and inflation level, with those spending the least having the highest inflation rate – varying from 3.7 per cent to 2.3 per cent. It found a similar, but less pronounced, effect with regard to income deciles, with the highest inflation rate being faced by those in the poorest decile, at 2.9 per cent, and the lowest in the seventh (or fourth richest) decile, at 2.4 per cent. Most of the difference in inflation rates was accounted for by changes in the costs of utilities, food and drink, which form a higher proportion of the spending of those with lower incomes or expenditure.

Average price inflation can therefore mask significant variations between households, depending on their spending habits. The cost of essentials has risen faster than general inflation at various points (for example on either side of the 2008/09 financial crisis) and looks likely to do so again, following the depreciation of the pound. Low-income families, with little wriggle room in their budgets and a higher proportion of their income spent on essentials, are particularly vulnerable in these circumstances.

Figure 5.8:

Average annual inflation rates by expenditure decile, 2003 to 2013

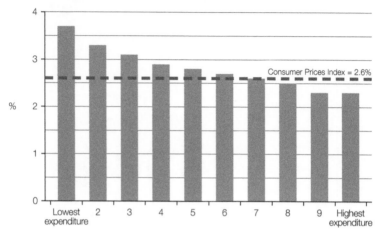

Source: T Flower and P Wales, *Variation in the Inflation Experience of UK Households: 2003–2014*, Office for National Statistics, 2014

Conclusions

While poverty is ultimately about the absence of the resources needed to meet material needs and participate in society, and thus poverty prevention must focus on increasing incomes for those in poverty, that income must always be considered relative to costs. And there are strong arguments in some cases for offering government support in the form of protection against specific costs – particularly for housing, childcare, disability and the costs associated with children.

Such support can take a number of forms: support through social security to help individuals meet these costs; government action in markets to reduce the costs directly; and direct provision by government, known as the 'social wage', or a universal basic services approach.

Each has its limitations. First, support through social security is weaker in cases where costs are variable and has been under attack as part of the austerity agenda, as demonstrated by large real-terms cuts in child benefit (for example). Yet it can also be appropriate where additional costs are shared by a predictable group, as is the case with children.

Second, intervention in markets works only where there are specific additional costs that can be addressed, and so is limited in the impact that it could have on, for example, child poverty. But in areas where costs contribute directly and substantially to poverty – notably through the housing market – a policy approach that does not attempt to tackle those costs directly is swimming against the tide.

And, third, a 'social wage' approach shares similar limitations, in that it cannot account for all the myriad costs faced by households and, importantly, taking the approach too far would limit the autonomy enjoyed by individuals and families in determining and responding to their own priorities. Meanwhile, not all subsidies are targeted at those on low incomes – for example, subsidies on train travel and culture (even if they may be beneficial in other ways). But this approach can also be efficient, as well as popular, with health and education provision enjoying widespread public and political support.

As we move on to consider who is at risk of poverty, and consider what can be done to reduce those risks, it is important to bear in mind these cost dimensions, even while recognising that income is central to the experience – and reduction – of poverty.

Notes

1   A Davis and others, *A Minimum Income Standard for the UK in 2016*, Joseph Rowntree Foundation, 2016

2   Author's calculations, based on RPI inflation and retrospective uprating in line with the previous September's inflation figure (child benefit for the first child would be £24.97 rather than £20.70, and for second and subsequent children, £16.48 rather than £13.70, a 20.3 per cent shortfall). Based on CPI inflation, child benefit would need to be 14 per cent higher for first children (£23.60), and 13.7 per cent higher for second and subsequent children (£15.58).

3   WH Beveridge, *Social Insurance and Allied Services: report by Sir William Beveridge*, HM Stationery Office, 1942

4   Joseph Rowntree Foundation, *UK Poverty: causes, costs and solutions*, 2016, Chapter 5a

5   See JC Brown, *Child Benefit: investing in the future*, Child Poverty Action Group, 1988

6   Figures are for 2014/15: HM Revenue and Customs, *Child Benefit, Child Tax Credit and Working Tax Credit: take-up rates 2014–15*, December 2016

7   See for example, JC Brown, *Child Benefit: investing in the future*, Child Poverty Action Group, 1988

8   Seebohm Rowntree was one of the first to highlight this 'lifecycle' argument:

'The life of a labourer is marked by five alternating periods of want and comparative plenty. During early childhood... he will probably be in poverty... there then follows a period during which he is earning money and living under his parents' roof... This period of prosperity may continue after marriage until he has two or three children when poverty will overtake him. This period of poverty will last perhaps for ten years until the first child is fourteen years old and begins to earn wages... the man enjoys another period of prosperity only to sink back again into poverty when his children have married and left him, and he himself is too old to work.' S Rowntree (1902), quoted in H Glennerster, 'The life cycle: public or private concern', in J Falkingham and J Hills (eds), *The Dynamic of Welfare: the welfare state and the life cycle*, Prentice Hall, 1995

9   P Levell, B Roantree and J Shaw, *Redistribution from a Lifetime Perspective*, Working Paper W15/27, Institute for Fiscal Studies, 2015. See also J Hills, *Good Times, Bad Times: the welfare myth of them and us*, Policy Press, 2017

10 For April to June 2017, based on the harmonised standard definition of 'disabled'; the proportion based on the Equality Act definition is 50 per cent, and for self-reported disability, 44.8 per cent. Office for National Statistics dataset, *A08: Labour market status of disabled people*, August 2017

11 For April to June 2017, Office for National Statistics Statistical Bulletin, *UK Labour Market: August 2017*, 2017

12 Papworth Trust, *Disability in the United Kingdom 2016: facts and figures*, 2016

13 T MacInnes and others, *Disability, Long-term Conditions and Poverty*, New Policy Institute, 2014

14 C Wood and E Grant, *Counting the Cost*, Demos, 2010

15 C Harding, B Wheaton and A Butler, *Childcare Survey 2017*, Family and Childcare Trust, 2017

16 D Hirsch and L Valadez, *How Much Does the Official Measure of Child Poverty Under-estimate its Extent by Failing to Take Account of Childcare Costs?*, Centre for Research in Social Policy, Loughborough University, 2015

17 Summarised from C Harding, B Wheaton and A Butler, *Childcare Survey 2017*, Family and Childcare Trust, 2017

18 D Hirsch, *The Cost of a Child in 2014*, Child Poverty Action Group, 2014

19 E Lloyd and S Potter, *Early Childcare Education and Care and Poverty*, University of East London for Joseph Rowntree Foundation, 2014; K Sylva and others, *The Effective Provision of Pre-School Education (EPPE) Project: final report, a longitudinal study funded by the DfES 1997–2004*, The Institute of Education, 2004

20 For further discussion of the relationship between poverty and childcare, see A Butler and J Rutter, *Creating an Anti-poverty Childcare System*, Joseph Rowntree Foundation, 2016

21 Department for Work and Pensions, *Households Below Average Income: an*

analysis of the income distribution 1994/95 to 2015/16, 2017, Table 4.5db

22 A Hood and T Waters, *Living Standards, Poverty and Inequality in the UK: 2016–17 to 2021–22*, Institute for Fiscal Studies, 2017

23 Report for the Department for Communities and Local Government, J Hills, *Ends and Means: the future roles of social housing in England*, CASEreport 34, ESRC Research Centre for Analysis of Social Exclusion, 2007

24 Office for National Statistics, *Index of Private Housing Rental Prices (IPHRP) in Great Britain: March 2017*, April 2017

25 Technically, the reduction was phased in across the country between November 2016 and February 2017

26 See A Westlake, *The UK Poverty Rip-Off: the poverty premium 2010*, Save the Children, 2011

27 S Davies, A Finney and Y Hartfree, *Paying to be Poor: uncovering the scale and nature of the poverty premium*, University of Bristol Personal Finance Research Centre, 2016

Six

Who is at risk of poverty?

Summary

- Families with children face higher risks of poverty because of the extra costs of children and because of the impact children have on the number of hours parents can work.
- Pensioner poverty (at 16 per cent) has fallen as a result of increases in benefits to pensioners, the growth of private pension incomes and rising pensioner employment.
- Although children in lone-parent families have the highest risk of poverty (at 47 per cent), most poor children live in couple families (62 per cent) because this type of family is much more common.

% OF DIFFERENT GROUPS IN POVERTY

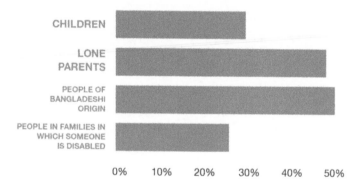

- The more paid work that is carried out by a family, the lower the chances of its being in poverty – if all adults work full time, the poverty risk is 7 per cent.
- Most adults in the bottom fifth of the income distribution who are working are low paid (around 65 per cent), but most adults who are low paid are not in the bottom fifth of the income distribution.

- The overall number (3 million) of women who are low paid is still much higher than the overall number (1.9 million) of men who are low paid.
- A quarter (26 per cent) of people living in families in which someone is disabled have a low income, compared with 20 per cent of people in families without someone in this situation.
- People of White ethnic origin are the least likely to be living in a low-income household (19 per cent). In contrast, 50 per cent of Bangladeshi people are in poverty.
- Scotland has a lower poverty rate (at 19 per cent) than England (22 per cent), Wales (23 per cent) and Northern Ireland (20 per cent).
- London has a similar poverty rate to the rest of England before housing costs. On an after housing costs basis, London's poverty rate is six percentage points higher than the rest of England.

Introduction

Some groups of the population are more likely to experience poverty than others. In this chapter we examine the variations in the likelihood of poverty – which we call the 'risk' of poverty. The concept of 'risk' in this chapter is applied to certain groups in the population – for example, lone parents. However, just because a group has a high risk of poverty, this does not mean it constitutes a large 'share' of the total population in poverty in the UK (the composition of overall poverty, in other words).

This is explored for some groups in Table 6.1. For example, 47 per cent of people in a lone-parent family are in a household in poverty. But because this is a relatively small group, only 17 per cent of people in poverty are in a lone-parent family.

This chapter considers the different risks faced by various groups in the population, and how these risks have changed over time. We examine poverty risk by age, different family types, the amount of paid work carried out across the family, gender, disability, ethnicity and region of the UK. When looking at each characteristic, it becomes evident that the burden of poverty is not spread evenly across the population and that certain people are much more likely to find themselves in poverty than others.

The poverty line used here is a 'relative poverty rate', which includes all households whose net income (ie, income after all taxes and national insurance contributions have been deducted) falls below 60 per cent of the contemporary median income. As throughout this book, incomes are adjusted (equivalised) for household size. We use income after housing costs, as this recognises that low-income families have little choice when it comes to the level of their housing costs, and more realistically reflects the income that families have at their disposal. (See Chapter 3 for a discussion about income before and after housing costs.) In 2015/16, the relative poverty line after housing costs for a single person without children was £144 a week, and for a couple with two children (one aged 14 or over, one aged under 14) it was £402.

We report 'risks' as the proportion of people in different family types with household incomes below the poverty line. A key difference is between the family and the household. A family is made up of an adult and her/his partner (if s/he has one) and any dependent children they are living with. While a household is a group of people living at the same address who share communal areas – in other words, everyone who lives behind the same 'front door'. For example, a couple living with their two children and the maternal grandparents would be one household of six people, made up of two families. Many of the characteristics we are interested in are measured at the family level, such as work status or family composition. Poverty is determined at the household level, and multiple families can live in the same household.

Table 6.1:
The risk and share of poverty

	Risk (proportion of group in poverty) %	Share (number in poverty in that group as a proportion of all in poverty) %
Children	30	29
Working-age adults	21	58
Pensioners	16	13
Lone parents	47	17
Single adults	25	21
Couples with children	23	37
Couples without children	12	11
Pensioner families	16	15
Working families	16	53
Workless families	35	47

Note: a pensioner family can contain one working-age adult, so this share figure differs from pensioners elsewhere in the table.

Source: Department for Work and Pensions, *Households Below Average Income: an analysis of the income distribution, 1994/95 – 2015/16*, 2017

Age

Figure 6.1 looks at the risk of poverty by age. It shows that, in 2015/16, children were the group with the highest proportion in poverty, at 30 per cent. This has increased by one percentage point when compared with 10 years earlier, and is higher than in 2010/11 when it was 27 per cent. Those aged 65 years and above are the age group least likely to be in poverty, at 16 per cent. The proportion in poverty decreased in 2015/16 compared with 10 years earlier, though is higher than in 2010/11, when it was 14 per cent. The proportion of people from all other age groups who are in poverty has increased in the 10 years since 2005/06 with the exception of 16–24-year-olds. However, this group has the second highest poverty rate.

Families with children face a particular set of poverty risks. Each child needs food, clothing, warmth and shelter. They also need access to books, toys, school trips and places to play so they can participate in society and thrive. This means each additional child costs money. At the same time, the arrival of a child means that parents must either reduce their working hours, and therefore their pay, or they must pay for childcare

Figure 6.1:

Percentage of children and adults in poverty in each age group, 2005/06, 2010/11 and 2015/16

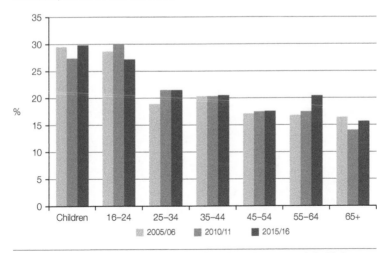

Source: Department for Work and Pensions, *Households Below Average Income: an analysis of the income distribution, 2005/06, 2010/11 and 2015/16*

– either presenting another cost or reducing household earnings. This is why families with children, and therefore children, face higher risks of poverty than other age groups.[1]

There are other reasons why the risk of poverty varies by age. Pension age was historically associated with low income. However, increases in the level of state benefits to pensioners, the growth in private pension incomes and rising employment in this age group have all contributed to reducing pensioner poverty.[2] For working-age groups, poverty risk is influenced by a number of factors. As well as the presence of children, these include the amount of paid work carried out in a household, housing tenure (for example, younger working-age adults are more likely to be in the higher cost private rented sector), and the increasing prevalence of disability in older age groups.[3,4]

Figure 6.2 shows the number of people in each age group living in a household in poverty and in a household not in poverty. Not only are children at the highest risk of poverty, they also make up the largest share of the population living in poverty, at 4 million. Adults aged 65 years and over have the lowest risk of poverty, but they still make up 1.8 million of those living in poverty.

Figure 6.2:

Number of children and adults in each age group living in a household in poverty, 2015/16

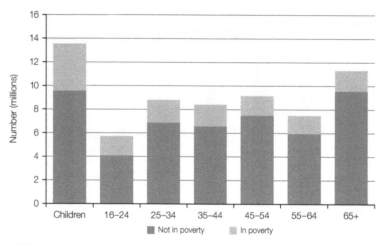

Source: Department for Work and Pensions, *Households Below Average Income: an analysis of the income distribution 1994/1995–2015/16*, 2017

Figure 6.3 shows child, pensioner, and working-age parent and non-parent poverty rates from 1961 until 2015/16. This graph shows that since the early-1980s there has been an increase in the proportion of people in relative poverty in all age groups apart from pensioners.

Child and working-age parent poverty increased especially steeply during the 1980s, reaching a peak in the late-1990s before decreasing again. In 1998, the Labour government adopted child poverty targets, aiming to eliminate child poverty by 2020. Although the midway milestone of halving child poverty by 2010/11 was missed,[5] the falls visible in the early-2000s were rapid and were driven by policies which, by 2010, had allocated an additional £18 billion a year in cash benefits to families with children.[6] Progress was stalled by the 2007/08 recession. In the period since then, the child poverty rate decreased, but then began to rise again over the last few years to reach 30 per cent in 2015/16.

Pensioner poverty rates have been on a downwards trend since the late-1980s and pensioners have gone from being the group with by far the

Figure 6.3:

Percentage of adults and children in poverty, 1961 to 2015/16

Note: the data is for Great Britain to 2001/02 and for the UK thereafter.

Source: Institute for Fiscal Studies data, based on a synthesis of Family Expenditure Survey and Family Resources Survey data

highest rate of poverty in the 1960s to being the group with the lowest poverty rates in 2015/16. This downward trend may have begun to reverse as pensioner poverty has risen slightly in the last few years. Historically, pensioner poverty has been high, given that pensioners generally do not receive income from employment, but instead rely on relatively low private and state pensions. The continued fall until 2012/13 in pensioner poverty was aided by pensioner benefits increasing more quickly than working-age benefits.[7] There have also been increases in the amount of private pension entitlements and the number of older people in employment has risen.[8]

Family type

Figure 6.4 shows that lone parents have the highest risk of poverty: nearly half (47 per cent) are living in poverty. Poverty rates are lowest for couples without children and pensioner couples, at 12 and 14 per cent respectively. The proportion of lone parents, female pensioners, male pensioners

Figure 6.4:

Percentage of people living in poverty by different family type

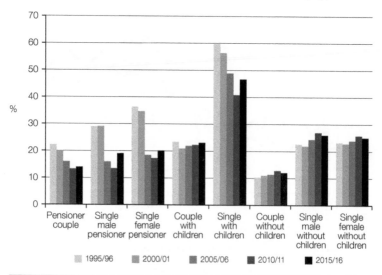

Source: Department for Work and Pensions, *Households Below Average Income: an analysis of the income distribution* for 1995/96, 2000/01, 2005/06, 2010/11 and 2015/16

and pensioner couples living in a household in poverty has decreased when compared with 1995/96, whereas for all other family types the proportion in poverty has stayed the same or increased slightly.

What explains the variations in poverty by family type? We have already touched on this in relation to pensioners. The other main dimensions are whether there are one or two adults, and whether the family has children. The first is important because it is related to income generation and economies of scale. A family with two adults can potentially have double the income of a one-adult family, but it has less than twice the costs. The data contain adjustments to income to reflect this, a process called 'equivalisation'. Couple families also have, for example, lower per person housing costs, and this can provide a buffer in the event of a loss of one these incomes (although losing an earner does increase the poverty risk, as we discuss later). Children increase the costs a household faces, while also potentially reducing earnings through childcare costs or reduced labour market participation.

Figure 6.5 shows the *number* of people in poverty in each family type, rather than the proportion. This is to emphasise that high risk of poverty

Figure 6.5:
Number of people living in poverty by different family type, 2015/16

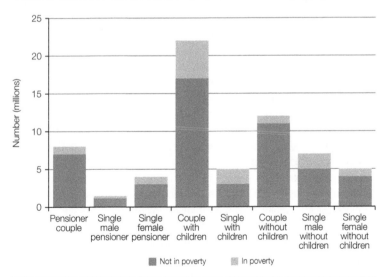

Source: Department for Work and Pensions, *Households Below Average Income: an analysis of the income distribution, 1994/95–2015/16*, 2017

among a group does not necessarily translate into significant numbers overall. For example, although 47 per cent of people in lone-parent families are living in poverty, they do not make up a large proportion of those living in poverty overall: there are 5.2 million people in lone-parent families in the UK (2 million lone parents and 3.2 million children), 2.4 million of whom are living in poverty. The largest number of people living in low-income households are couples with children. Even though couples with children have a lower poverty rate than lone parents with children, because they are the largest group in the population (22.1 million), they are also the largest group of people living in a household in poverty, at 5.1 million.

The amount of paid work

Work is an important route out of poverty, and how much work the adults in a family can do has an impact on the family's risk of poverty. Figure 6.6 shows the poverty rate of people in families by different levels of 'work intensity', or how much paid work is carried out by the adults in the family. All the adults could be working full time or all the adults could be out of work, with various combinations in between. The graph shows that families with all adults in work (whether one or two), with at least one working full time, have the lowest poverty rates. In other words, the more paid work that is carried out by a family, the lower the chances of its being in poverty.

For families with all adults (whether a single adult or a couple) working full time, the poverty rate is 7 per cent. For families with one full-time and one part-time worker, the rate is 8 per cent. These rates are much lower than the overall poverty rate of 22 per cent. Families in which one or more adult is self-employed, couples with one adult working full time and one not working, and families with one or more adult working part time and no one working full time, all have higher poverty rates than the overall poverty rate. This is despite their all having at least one adult doing some form of paid work. But because these families are relying either on part-time earnings (which also tend to have lower hourly rates) or one set of earnings for two adults, they have relatively higher poverty risks.

Families in which no adults are in paid work and at least one adult is unemployed, and families in which no adults are in paid work because they are economically inactive, have the highest rates of poverty, at 70 per cent and 55 per cent respectively. 'Economic inactivity' refers to those who are not in employment and who are not seeking work and who are unavailable to start work. For example, this includes those who are caring

Figure 6.6:

Percentage of people living in poverty by the amount of paid work carried out across the family

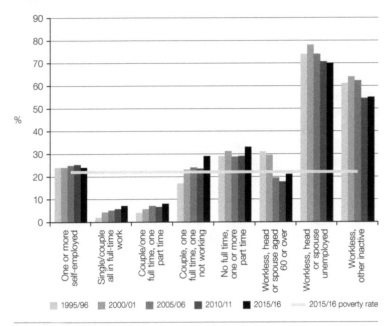

Source: Department for Work and Pensions, *Households Below Average Income: an analysis of the income distribution, 1994/95–2015/16*, 2017

for children or a partner and who are therefore unavailable to work, and those who are too ill to work. This category is different from those who are unemployed because the latter are actively seeking work and are available to start if they find a job. Households in which no adults work are at much greater risk of poverty than other households: when out-of-work benefits are set at too low a level, they fail to act as a safety net for these families.

Since 1995/96, the poverty rate for all families with at least one adult in paid work has increased. It has increased the most for families with one adult working full time and one adult not working – by 12 percentage points, from 17 per cent in 1995/96 to 29 per cent in 2015/16. There are around 1.1 million non-working adults who are in a family in which the other adult is in paid work. One in five are unemployed, which means they are actively seeking and available for work. The large majority of these non-working adults are economically inactive for a number of different reasons. Forty-five per cent are looking after the home or family. One in 10 of these non-working adults in a working family in poverty are retired or a student, and 16 per cent are sick, disabled or injured.[9]

Figure 6.7 shows the size of these groups for comparison. Singles or couples in full-time work are by far the largest group, at 17.9 million, with just a small proportion in poverty. Those in families with no one in paid work and in which the head or spouse is unemployed (rather than economically inactive) are a comparatively small number of the population. There are 1.4 million people in this group, with a large majority in poverty. Although Figures 6.6 and 6.7 can illustrate that households in which no adults are in paid work are at greater risk of poverty, overall there are more people (7.4 million) in families living on a low income with someone in paid work than people (6.5 million) in families living on a low income in which no one is working, including pensioners.

Figure 6.7:

Number of people living in poverty by the amount of paid work carried out across the family, 2015/16

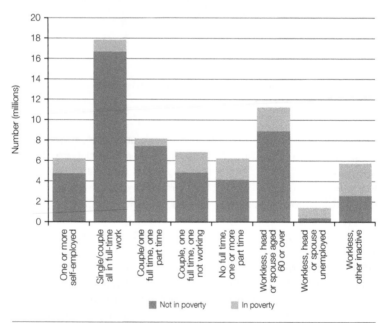

Source: Department for Work and Pensions, *Households Below Average Income: an analysis of the income distribution, 1994/95–2015/16*, 2017

Low pay

Another factor which can have an impact on poverty is low pay. The relationship between poverty and low pay is complicated. Low pay alone does not guarantee poverty – there are other factors, such as the amount of in-work benefits being received by the family, the income of a partner, family size and housing costs.[10] It is also possible to work enough hours at low rates to avoid poverty. However, it may be hard to avoid living in poverty if you are low paid and have children and a partner who is not working.

Figure 6.8 looks at low pay. 'Low pay' here is defined as having an hourly pay rate below two-thirds of the median. Both male and female part-time workers have much higher rates of low pay than full-time workers. The proportion of men who are working full time and who are low paid has remained fairly consistent since 2002, and in 2016 it was 10 per cent. The proportion of women who are working full time and are low paid has decreased from 18 per cent in 2002 to 14 per cent in 2016.

In 2002, half (50 per cent and 49 per cent) of both men and women working part time were low paid. By 2016, for women working part time

Figure 6.8:

Percentage and number of women and men in low-paid work

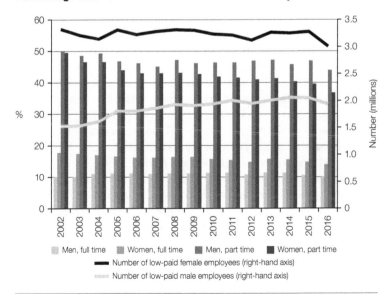

Men, full time   Women, full time   Men, part time   Women, part time
— Number of low-paid female employees (right-hand axis)
Number of low-paid male employees (right-hand axis)

Source: Office for National Statistics, *Annual Survey of Hours and Earnings*, via www.nomisweb.co.uk

this had fallen to 37 per cent, while for men it was 44 per cent. Many more women work part time than men, however: 5.4 million women, compared with 1.8 million men.

One way of thinking about the interaction between low hourly pay and poverty is this: most adults in the bottom fifth of the income distribution who are working are low paid (around 65 per cent for 2008/09 to 2010/11).[11] However, most adults who are low paid are not in the bottom fifth of the income distribution. Low pay is an issue for workers in poverty, but is not a risk factor for workers overall. This is because of other factors, such as second earners.

The proportion of all female employees who are low paid has been falling, from 31 per cent in 2002 to 24 per cent in 2016. In contrast, the proportion of male employees who are low paid has increased slightly, from 14 per cent in 2002 to 15 per cent in 2016. The overall number of women who are low paid – 3 million – is still much higher than the overall number of men who are low paid – 1.9 million, partly explained by the fact that there is a much larger number of women who are working part time (work which tends to be lower paid, on average).

Gender

In all the years shown in Figure 6.9, women are slightly more likely to live in a low-income household than men. The difference in these figures is relatively minor, however. One of the reasons why there is only a small difference in poverty rates between the two is that the majority of men and women live in a couple – and this means it is assumed they share a household income and so are counted as either both living in poverty or both not living in poverty. The small gap can, in part, be accounted for by the fact that lone parents are at high risk of being in poverty compared with other groups, and women make up 90 per cent of lone parents.

However, these statistics do not say anything about the distribution of income *within* households between men and women. There is the potential for 'hidden' poverty in the household, given the tendency of women often to bear the responsibility of managing limited income, and to bear the costs of this.[12]

Male and female relative poverty rates both increased in the years from 2004/05 to 2007/08, and then fell until 2014/15 for men and 2012/13 for women. Since 2012/13, the male poverty rate has only marginally changed, whereas the female rate has increased by 1.3 percentage points.

Figure 6.9:
Percentage of women and men in poverty

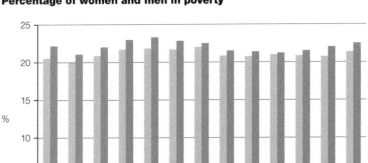

Source: Department for Work and Pensions, *Households Below Average Income: an analysis of the income distribution, 1994/95–2015/16,* 2017

Disability

In this section, the definition of disability is taken from the Equality Act 2010. You are disabled:[13]

> ... if you have a physical or mental impairment that has a 'substantial' and 'long-term' negative effect on your ability to do normal daily activities.

Households with a disabled family member are at higher risk of poverty than those in which no one is disabled. A quarter (26 per cent) of people in families in which someone is disabled have a low income, compared with 20 per cent of people in families without someone in this situation.

It is important to note that these figures are likely to underestimate the number of disabled people living in poverty. This is because any 'extra' income they get through social security because of their disability is included in their income and this may lift them above 60 per cent of the median. But this extra money is needed to cover the extra costs that can

Figure 6.10:

Percentage of people living in poverty in households with at least one family member who is disabled, 2015/16

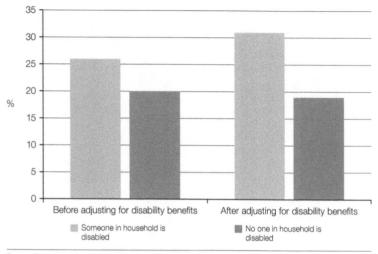

Source: Department for Work and Pensions, *Households Below Average Income: an analysis of the income distribution, 1994/95–2015/16*, 2017

arise from their having a disability. This includes both 'enhanced costs', which are things that everyone needs but which are more expensive for disabled people, and 'special costs', which are things that only disabled people need. It is difficult to adjust for these costs as they vary for each person, but previous research has found that, when disability benefits (disability living allowance or attendance allowance) are excluded, an extra 1 million people are in poverty.[14] The poverty rate for people in a family with a disabled person rises to 31 per cent if disability benefits are adjusted for. As well as having a high risk of poverty, those with disabilities also make up a large share of the total. When benefits that are awarded for disability are removed, disabled people make up 28 per cent of people in poverty, and a further 20 per cent of people in poverty live in a household with a disabled person.[15]

People in families with someone with a disability are more likely to be living in poverty for a number of reasons. As well as the extra costs of having a disability, such as the cost of equipment to manage a condition,[16] people with a disability are less likely to be in employment. Of those who are working age, 39 per cent of disabled people are employees and a further 7 per cent are self-employed, giving an employment rate of 46 per cent. This is 34 percentage points below the employment rate of non-disabled people, 69 per cent of whom are employees and 11 per cent are self-employed. Among disabled people, around one in five (21 per cent) want to work but do not have any work: 6 per cent are unemployed and 15 per cent are economically inactive but would like to work. Among non-disabled people, the figure is 8 per cent, half of whom are unemployed and half are inactive but wanting to work. Much of the difference in employment rates is explained by those who are inactive and would not like to work, which is the case for just over a third of working-age disabled people (34 per cent) and only 13 per cent of non-disabled people. Looking only at people in work, 65 per cent of disabled workers are full time, compared with 76 per cent of non-disabled workers.[17] When they are in work, people with a disability are more likely to be low paid than people without a disability, even when they have the same level of qualifications.[18]

Ethnicity

Figure 6.11 shows that the proportion of people living in a household in poverty varies greatly by ethnic group. The ethnic groups that have the highest risk of being in a low-income household are Pakistani, Bangladeshi and 'other ethnic groups'. These three groups are more than twice as likely as people from a White background to be living in a household in poverty. People from a White background are the least likely to be living in a low-income household, with one in five (19 per cent) doing so.

The proportion of children in poverty is higher than the overall proportion of people living in poverty for all ethnic groups, with the exception of families with a Chinese head of household. This follows a broadly similar pattern to the overall number of people from each ethnic group living in a low-income household. For Bangladeshi and Black/African/Caribbean/ Black British families, the child poverty rate is 7 percentage points higher than the total.

Although those of White ethnic origin have a low risk of poverty, they make up by far the largest share of those in poverty, at 10.6 million. The next largest group in terms of numbers of people in poverty are those from a Black/African/Caribbean/Black British background, at 800,000. Those of Bangladeshi origin have the highest risk of poverty, but they make up a small share of those living in poverty, at 300,000.

Figure 6.11:

Percentage of adults and children in poverty by ethnicity of the head of household, 2013/14 to 2015/16

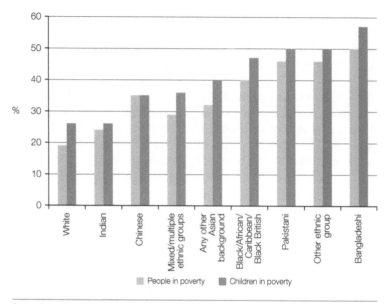

Source: Department for Work and Pensions, *Households Below Average Income: an analysis of the income distribution*, three-year average 2013/14, 2014/15 and 2015/16

Figure 6.12 shows that those of White ethnic origin have the highest rates of employment, at 75 per cent, whereas those of Pakistani origin have the lowest rates of employment, at 55 per cent.

Those of Black, African, Caribbean and Black British origin have rates of unemployment that are three times those of people of Chinese origin. These different levels of employment can, in part, explain some of the variation in levels of poverty seen in Figure 6.11. Those of Pakistani and Bangladeshi origin have low levels of employment and high levels of low pay, at 34 and 50 per cent respectively. Those from any other Asian background have high levels of employment, but also high levels of low pay, at 36 per cent.

Figure 6.12:

Percentage of people of different ethnic origins who are employed or unemployed, and proportion of employees who are low paid, January to March 2016

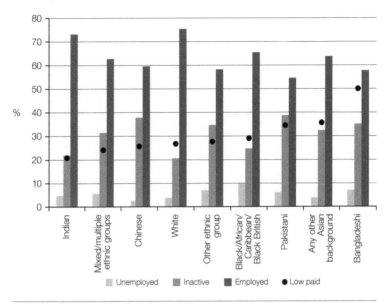

Source: Office for National Statistics, *Labour Force Survey*. The data is for quarter one 2016.

Geography

Figure 6.13 shows that the highest proportion of people living in a low-income household is found in London, at 27 per cent. For this measure, taking housing costs into account makes a big difference. When looking at the poverty rates before housing costs, London has a poverty rate similar to the rest of England.[19] Once the cost of housing is taken into account and the after housing costs poverty measure is used, the gap between London and the rest of England is six percentage points. Despite the fact that household incomes are higher in London than in the rest of England, the high cost of housing results in a large number of people who are left with an income below 60 per cent of the median.

The proportion of people in the rest of England in a low-income household is low in the South East, the East of England, the South West

Figure 6.13:

Percentage of adults and children in poverty by region, 2013/14, 2014/15 and 2015/16

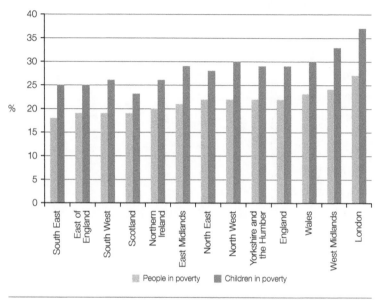

Source: Department for Work and Pensions, *Households Below Average Income: an analysis of the income distribution*, three-year average 2013/14, 2014/15 and 2015/16

and Scotland, at 18 per cent, 19 per cent, 19 per cent and 19 per cent respectively. Apart from London, it is highest in the West Midlands and Wales at 24 per cent and 23 per cent respectively.

Figure 6.13 also shows that, in London and the West Midlands, more than two-thirds of children (37 per cent and 33 per cent respectively) are living in a low-income household, while in Scotland, the figure is just 23 per cent.

There are multiple factors that explain the variation in poverty rates. These include demography (some regions have higher incidences of disability, for example), employment rates (the regions with the highest employment rates are the South West, the South East and the East of England), and housing stock and cost (London's large private rented sector and higher general housing costs contribute to its high poverty rate). The regions with the highest poverty rates tend to be urban (London, the West Midlands and the North West).

Conclusions

This chapter has shown that certain groups of people are more likely to experience poverty. This is especially true for children, women, those with a disability and some minority ethnic groups. Furthermore, the characteristics which can put you at greater risk of poverty can interact with one another, meaning that, for some groups, the risk of living in poverty is extremely high. For example, nearly two-thirds (63 per cent) of Bangladeshi children are living in a low-income household. Being in a group that is at greater risk of poverty is not, in itself, a cause of high rates of poverty – it is the reduced access to adequate income, as the labour market disproportionately excludes them from wages above the poverty line and benefits do not make up the difference.

Targeted government policies succeeded in reducing child poverty in the early- to mid-2000s, and in causing the long-term fall in pensioner poverty that has now resulted in their being the group with the lowest rates of poverty. This shows that policies can have a big impact on reducing poverty: the risk of poverty is not inevitable.

Notes

1 M Haddad, 'The cost of children', *Poverty*, 155, 2016, Child Poverty Action Group, pp6–10

2 C Belfield and others, *Living Standards, Poverty and Inequality in the UK: 2016*, Institute for Fiscal Studies, 2016

3 H Aldridge, *Why Has Poverty Risen So Much For Young Adults?* New Policy Institute, 2015

4 A Tinson and others, *Disability and Poverty: why disability must be at the centre of poverty reduction*, New Policy Institute, 2016

5 L Judge, 'Introduction', in *Ending Child Poverty by 2020: progress made and lessons learned*, Child Poverty Action Group, 2012

6 R Joyce, *Child Poverty in Britain: recent trends and future prospects*, Institute for Fiscal Studies, 2015

7 R Joyce, *Child Poverty in Britain: recent trends and future prospects*, Institute for Fiscal Studies, 2015

8 R Joyce, *Child Poverty in Britain: recent trends and future prospects*, Institute for Fiscal Studies, 2015

9 A Tinson and others, *Monitoring Poverty and Social Exclusion 2016*, New Policy Institute for Joseph Rowntree Foundation, 2016

10 T MacInnes and others, *Monitoring Poverty and Social Exclusion 2013*, New

Policy Institute for Joseph Rowntree Foundation, 2013

11 T MacInnes and others, *Monitoring Poverty and Social Exclusion 2013*, New Policy Institute for Joseph Rowntree Foundation, 2013

12 F Bennett, *Poverty in the UK: the need for a gender perspective*, UK Women's Budget Group, 2015

13 The Equality Act 2010, available at www.gov.uk/definition-of-disability-under-equality-act-2010

14 T MacInnes and others, *Disability, Long-term Conditions and Poverty*, New Policy Institute, 2014

15 A Tinson and others, *Disability and Poverty: why disability must be at the centre of poverty reduction*, New Policy Institute, 2016

16 A Tinson and others, *Disability and Poverty: why disability must be at the centre of poverty reduction*, New Policy Institute, 2016

17 A Tinson and others, *Disability and Poverty: why disability must be at the centre of poverty reduction*, New Policy Institute, 2016

18 A Tinson and others, *Disability and Poverty: why disability must be at the centre of poverty reduction*, New Policy Institute, 2016

19 H Aldridge and others, *London's Poverty Profile 2015,* New Policy Institute, 2015

Seven
Child poverty in the UK

Summary

- Children living in lone-parent families have a material deprivation rate (at 40 per cent) more than three times that of children living in two-parent families (13 per cent).
- Lone parents face a higher risk of poverty due to a lack of an additional earner and low rates of maintenance payments, gender inequality in employment and pay and childcare costs.
- A quarter of children living in households with one or two dependent children are in poverty (27 per cent and 26 per cent respectively). This increases to 39 per cent in families with three or more children.

39%
OF CHILDREN LIVING
IN FAMILIES WITH
THREE OR MORE CHILDREN
ARE IN POVERTY

43%
OF CHILDREN
LIVING IN MINORITY
ETHNIC FAMILIES
ARE IN POVERTY

47%
OF CHILDREN
IN LONE-PARENT
FAMILIES
ARE IN POVERTY

67%
OF POOR
CHILDREN ARE
IN WORKING
FAMILIES

68%
OF CHILDREN IN
FAMILIES WITH NO
WORKING ADULTS
ARE IN POVERTY

- Almost seven in 10 (68 per cent) of children in families with no working adults are in poverty, compared with less than a quarter (23 per cent) of children in families in which someone works.
- Although lone-parent employment rates have increased by almost 20 percentage points since the 1990s, single mothers still have the lowest employment rate among parents, with slightly more than six in 10 (62 per cent) employed.

- Children from Black and minority ethnic groups are more likely to be in poverty: 43 per cent of children living in minority ethnic families are in poverty, compared with 26 per cent of children in White British families.

Introduction

This chapter explores further how a child's risk of poverty is affected by the family in which s/he lives. Families with children face particular risks of poverty because children bring additional costs, but with no expectation that they will contribute towards those costs. Parents' ability to bring earned income into the household is also affected by their caring responsibilities, meaning that family-friendly employment and affordable, accessible, high-quality childcare take on particular importance. Child poverty is thus particularly sensitive to government policy, to which its variation over time attests. (For a discussion of child poverty over time, see Chapter 6.)

Our main measures of poverty are at a household or family level, based on the assumption that families pool resources, so, for children to be in poverty, their parents must be in poverty. As we saw in Chapter 6, a family's risk of poverty (and so a child's risk of poverty) is affected by a number of things: lone parenthood, the number of children in the family, how much paid work is carried out by the adults in the family, its ethnicity and whether anyone has a disability. These characteristics are not, in themselves, *causes* of poverty. Rather, wider societal factors such as gender inequality and structural racism mean that a higher proportion of certain parents, and therefore certain children, are in poverty, which we refer to as a greater 'risk' of poverty. However, just because a group has a high risk of poverty, this does not mean it constitutes a large 'share' of the total population in poverty in the UK (the composition of overall poverty, in other words).

In this chapter, we use the 'relative poverty' measure of child poverty. This means that the child poverty rate includes all the children who live in households whose net income (ie, after taxes, national insurance and certain other payments (like student loan repayments) have been deducted) falls below 60 per cent of the contemporary median income. Larger households need a larger income than smaller households to be able to have the same standard of living, so incomes have been adjusted (equivalised) to reflect different household compositions. We use income after housing costs, which recognises that low-income households have little choice over these, so this gives us a better idea of their real disposable income. (See Chapter 3 for a discussion about using income before and after housing costs.)

A child is considered to be 'materially deprived' if s/he lacks essential children's items, activities and services because her/his family cannot afford them. Some of the items used to judge whether a child is materially deprived include a safe outdoor space in which to play, celebrations on special occasions and leisure equipment, such as a bicycle. (See Chapter 4 for more on this.)

The number of parents and children in a household

Number of parents

Family structure and family size have a considerable impact on children's risk of poverty and material deprivation. Most families (75 per cent) in the UK have two parents, so most of the families in poverty (59 per cent) have two parents. However, lone-parent families have a much higher risk of poverty than two-parent families. Almost half of children in lone-parent families are in poverty (47 per cent), while less than a quarter of children living with two parents are in poverty (24 per cent). Children living in lone-parent families have a material deprivation rate (40 per cent) more than three times that of children living in two-parent families (13 per cent). Parents in poverty seek to shield children from deprivation by depriving themselves,[1] so children in material deprivation are likely to be living with parents who are even more materially deprived.

The causes for the high poverty rates among lone-parent families are more complicated than just the lack of an additional earner. Gender inequality in employment and pay is a key driver, as the vast majority of lone parents (90 per cent) are women.[2] Lone parents also face higher childcare penalties (another form of gender inequality) – either because they must work fewer hours because of their childcare responsibilities or because they need childcare while they work.[3] These issues are not inevitable, but rather the result of structural and policy failures, such as the shortfall between the cost of children and the rate of children's benefits paid to lone parents,[4] the lack of enforcement of child maintenance payments,[5] and the lack of affordable childcare.

Number of dependent children

Figure 7.1 shows that the number of dependent children in a family also affects the child poverty rate. A quarter of children living in households with one or two dependent children are in poverty (27 per cent and 26 per cent respectively). This increases to 39 per cent in households with three or more children. The material deprivation rate increases from 15 per cent for two-child families to 27 per cent for families with three or more children. Large families (three or more children) have a higher material deprivation risk and a higher severe child poverty risk.[6]

Parents of large families are more likely to have characteristics that are associated with higher poverty risks, such as unemployment, lower educational attainment, having had their first child at a younger age, and having a young child.[7] Large families are also more common among minority ethnic communities, which also have a higher poverty risk.[8] However, even when these characteristics are controlled for, large families still have a higher risk of poverty.[9] There are several factors behind this.

Figure 7.1:

Child poverty and material deprivation rates by number of children in family, 2015/16

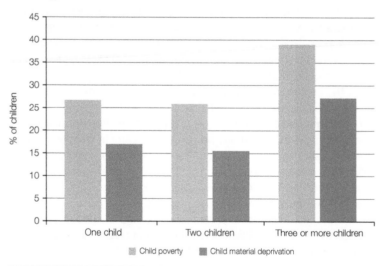

Source: New Policy Institute analysis of *Households Below Average Income* data

One is that every additional child brings additional costs without a compensating increase in earnings, meaning that a family's earnings are spread more thinly. The social security system addresses this to some extent, though there is still a shortfall between the income families receive from children's benefits and the cost of children (the shortfall increases the more children a family has).[10] From April 2017, this shortfall will increase as most new claimants will only get child tax credit or universal credit for two children. High childcare costs, as well as the time cost to parents for coordinating childcare and education for multiple children (meaning they have less time for employment) also stretch larger families' resources, which can lead to material deprivation.[11]

Employment

Income from employment, rather than social security, is a key route out of poverty and a key way to remain out of poverty. (See Chapter 8 for a fuller discussion on this.) More than three-quarters (68 per cent) of children in families with no working adults are in poverty, compared with less than a quarter (23 per cent) of children in families in which someone works. However, the risk of child poverty increases to almost half (46 per cent) in families with no full-time workers. The employment status of parents therefore has a significant impact on a child's risk of poverty.

There are around 14 million working-age parents in Britain, the majority of whom live with a partner. Among the 2 million lone parents, more than nine in 10 are women.[12] As Figure 7.2 shows, the vast majority of fathers in couple families are employed[13] (92 per cent), with 85 per cent employed full time. A smaller majority of mothers in couple families are employed (72 per cent), and only a third (33 per cent) work full time. In numbers, in 2015 there were 5.6 million employed fathers in couple families, 5.2 million of whom are employed full time, and 4.2 million employed mothers in couple families, two million of whom work full time. The smallest group are single fathers, at 140,000, 110,000 of whom work full time. Of the 1.2 million employed single mothers, 510,000 worked full time.

Although lone-parent employment rates have increased by almost 20 percentage points since the 1990s,[14] single mothers still have the lowest employment rate among parents, with slightly more than six in 10 (62 per cent) employed. Like mothers in couples, more than half of single mothers in employment work part time (36 per cent of all single mothers). Childcare costs and childcare responsibilities are key barriers to lone-par-

Figure 7.2:

Parental employment rates by family status

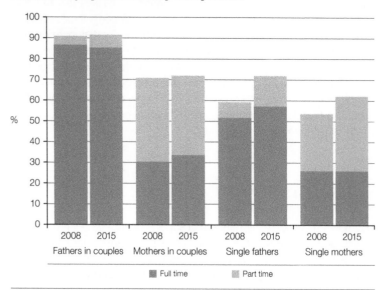

Source: A Tinson, H Aldridge and G Whitham, *Women, Work and Wages in the UK*, New Policy Institute, 2016

ent employment. Sweden, a country with high lone-parent employment, demonstrates the difference that affordable childcare and flexible parental employment can make to access to employment for lone parents.[15] These contribute to the country's overall lower poverty rate relative to the European Union average.

Minority ethnic families

Children from Black and minority ethnic groups are more likely to be in poverty: 43 per cent of children[16] living in minority ethnic families are in poverty, compared with 26 per cent of children in White British families.[17] People from minority ethnic groups are more likely to be in poverty across work statuses, geographic locations in the UK and types of family,[18] indicating that there are additional obstacles keeping them in poverty that go beyond differences in employment and low pay rates.

Almost half (45 per cent) of children with foreign-born parents are in poverty.[19] Some of the reasons for this include the fact that these families are more likely to live in the private rented sector (where poverty rates are higher than in other tenures due to high housing costs) and because foreign-born adults are more likely to be employed part time rather than full time.[20] Many foreign-born people are also from a minority ethnic group, so there is a strong connection between the barriers outlined here and above.

The reasons for the increased child poverty are complex. Some of the increased risk can be attributed to differing levels of employment or the likelihood of living with a particular housing tenure. However, these correlations, in themselves, do not paint a full picture – they indicate, but cannot fully illuminate, the cumulative impact of limitations caused by prejudice in multiple areas of society, from educational outcomes, to employment, to access to different housing tenures (see Chapter 6 for a full discussion).

Conclusions

Children currently have a higher risk of poverty in the UK than working-age people or pensioners.[21] This is not uniformly true across Europe, showing that this is not inevitable, but rather the result of societal and policy decisions. Denmark has the lowest child poverty rate in the OECD.[22] A range of policies, such as affordable childcare, generous welfare benefits and a highly effective child maintenance system keep child poverty low, despite the country having large proportions of children living in lone-parent and in large families.

Among the factors that contribute to children's higher poverty risk are the higher living costs of families with children (which are not covered by children's benefits), and lack of support for parents (particularly lone parents) in employment, which forces them to take lower paid work than they would otherwise have liked in order to manage their childcare responsibilities. Having parents from a minority ethnic background, or being born abroad, also raises the likelihood that a child will be in poverty.

Child poverty is not inevitable. Child poverty fell between 1998 and 2010, has plateaued since and is now projected to rise, reflecting successive changes in priorities. With the right interventions, child poverty can be reduced in the same way as pensioner poverty rates, which we have seen more than halved since the 1980s.[23]

Notes

1 Child Poverty Action Group, *Poverty Gaps and Material Deprivation*, 2016

2 A Tinson, H Aldridge and G Whitham, *Women Work and Wages in the UK*, New Policy Institute, 2016

3 G Cory and A Stirling, *Pay and Parenthood: an analysis of wage inequality between mums and dads*, TUC, 2016

4 D Hirsch, *The Cost of A Child in 2016,* Child Poverty Action Group, 2016

5 Gingerbread, *Missing Maintenance,* 2016

6 M Culliney and others, *Family Structure and Poverty in the UK: an evidence and policy review*, Joseph Rowntree Foundation, 2014

7 J Bradshaw and others, *Child Poverty in Large Families*, Policy Press for the Joseph Rowntree Foundation, 2006

8 F Bennett with P Dornan, *Child Benefit: fit for the future: 60 years of support for children,* Child Poverty Action Group, 2006

9 J Bradshaw and others, *Child Poverty in Large Families*, Joseph Rowntree Foundation, 2006

10 D Hirsch, *The Cost of A Child in 2017*, Child Poverty Action Group, 2017

11 N Sharma, *It Doesn't Happen Here: the reality of child poverty in the UK*, Barnardo's 2007

12 A Tinson, H Aldridge and G Whitham, *Women, Work and Wages in the UK*, New Policy Institute, 2016

13 Including people who are self-employed.

14 T MacInnes and others, *Monitoring Poverty and Social Exclusion 2015*, New Policy Institute for Joseph Rowntree Foundation, 2015

15 OECD, *Babies and Bosses: reconciling work and family life*, 2007

16 Children living in families in which the head of household identifies as 'Black or Minority Ethnic'.

17 New Policy Institute analysis of *Households Below Average Income*, 2016.

18 G Palmer and P Kenway, *Poverty Among Ethnic Groups: how and why does it differ?*, Joseph Rowntree Foundation, 2007

19 C Hughes and P Kenway, *Foreign-born People and Poverty in the UK*, Joseph Rowntree Foundation, 2016

20 C Hughes and P Kenway, *Foreign-born People and Poverty in the UK*, Joseph Rowntree Foundation, 2016

21 A Tinson and others, *Monitoring Poverty and Social Exclusion 2016*, New Policy Institute for Joseph Rowntree Foundation, 2016

22 OECD Directorate of Employment, Labour and Social Affairs, *C02.2: Child Poverty,* OECD, 2016

23 A Tinson and others, *Monitoring Poverty and Social Exclusion 2016*, New Policy Institute for Joseph Rowntree Foundation, 2016

Eight
The dynamics of poverty

Summary

- Children, lone parents, disabled people and people in households in which no one works have a higher risk of falling into poverty, remaining in poverty for longer and experiencing deeper poverty, than other people.
- Slightly more than one in 15 (7 per cent) of people who were not in poverty in 2013 fell below the poverty line in 2014, while half (50 per cent) of people who had been in poverty in 2013 were not in poverty in 2014.

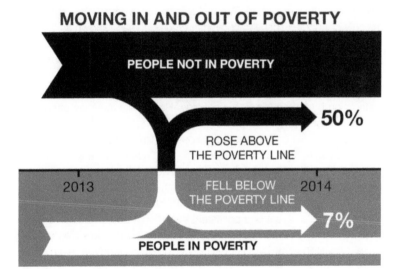

MOVING IN AND OUT OF POVERTY

PEOPLE NOT IN POVERTY

50%

ROSE ABOVE THE POVERTY LINE

2013   FELL BELOW   2014
THE POVERTY LINE

7%

PEOPLE IN POVERTY

- In 2015, 7.3 per cent of the UK population, or approximately 4.6 million people, were living in persistent poverty.
- About one in 16 working-age people experienced persistent poverty in 2014. Children and pensioners are significantly more likely to remain in poverty than working-age people.
- Nine in 10 lone-parent households (of which 16 per cent were in persistent poverty) are headed by women.

- There is no official definition of destitution. According to a new definition developed by researchers from Heriot-Watt University for the Joseph Rowntree Foundation, there were an estimated 670,000 households, containing 1.3 million people, who were destitute and in contact with support services during 2015.

Introduction

Slightly more than one in five people were in poverty in the UK in 2015/16, a poverty rate that has not changed significantly for more than a decade. This leads many people to assume that the same one-fifth of people have been poor consistently every year during this time. Political and media portrayals of poor people as 'skivers', who spend their entire lives reliant on benefits and never working, support this view that the UK has a fixed 'underclass' of poor people. The reality is far more complex: a significant minority of people experience poverty in multiple years (known as 'persistent poverty'), but half of the people who are living in poverty this year will not be living in poverty next year. New people will also be in poverty next year who are not in poverty at the current time.

Income dynamics describe these movements around the income distribution by individuals or households. Household incomes often vary across the year (for example, if someone becomes unemployed or gets a pay rise) and will certainly change across the life course (as new families form or break up, as children are born or leave home, as people enter the workforce or retire, or as people progress in work).[1] Some of these changes may cause people to fall into poverty, or may lift them out of poverty.

The experience of poverty is different depending on whether it is a fleeting, one-time event or a persistent condition. People can also experience recurrent, or repeating, poverty, illustrated by the 'low-pay, no-pay cycle'.[2] Analysing how long people remain in poverty (and the depth of the poverty they experience) is important because persistent poverty has been shown to increase the likelihood of negative consequences of low income, such as mental and physical health issues,[3] poor performance in school,[4] lack of savings, and debt.[5] Growing up in persistent poverty has also been shown to negatively affect the life chances of children.[6] Identifying how widespread the experience of poverty is over time, and how likely it is that people experiencing poverty can escape it, is also critical to understanding levels of insecurity across society.[7]

Some people also fall further below the poverty line than others.

And this deeper poverty is associated with worse outcomes for future prospects and current wellbeing.[8]

This chapter examines the key factors that contribute to people entering or exiting poverty, the length of time people experience poverty (the persistence of poverty), and the characteristics of those who remain in poverty for extended periods. It also explores the differences between those people who are living in poverty.

Box 8.1:

Key terms

Poverty rate

In this chapter, the poverty rate includes people who live in households whose net income – ie, income after all taxes and national insurance contributions (along with other payments such as maintenance payments and student loan repayments) have been deducted – falls below 60 per cent of the contemporary median income. Larger households need a larger income than smaller households to be able to have the same standard of living, so incomes are equivalised – ie, adjusted to reflect different household compositions. Unless otherwise noted, income *before* housing costs is used for comparability with the persistent poverty measure.

Persistent poverty

This chapter uses the same measure of persistent poverty as that used by Eurostat across the European Union. This is defined as having an income of less than 60 per cent of the contemporary national median household equivalised income *before* housing costs in both the current year and in at least two of the three preceding years.[9] Income before housing costs is used in this chapter for international comparability.

Material deprivation

This chapter uses the same measure of material deprivation as that used by Eurostat across the European Union as an indication of the living standards of people in poverty. This is defined as being unable to afford to have three of nine essential items (such as a meal with protein every second day or a telephone). Material deprivation provides us with an insight into the consequences of persistent poverty – those living in poverty for longer are more likely to be materially deprived.

Severe child poverty

Children are defined as being in severe poverty if they are in a household with an after housing costs income below 50 per cent of the median and they are materially deprived.

Destitution

There is no official measure or definition of, or government statistic for, destitution. In this chapter, we use the measure based on recent research from Heriot-Watt University for the Joseph Rowntree Foundation. This defines a household as destitute if either:

- it has a low income (below 60 per cent of median income after housing costs) and no savings and has gone without at least two of six essential items (such as shelter, food and basic toiletries) over the past month; *or*
- it has a household income below the destitution threshold set by the research. This is currently £140 a week for a couple with two children.

Entries and exits

The proportion of people in households whose income falls below the poverty line (the entry rate) and the proportion of people previously in poverty who escape each year (the exit rate) are important indicators of how much 'churn' occurs to the population living in poverty.

The UK has high entry and exit rates for poverty, compared with other European countries. This is consistent with the UK's relatively low persistent poverty rate and average overall poverty rate, and means that while people in the UK have a fairly high risk of falling into poverty, they also have a high chance of escaping it.

About one in 15 (6.5 per cent) of people who were not in poverty in 2013 fell below the poverty line in 2014, while half (50 per cent) of people who had been in poverty in 2013 were not in poverty in 2014 (Figure 8.1). A similar number of people enter and exit poverty every year. As there are far fewer people in poverty than not in poverty, the proportion of people exiting poverty every year is larger than the proportion entering poverty.

Figure 8.1:

UK poverty exit and entry rates, 2008 to 2014

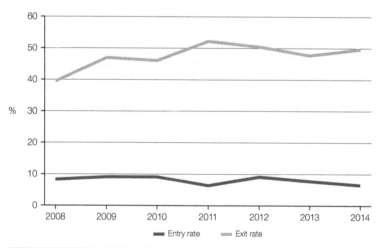

Note: About half of people in poverty in 2013 were not in poverty in 2014, while one in 15 (6.5%) people not in poverty fell below the poverty line.

Source: Office for National Statistics and Eurostat, *Persistent Poverty in the UK and EU: 2014*, 2016, Figure 5

The persistence of poverty

Persistent poverty is defined as having an income of 60 per cent or less of the median income in both the current year and in at least two of the three preceding years.[10] In other words, people in persistent poverty do not dip into poverty once for a brief time, but rather experience poverty either consistently or at multiple times over the course of several years (at least).

Figure 8.2:

Persistent poverty rates across the European Union, 2015

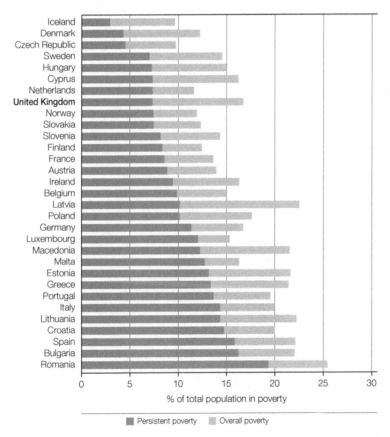

% of total population in poverty

■ Persistent poverty   ▨ Overall poverty

Source: Office for National Statistics and Eurostat, *Persistent Poverty in the UK and EU: 2015*, 2017

Persistent poverty in the UK declined for people of all ages between the early 1990s and the early 2000s. Since then, persistent poverty has fallen slightly for pensioners and risen slightly for children and working-age adults.[11] In 2015, 7.3 per cent of the UK population, or approximately 4.6 million people, were living in persistent poverty.

As Figure 8.2 shows, in 2015 the UK had the joint sixth lowest persistent poverty rate in the European Union (EU): the EU average was 10.9 per cent.[12] However, the UK's overall poverty rate (16.7 per cent[13]) was close to the EU average for overall poverty (17.3 per cent). This indicates that the UK had a similar proportion of people in poverty as the EU as a whole, but fewer people experience poverty for multiple years. A key driver of this is likely to be the fact that the UK has a fairly high turnover rate of people losing and finding work relative to the rest of the EU – on average, one million people find a job, and one million lose their job, every three months in the UK.[14] The increase in zero-hour contracts and self-employment over the past decade is also making some people's income more variable.[15] This volatility seems more concentrated at the bottom of the income distribution,[16] meaning poorer people are more likely to cycle in and out of poverty than people further up the income scale.

Who is most likely to remain in poverty?

There are two key factors that are strongly correlated with entering and exiting poverty: changes in earned income, and changes in family structure. Between 2009 and 2012, almost three-quarters of children in households in which previously no one had been working exited poverty when their parents moved into full-time employment.[17] Changes in family structure affect poverty rates as they can increase or decrease costs (the birth of another child or a child leaving home), or they can affect the earning potential of a household (by gaining or losing adult earners). For a full discussion of children's higher poverty rates relative to adults, see Chapter 7.

It is important to keep these factors in mind when considering the characteristics of those people who are more likely to remain in poverty: around one in 16 working-age people (6.3 per cent) experienced persistent poverty in 2015. Children (under the age of 18) and pensioners (65 and older) are significantly more likely to remain in poverty than working-age people.

The number of adults in a family is also critical. As Figure 8.3 shows, both single-adult households without children and lone-parent households are more likely to experience persistent poverty than households with two

Figure 8.3:

Persistent poverty by family type, UK, 2014

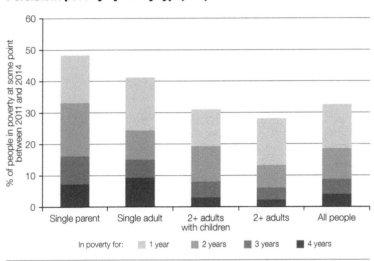

Note: At some point between 2011 and 2014 a third of people were in poverty; almost half of those in single-parent families experienced poverty in that period.

Source: Office for National Statistics and Eurostat, *Persistent Poverty in the UK and EU: 2014*, 2016

adults (with or without children). Two-adult households benefit from being able to generate two incomes – or, to put it another way, the loss of one adult's earnings is less consequential than it would be for a one-adult family.

People who left education without formal qualifications were twice as likely to have experienced poverty in the three years to 2015 than people with a degree or higher,[18] due to lower earnings and higher rates of unemployment.[19]

People with disabilities have a higher rate of persistent poverty than non-disabled people.[20] People with disabilities are disadvantaged in multiple ways, including having lower rates of educational attainment, lower employment rates and higher rates of low pay than non-disabled people.[21] They also face higher living costs, which current social security disability benefits do not adequately cover, meaning that they are likely to have a lower standard of living than non-disabled people on a similar income.[22] Much of disability is chronic, meaning that people face higher living costs and employment challenges for a long period of time, making it more likely that they will experience persistent poverty.

The persistent poverty rate for women in the UK was 1.9 percentage points higher than for men in 2015 (8.2 per cent of women compared with 6.3 per cent of men).[23] Men and women who live together are deemed to have the same household income (even though this may not been equally shared), and therefore the same poverty rate, so this statistical gender gap is driven by gender differences in single-adult households. Nine in 10 lone-parent households (of which one-fifth were in persistent poverty) are headed by women. Women are also more likely to be low paid than men,[24] putting single women at greater risk of falling below the poverty line than single men.

Almost seven in 10 working-age lone parents who were not in work were in poverty in 2015. The poverty rate was almost a third for working-age lone parents in work, indicating that lone parents' ability to get, and maintain, work plays a key role in their exiting or remaining out of poverty. However, the high rate of poverty among lone parents in work indicates that income from one adult's work is often not enough to stay above the poverty line for many families.

Movements below the poverty line: destitution and severe child poverty

Just as the experience of persistent poverty is different from the experience of shorter term poverty, so too is the depth of poverty experienced. Since 2010, the average gap between the poverty line and the income of families in poverty has grown; in other words, the poor are growing poorer.[25] There are various ways to analyse the depth of poverty. The measures used here are: material deprivation, which captures how many essential items people in poverty lack; and severe child poverty and destitution, which combine income and material deprivation measures.

Material deprivation is a measure used as an indication of the living standards of people in poverty. A person is materially deprived if s/he does not have three of nine essential items (such as a meal with protein every second day or a telephone) because s/he cannot afford them. In 2015, 14.1 per cent of people in the UK were materially deprived (lacking at least three of the nine), while 6.1 per cent lived in severe material deprivation (lacking at least four of the nine).[26] While the proportion of children in material deprivation has remained fairly stable over the past decade, there are indications that parents have become more so in order to shield their children.[27]

A related concept is severe child poverty. The measure used here is based on work by Save the Children, and is defined as having a household income after housing costs below 50 per cent of the median and being materially deprived.[28] Children in these families often miss out on things important to their development like attending school trips or having hobbies. In 2015/16, there were 1.1 million children living in severe poverty on this basis, 8 per cent of all children.

The risk factors for severe child poverty include having disabled parents, being in a workless family, living in the social-rented sector, being from certain minority ethnic backgrounds (Pakistani, Bangladeshi and Black African), and being in a larger family.[29]

The Immigration and Asylum Act 1999 defines an asylum seeker as destitute if s/he lacks adequate accommodation or any means of obtaining it and/or s/he cannot meet her/his essential living needs.[30] But leaving aside asylum seekers, there is no official definition or government measure capturing this extreme end of poverty. Recent research from Heriot-Watt University for the Joseph Rowntree Foundation attempted to estimate how many people in the UK experience destitution by combining income and the lack of essential items.[31] This research defines a household as destitute if it:

- has a low income and no savings and has gone without at least two of six essential items (such as shelter, food and basic toiletries) over the past month; *or*
- has a household income below the destitution threshold set by the research. This is based on an average of the actual spend of bottom decile households on these essential items, 80 per cent of the Joseph Rowntree Foundation minimum income standard for equivalent items, and the amount the general public thought was necessary to avoid destitution. The threshold is currently £140 a week for a couple with two children.

Based on this definition, there were an estimated 670,000 households, containing 1.3 million people, who were destitute and in contact with support services during 2015. This estimate was based on data from support services, so it is an underestimation that does not take into account households who are not receiving such support.[32]

Ways of measuring poverty solely based on income will never be perfect, but in a market economy, they are critical to understanding poverty. To drill deeper into what life looks like for people living on low incomes, measures such as material deprivation and destitution can provide insight into the experience of poverty. Table 8.1 illustrates the hugely different levels of income that can exist below the poverty line – a single person who was destitute in 2015 is surviving on half the income of some-one at the poverty line. While both are in poverty, their lived experience may be very different. Someone at the poverty line may well lack the ability to adequately heat their home, while the destitute person may be unable to afford shelter at all, and be forced to sleep rough. While both people have living standards far below what most people in the UK believe is acceptable,[33] the level of hardship they face is likely to be different. Note that the destitution threshold is not designed to be a new poverty line, but instead the income level at which people are no longer able to meet basic material needs for functioning.[34] This might help explain why it is a rela-tively smaller proportion of the poverty line for a couple with two children than for a single adult, due to the economies of scale for basic items.

Table 8.1:

Poverty thresholds

Weekly amounts	Single adult	Lone parent with one young child	Couple with no children	Couple with two children, one 14 or over, one under 14
2015/16 'relative' low-income threshold (the poverty line), after housing costs	£144	£193	£248	£402
UK destitution threshold 2015	£70	£90	£100	£140

Source: A Tinson and others, *Monitoring Poverty and Social Exclusion 2016*, New Policy Institute, 2016

Conclusions

Income dynamics show that there is no fixed pool of people living in poverty in the UK, but rather a constant churn of people entering and exit-ing poverty. Every person's income varies across their lifetime, although some people's income varies more from year to year or even month to month. Volatility in income can have a profound effect on those at the bot-tom of the income distribution, when it can result in people entering or exiting poverty. People's experience of poverty depends on the length of time they have a low income and on how low that income is, together with the impact this has on their living standards – what they cannot buy (such as nutrition-rich food or warm clothing for winter), and the experiences from which they are excluded (such as annual holidays, meals with friends and after-school activities). A third of people in the UK experienced poverty at some time in the four years to 2014,[35] showing that the risk of poverty is widespread throughout society. However, through analysing who moves into and out of poverty and why, and the different experiences of poverty, it becomes clear that the risk of entering and remaining in poverty and the experience of poverty is not evenly distributed across society. Children, lone parents, disabled people and people in households in which no one works have a higher risk of falling into poverty, remaining in poverty for longer and experiencing deeper poverty than other groups of people.

Notes

1   J Hills, *Good Times, Bad Times: the welfare myth of them and us*, Policy Press, 2015

2   T Shildrick and others, *The Low-pay, No-pay Cycle: understanding recurrent poverty*, Joseph Rowntree Foundation, 2010

3   D Buck and J Jabbal, *Tackling Poverty: making more of the NHS in England*, The King's Fund for the Joseph Rowntree Foundation, 2014

4   P Serafino and R Tonkin, *Intergenerational Transmission of Disadvantage in the UK and EU,* Office for National Statistics, 2014

5   *The Debt Trap: exposing the impact of problem debt on children*, StepChange and The Children's Society, 2014

6   J Tucker (ed), *Improving Children's Life Chances,* Child Poverty Action Group, 2016

7   G Standing, *The Precariat: the new dangerous class*, Bloomsbury, 2011; M Orton, *Something's Not Right: insecurity and an anxious nation*, Compass, 2015

8   J Strelitz, *Ending Severe Child Poverty*, Joseph Rowntree Foundation, 2008

9   The definition of persistent poverty used in the Child Poverty Act 2010 (abolished in 2016) had a longer time frame of three out of the previous four years.

10 Eurostat uses a relative poverty measure of 60 per cent of median equalised disposable income before housing costs, so we use this indicator here. The overall poverty rate used is also based on income before housing costs for comparability.

11 Department for Work and Pensions, *Low Income Dynamics*, 2013

12 Data not available for Ireland.

13 Before housing costs.

14 J Hills, *Good Times, Bad Times: the welfare myth of them and us*, Policy Press, 2015

15 A Tinson and others, *Monitoring Poverty and Social Exclusion 2016,* New Policy Institute for Joseph Rowntree Foundation, 2016

16 J Hills, *Good Times, Bad Times: the welfare myth of them and us*, Policy Press, 2015

17 T MacInnes and others, *Monitoring Poverty and Social Exclusion 2015,* New Policy Institute for Joseph Rowntree Foundation, 2015

18 Office for National Statistics, *Persistent Poverty in the UK and EU: 2015*, 2017

19 A Tinson and others, *Monitoring Poverty and Social Exclusion 2016,* New Policy Institute for Joseph Rowntree Foundation, 2016

20 Department for Work and Pensions, *Low Income Dynamics*, 2013

21 A Tinson and others, *Disability and Poverty in the UK*, New Policy Institute, 2016

22 A Tinson and others, *Disability and Poverty in the UK*, New Policy Institute, 2016

23 Office for National Statistics, *Persistent Poverty in the UK and EU: 2015*, 2017

24 H Aldridge, A Tinson and G Whitham, *Women, Work and Wages in the UK*, New Policy Institute, 2016

25 H Aldridge, A Tinson and G Whitham, *Women, Work and Wages in the UK*, New Policy Institute, 2016

26 Eurostat, *Material Deprivation Statistics*, 2016

27 Child Poverty Action Group, *Poverty Gaps and Material Deprivation*, 2016

28 Here defined as a material deprivation score of 25 or more. M Magadi and S Middleton, *Severe Child Poverty in the UK,* Save the Children, 2007

29 Save the Children and the New Policy Institute, *Severe Child Poverty: nationally and locally*, 2011

30 Home Office, *Assessing Destitution*, 2011

31 S Fitzpatrick and others, *Destitution in the UK*, Joseph Rowntree Foundation, 2016

32 S Fitzpatrick and others, *Destitution in the UK*, Joseph Rowntree Foundation, 2016

33 S Fitzpatrick and others, *Destitution in the UK*, Joseph Rowntree Foundation, 2016

34 S Fitzpatrick and others, *Destitution in the UK*, Joseph Rowntree Foundation, 2016

35 A Tinson and others, *Monitoring Poverty and Social Exclusion 2016,* New Policy Institute for Joseph Rowntree Foundation, 2016

Nine

Poverty in the UK and other countries

Summary

- In terms of relative disposable incomes, and taking into account both median household incomes and the relative price of goods and services in each country, the UK's position as a wealthy country remains unchallenged.
- UK child poverty rates are around the average among European Union countries. Scandinavian countries have the lower rates and some Mediterranean countries and former Soviet bloc countries the higher rates. The United States, the richest country in the world, has the highest child poverty rate.

CHILD POVERTY RATES
BEFORE AND AFTER TAX AND BENEFITS

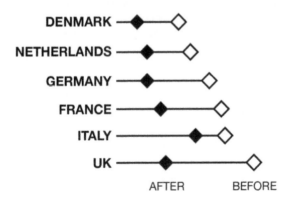

- The rank order of countries by the extent of child deprivation (ie, children going without essentials in each country) aligns well with the rank order by the proportion of each country's children found in relative income poverty.

- The UK's initial child poverty rate before cash transfers in benefits and tax credits is among the very highest in Europe: higher even than Greece, Italy and Spain. Initial income poverty in the UK is very high, driven mainly by large disparities in wages.
- Compared to most other countries, the UK's tax and benefits system has to work exceptionally hard to reduce very high initial poverty rates down to near the European average.
- Poverty rates among UK pensioners almost halved (from 30 per cent to 17 per cent) in the 20 years up to 2014 and are now almost exactly equal to the OECD average.

Introduction

There is a lot to be learned from comparing poverty rates between different countries. It is possible to see more clearly, for example, how different countries' approaches to income redistribution have an impact on their rates of relative income poverty. On the other hand, such comparisons in standards of living are made difficult by differences in what similar amounts of money can buy in different countries, by changes in exchange rates, and by differences in how much of the total economy in one country is captured by its official statistics.[1] Often figures are given on a a 'purchasing power parity' basis, to help account for differences in what money can buy in different countries. This chapter compares the UK with other countries within the Organisation for Economic Cooperation and Development (OECD) and the European Union (EU).

A world of inequality

The overall income levels and the degrees of income inequality in each country are not, in themselves, measures of relative poverty. But these measures set the frame for measuring relative poverty levels and need to be compared first.

Overall incomes

In terms of relative disposable incomes, which take into account both median household incomes and the relative price of goods and services in each country, the UK's position as a wealthy country remains unchallenged (Figure 9.1) This alone should inform the debate about how much the UK can 'afford' to assist low-income families with cash transfers. The IMF, Word Bank and United Nations all rank the UK as the world's fifth largest economy, although it falls to ninth, tenth and ninth place respectively on a purchasing power parity basis.

The UK's disposable household income, surprisingly perhaps, remains similar to that of Scandinavian and some other northern European countries, while below it are southern European countries such as Italy and Spain and then, further down, the former Soviet bloc nations. While it is no surprise that the UK is more than twice as rich as Mexico, not everyone would expect that relative UK incomes, when adjusted for domestic costs of living, are still similar to those in Japan.

Income inequality

The most commonly used measure by which countries may be compared in their degrees of income inequality is the Gini coefficient (Figure 9.2).[2] (See Chapter 3 for an explanation of how the Gini coefficient is calculated.)

In this analysis, the UK parts company with the Scandinavian countries, which have less inequality, redistributing income to a greater extent though their tax and benefit regimes. Some of the former Soviet bloc countries (Slovenia, Slovakia and the Czech Republic) also retain greater income equality, though they have lower overall incomes too, while others (Bulgaria and the Baltic republics) have emerged with much greater inequality. Other northern European countries tend towards the lower range of inequality and the southern Europeans towards the higher range. Among the larger countries, the UK and Italy slightly exceed the EU average, while the United States, among all the developed nations, is both the richest and the least equal.

Inequality has grown in most OECD countries, but has grown fastest among countries that have rowed back most from their earlier, more redistributive, fiscal regimes – notably New Zealand and Sweden and, to a lesser degree, Germany. Countries that have done more to retain their earlier degrees of social protection, especially France, have seen little or no increase in income inequality.[3] Overall, the contribution to household income from social transfers across the OECD countries actually rose during the 1980s, but was retrenched in the 1990s and has again been reduced since 2008. The OECD reports:[4]

Figure 9.1:

Adjusted annual disposable household incomes across the OECD countries, US $, 2016

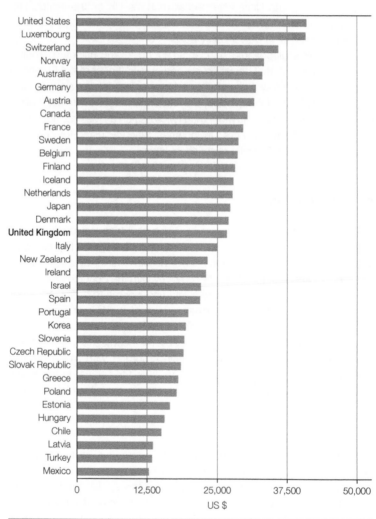

Source: OECD Better Life Index, 2016

As a result, tax-benefit policies offset some of the large increases in market-income inequality, although they appear to have become less effective at doing so since the mid-1990s. Until the mid-1990s, tax-benefit systems in many OECD countries offset more than half of the rise in market-income inequality. However, while market-income inequality continued to rise after the mid-1990s, much of the stabilising effect of taxes and benefits on household income inequality declined.

Figure 9.2:

Gini coefficient across Europe, 2015

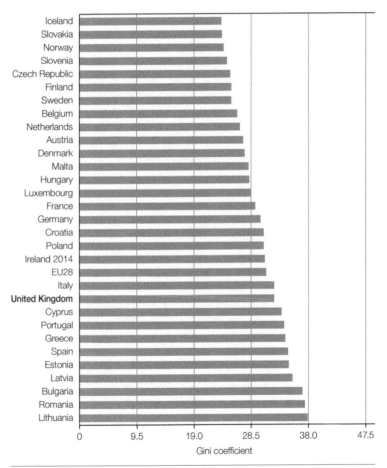

Source: Eurostat, *Equivalised disposable income 2015*, EU-SILC Survey, 2016

We examine the impact of social transfers on poverty rates below.

Child poverty and deprivation in rich countries

Table 9.1 shows five key indicators of child poverty for most of the richer countries in the world.

Relative income poverty

In 2015, almost half of the 35 richer countries had between a fifth and quarter of their children living in households below 60 per cent of their national median income. This middle range is quite narrow, ranging between France at 17 per cent and Latvia at 25 per cent and includes the UK at 21 per cent. Outside this middle range, the Scandinavian countries are at the more favourable end, though it is surprising that Cyprus is among them.[5] But it is remarkable that the richest country, the United States, shares with one of the poorest, Romania, the outlying position of having the largest proportions of children in relative income poverty, at 31 per cent and 32 per cent respectively.

Not all the families below 60 per cent of median income are found just below that threshold; some are much further down the income scale. By comparing the proportion below 60 per cent of national median income with the proportion below 50 per cent we can get some idea of the *depth* of poverty in each country. If the proportions are similar, this implies that most of those in poverty are deep in poverty.

In this respect, the UK does better than most other countries: the remaining effect of the increased cash transfers to families with children that began in 1999 still leaves fewer than half of those below 60 per cent in the greater poverty below 50 per cent. In fact, from the mid-1990s until 2011, child poverty fell fastest in the UK. Finland, though, still manages to keep all but 4 per cent of its children above the 50 per cent mark, compared with 9 per cent in the UK. The US does less well – two-thirds of children in poverty are below 50 per cent of the American median – while in the southern European countries, especially Greece, most of those in households living on below 60 per cent of median income are, in fact, on incomes below 50 per cent.

Table 9.1:

Key indicators of child poverty, 2015

	Below 60% of median income %	Below 50% of median income %	Poverty gap %	Relative income gap %	Deprived of two or more essential items %
Iceland	10	6	13	38	1
Norway	11	5	21	37	2
Slovenia	11	8	18	48	8
Denmark	11	5	33	40	3
Finland	12	4	11	38	3
Cyprus	12	9	18	47	7
Sweden	13	9	21	46	2
Czech Republic	13	6	21	40	9
Austria	14	10	16	42	9
Germany	15	7	22	43	9
Netherlands	15	6	18	40	3
France	17	9	15	44	10
Belgium	17	10	18	48	9
Slovakia	17	14	27	54	19
Switzerland	18	7	16	40	n/a
Australia	18	9	14	45	n/a
Ireland	19	7	13	42	5
New Zealand	19	11	16	47	n/a
Malta	20	15	16	48	9
Hungary	21	15	12	48	32
Japan	21	16	31	60	n/a
Estonia	21	12	20	56	12
United Kingdom	21	9	19	40	6
Luxembourg	22	13	15	41	4
Canada	22	17	21	53	n/a
Poland	23	15	21	52	21
Portugal	23	17	30	60	27
Lithuania	24	18	24	55	20
Italy	24	18	30	61	13
Greece	24	22	21	65	17
Spain	24	20	33	63	8
Bulgaria	24	23	32	67	57
Latvia	25	16	31	60	32
USA	31	20	38	59	n/a
Romania	32	24	35	67	73

Source: J Hudson and S Kühner, *Fairness for Children: a league table of inequality in child well-being in rich countries*, Innocenti Report Card 13, UNICEF Office of Research, 2016

The poverty gap and the relative income gap.

Another way of looking at the depth of poverty in each country is to compare the median incomes of those in poverty with the incomes received by those just on the national median. The 'poverty gap' does this for all those below 60 per cent of the median;[6] the 'relative income gap' does this for the income of those exactly on the 10th percentile of income – ie, nine out of 10 families are richer, while just one in 10 are poorer.

Box 9.1:

The poverty gap and the relative income gap

The **poverty gap** is the *difference* between the median income of those below the poverty line (below 60 per cent of the median) and the national median income, expressed as a percentage. Thus, the disposable income of French families in poverty falls 15 per cent short of the French national median income.

The **relative income gap** is the household income of children found exactly at the 10th percentile of income (10 per cent poorer, 90 per cent richer) expressed as a percentage of the national median income. Thus, the income of Romanian children at the 10th percentile is 67 per cent lower than the national median income in Romania.

Again, the figures for the UK are towards the more favourable end of the range of gaps calculated for each country, with a poverty gap about half those estimated for the southern European countries and the United States, slightly less even than that for Sweden and Germany, and the same as that of the Netherlands. Thus, the UK system does quite well in keeping families out of the direst poverty. Japan's figures are more surprising, having most children in poverty living on household incomes below the 50 per cent mark, with large poverty and relative income gaps.

However, as we show in Chapter 10, the cuts to the UK's family benefits, which will be completed by 2020, will expose more UK families to the risks of much deeper poverty.

Deprivation and hardship

The deprivation levels cited in Table 9.1 are from surveys using a 14-item scale, asking whether families have a range of basic goods and services familiar from Chapter 4, recording the proportion of children lacking two or more items. The rank order from favourably low to unfavourably high proportions of children going without essentials aligns well with the rank order of countries according to the proportions of children found in income poverty, though the UK does somewhat better on the deprivation index than predicted by its ranking on income poverty.

There are, though, some strange anomalies. Among the poorest countries, the former Soviet bloc nations of Bulgaria, Romania, Latvia and Hungary have alarmingly high levels of child deprivation, but Poland, Estonia, Slovakia and Slovenia have much lower levels. Among those in the middle range of national income, Italy, Greece and Portugal have higher levels; Spain and the UK rather lower. The Czech Republic has the same GDP per capita as Portugal, but has levels of child deprivation three times lower. And although the richest nations all have favourable levels below 10 per cent, they are much lower in the Scandinavian countries and the Netherlands compared with Germany, Austria and Belgium. In Iceland, child deprivation is almost unknown, at least in the terms that are measured by these items.

Again, some of these discrepancies in 2008/09 may well have reflected differences in technical developments in different countries. For example, one item asked whether children had an internet connection, whereas the national rate of connection varied widely across Europe at that time.[7]

The effect of social transfers

In each country, the national rate of child poverty is reduced by social transfers: cash benefits paid to families to increase their incomes. The UK, for example, spends about 3.5 per cent of its GDP on transfers to families with children, while the US spends about 1.5 per cent, though total social expenditure in the two countries is fairly similar (22 per cent compared to 19 per cent).

How hard is the tax and benefits system made to work in each country to transfer income to poorer families, lifting those with low initial incomes (or none) up above the poverty line? Figure 9.3 answers this question for the EU countries, with some quite surprising results.

Figure 9.3:

Child poverty rates before and after cash benefits, 2015

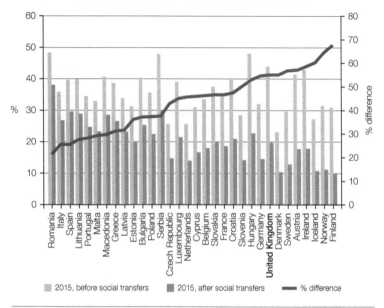

2015, before social transfers   2015, after social transfers   ▬ % difference

Source: J Hudson and S Kühner, *Fairness for Children: a league table of inequality in child well-being in rich countries*, Innocenti Report Card 13, UNICEF Office of Research, 2016

Again, some of the residual impact of the 1997–2010 Labour governments' increases in the UK's cash transfers to families with children carried through into 2015, despite reductions in benefits introduced in the wake of the financial crisis of 2008. The UK has had one of the more effective anti-poverty strategies in Europe, save for the Scandinavian countries, Austria and Ireland. The UK is almost alone (together with Ireland and Austria) in cutting a relatively high pre-transfer child poverty rate down to a relatively low one, reducing rates from more than 40 per cent to below (in this calculation) 20 per cent – thus reducing the pre-transfer poverty rate by about 60 per cent. Corresponding reductions in southern European and former Soviet bloc countries are far smaller.

While this seems like good news, it is fair to wonder why the tax and benefits system *has* to work so hard in the UK compared with elsewhere. The UK's initial child poverty rate before transfers is among the very highest in Europe: higher even than Greece, Italy and Spain. Initial income poverty in the UK is very wide, driven mainly by large disparities in *wages*.[8]

Higher earners in the UK pay less tax than high earners pay in most other EU countries. The Office for National Statistics reports that:[9]

> Qualitative analysis by the World Economic Forum (WEF) identifies the UK has [sic] having the 5th most efficient labour market (out of 148 countries), compared with the United States (4th), Canada (7th), Germany (41st), France (71st) and Italy (137th). The measure considers flexibility in wage determination, hiring and firing and redundancy costs among other labour market factors.

So, the effectiveness of the UK system lies in the use of family tax credits to try to lever some (though not all) of the worst paid working parents back over the poverty line. Even so, it still leaves two-thirds of children in relative income poverty in families in which at least one parent has a paid job. It also protects low-waged tenants from rapidly rising housing costs by transferring large amounts of housing benefit, though recently these have been cut for many.

A second illustration of the all-important impact of policy on child poverty is given in Figure 9.4, which shows by how much social transfers, mainly cash benefits, reduce the relative income gap for families with children in each country. In this analysis, the UK does best in all Europe – but again, this happens largely because the initial gap before transfers is so large – larger than anywhere else except Belgium and Bulgaria – reducing the UK's gap from 77 per cent to 40 per cent (a *reduction* of 48 per cent).[10] Other countries' systems have to work less hard in reducing the relative income gap. In Switzerland, for example, it is reduced from 49 per cent to 40 per cent – a reduction of just 19 per cent, to achieve exactly the same outcome that a reduction of 48 per cent achieves in the UK. And as we show elsewhere, the real value of social transfers to UK families has fallen recently and will continue to fall sharply under the new universal credit benefit regime.

In most of the southern European and former Soviet bloc countries, however, the picture is dismal. Benefits do almost nothing to improve the relative income gaps of the families with the lowest incomes. In Spain, Italy, Portugal and Greece, relative income gaps begin at over 60 per cent before transfers and remain so after.

The 2016 Unicef Innocenti Report Card 13, *Fairness for Children: a league table of inequality in child well-being in rich countries*, provides a complex and far-ranging comparison of child wellbeing in Europe, including, as well as income, estimates of inequality in education, health and life satisfaction.[11] It concludes that:

Countries with higher income gaps tend to have lower levels of overall child well-being [and that] ... large relative income gaps are not inevitable, that policy makers have tools at their disposal that are effective in reducing income inequality, and that smaller income gaps are better for all children...

Figure 9.4:

Income inequality and social transfers: the percentage by which social transfers in each country reduce the relative income gap for families with dependent children, 2015

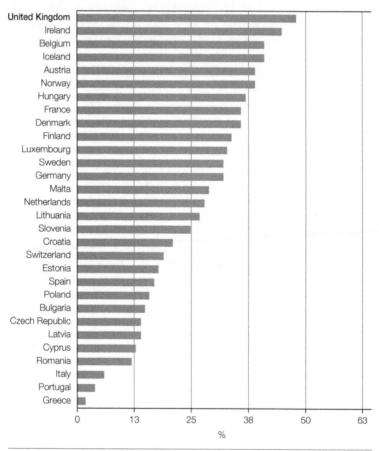

Source: J Hudson and S Kühner, *Fairness for Children: a league table of inequality in child well-being in rich countries*, Innocenti Report Card 13, UNICEF Office of Research, 2016

Pensioners

We saw earlier that the position of pensioners in the UK has improved as a result of the protection of their state pensions and the quite rapid spread of private pensions among the more recent age cohorts entering retirement. Pensioners as a group are also unique in not having poverty rates

Figure 9.5:
Pensioner poverty in Europe, 2007 and 2012

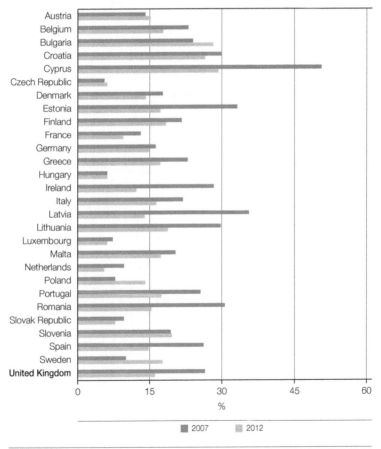

Source: OECD, *Pensions at a Glance 2013: OECD and G20 indicators*, OECD Publishing, 2013, http://dx.doi.org/10.1787/pension_glance-2013-en

higher after housing costs than before. Poverty rates among them almost halved (30 down to 17 per cent) in the 20 years up to 2015/16. Remarkably, this fall continued during the post-recession period. Overall, the UK now has a rate of pensioner poverty almost exactly equal to the OECD average (Figure 9.5). Among most other European countries, falls in pensioner poverty matched or exceeded those in the UK, though the falls recorded for some of the former Soviet bloc countries are so steep as to question whether changes in the methods of measurement or the data available may account for some of the differences. In Poland and Bulgaria, and, strangely, in Sweden, they rose.

Finally, Figure 9.6 compares the rates of child poverty and pensioner poverty in the EU in 2015. It is clear that, in most countries where there are significant levels of child poverty, pensioner poverty is lower.

Figure 9.6:

Child poverty and pensioner poverty in Europe, 2015

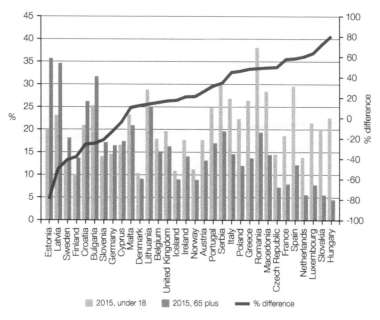

Source: Eurostat, *People at Risk of Poverty or Social Exclusion*, 2016

Conclusions

The UK remains one of the richest countries in the world. This alone should inform policy discussion about what the UK might or might not be able 'to afford' when setting the rates of benefits for those of its citizens with low incomes, or none. Such policy discussion is sharpened by evidence that the UK is among one of the more unequal among rich countries.

What these comparative data show most clearly is that income poverty is policy-responsive. For any nation to reduce poverty among its people, both the labour market and the system of social transfers and benefits should work well and in harmony. In the UK, a liberal market-led economy and government social policy do not combine well compared with many other developed countries. Social transfers in the UK have to work extraordinarily hard to overcome large initial inequalities caused by wide disparities in wages, widened by a tax regime less progressive than in most other European countries. Relatively low productivity and an over-reliance on low-paid labour has left the UK a country where for too many workers, the minimum wage has become the maximum wage while the rewards of educated labour have increased far faster. Continued reductions expected in the future in the value of UK social transfers, together with slow lower wage growth and more part-time work, will cause the UK to fall once more back down the league table towards the unfavourable end of the range of poverty rates found among rich countries.

Notes

1   There is a long list of other difficulties in comparing standards of living between countries, of course, some of them simply geographical. For example, no one living in the Virgin Islands ever has to switch on domestic heating or air conditioning or drive very far, so their disposable income is boosted by small energy costs. Water, though, is expensive.

2   It is fair to add that the Gini coefficient, devised more than a hundred years ago, is falling out of favour with some economists in this field, who prefer to emphasise the resource gap between the richest and poorest.

3   See 'An overview of growing income inequalities in OECD countries: main findings', in OECD, *Divided We Stand: why inequality keeps rising*, OECD Publishing, 2011, p24

4   OECD Better Life Index, 2016

5   Cyprus does have very low rates of lone parenthood – just 8 per cent compared with the UK's 25 per cent – and has a very low median income.

6   J Hudson and S Kühner, *Fairness for Children: a league table of inequality in child well-being in rich countries,* Innocenti Report Card 13, UNICEF, 2016; J Bradshaw and others, *Relative Income Poverty Among Children in Rich Countries,* Innocenti Working Paper IWP-2012-01, UNICEF, 2012

7   See 'Fixed and wireless broadband subscriptions per 100 inhabitants', Table 1.2.1 on OECD Broadband Portal, June 2016, available at www.oecd.org/sti/broadband/oecdbroadbandportal.htm

8   C Dreger and others, *Wage and Income Inequality in the European Union,* European Parliament, Directorate General for Internal Policies, 2014. The authors' analysis places the UK among the four countries with the widest dispersion of wages and also points out that: 'The UK, Ireland, and the Netherlands are characterised by a large share of part-time workers that drive inequality in labour earnings.'

9   A Jowett and others, *An International Perspective on the UK: labour market performance,* Office for National Statistics, 2014

10   J Hudson and S Kühner, *Fairness for Children: a league table of inequality in child well-being in rich countries,* Innocenti Report Card 13, UNICEF, 2016, p16, Figure 6

11   See J Bradshaw, 'Child poverty and child well-being in international perspective' in E Fernandez and others (eds), *Theoretical and Empirical Insights into Child and Family Poverty: cross national perspectives,* Children's Well-Being: indicators and research services, 10, Springer International, 2015, pp59–70; EU-SILC 2009

Ten

The causes of poverty

Summary

- The long-term deterioration of the terms of employment for workers at the lower paid end of the UK labour market – essentially the bottom 20 per cent – has been a major, possibly *the* major, cause of enduring poverty in the UK.
- Since 2006, there has been a 60 per cent rise in the number of people moving repeatedly between work and unemployment.
- Between 1975 and 2014, the real hourly wages of full-time employees in the middle of the income distribution doubled. Those above the middle increased up to 189 per cent among the best paid, while those below the middle rose typically by about 80 per cent.

LOW-PAID, INSECURE JOBS FUNDAMENTAL TO UK'S ENDURING POVERTY PROBLEM

BOTTOM 20%

- Among part-time workers, this wage difference is wider: those in the middle saw increases of 87 per cent over four decades; those below this, less. But part-time workers *at the top* tripled their real hourly wages.
- Benefit payments and tax credits are insufficient to keep people out of poverty.

- As a proportion of their income, those in the bottom fifth of the income distribution pay the most in direct and indirect taxes combined (at 40.7 per cent). Those among the richest fifth pay 37.8 per cent of their income as tax.
- Research shows that children brought up in poverty and hardship find it extremely difficult to respond to interventions intended to improve their 'life chances' if their parents are struggling to provide for them and they are going without basics at home. The government's recent emphasis on debt, drug and alcohol dependence as important causes of poverty are not supported by research.

Introduction

The causes of poverty in the UK are economic, structural and political. Enduring weaknesses in the UK labour market, especially those associated with industrial disinvestment, have resulted in low wages in insecure jobs that offer few prospects, accompanied by recurrent waves of unemployment. At the same time, inadequate social security transfers and the increasingly unequal distribution of incomes, power and resources have left many disadvantaged people without access to enough regular income to maintain an acceptable standard of living.

Unemployment and insecure work

Unemployment

During the first 30 years after the second world war, unemployment in the UK remained low. As late as the mid-1970s, the proportion of the workforce unemployed and seeking work remained between 3 per cent and 4 per cent (Figure 10.1) – which, for all practical purposes, is 'full employment', since there are always some people who need to change jobs as firms come and go, or as contracts end.

From the early 1980s onwards, however, unemployment rose rapidly, peaking at more than 11 per cent in 1983, with three million people unemployed and claiming benefits. The rate fell in the later 1980s,[1] but returned to the same level in 1996, when there was a wider difference between men and women (11 per cent unemployed versus 8 per cent).

Figure 10.1:

Unemployment in the UK, 1971 to 2017

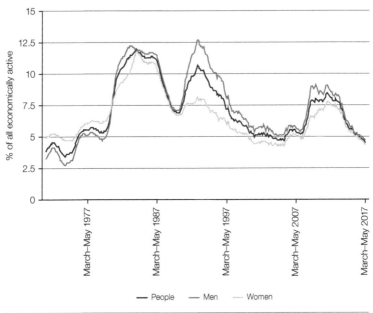

Sources: Office for National Statistics, Figure 11: UK unemployment rates (aged 16 and over), seasonally adjusted, January to March 1971 to August to February 2017

This difference was partly due to some unemployed women withdrawing from the labour market altogether. The pre-1980 full employment rate did not return, and unemployment fell only to 5 per cent. It then rose once more during the most recent recession from 2009 onwards, though rates did not rise as high as earlier, returning finally in 2016 to 5 per cent.

If these three waves of unemployment had passed through like bad weather, to be forgotten as fairer economic climates returned, then they might not have mattered quite so much. But, like storms, they left a trail of destruction. Research by Paul Gregg and others showed the 'scarring effect' of unemployment – that '... the best predictor of becoming unemployed is a recent history of unemployment'. More than that, periods of unemployment reduced future earnings, typically by about 10 per cent, resulting in workers becoming mired in a 'low-pay, no-pay cycle' of temporary and insecure work. By the end of the 1990s, it was already clear:[2]

... that repeat spells of unemployment go hand in hand with jobs that are low paid and unstable... interruptions to employment not only bring the obvious loss of current income during the period of unemployment, but inflict a longer term 'scar' through the increased future incidence of unemployment and lower subsequent earnings in employment... with lower earnings potential leading to an extended period of job search before a suitable job match is found or the person drifts into economic inactivity. Their effects will be particularly damaging in exacerbating lifetime inequality, bringing the threat of poverty and social exclusion.

Low wages

Even before the effects of the 2008/09 financial crisis took hold and the most recent recession began, a report by the Joseph Rowntree Foundation found that this process had become endemic in the UK, to the extent that low pay itself increases the risk of spells of unemployment.[3] The author's analysis of the British Household Panel Survey showed that, in a typical four-year period, about four in every 10 low-paid workers will spend at least one period out of work and claiming benefits. A third of these fail to return to work at all:

> Those working for low wages tend to also be working in jobs characterised by temporary contracts and low hours, and are also more likely to experience individual barriers to employment security such as work limiting health conditions and few qualifications.

And these data were based on employment data mostly before the 2008/09 crisis and recession struck. Subsequently, the Joseph Rowntree Foundation's programme of research has shown how the recession reinforced the role of poorly paid work, trapping workers in recurrent spells of poverty.[4] It draws attention to the growth of the 'peripheral labour market', contrasted with the 'core labour market', where those stuck on the periphery could expect little wage progression. It provides an important qualification to the principle of government anti-poverty policy for the past 30 years, that work is the surest way out of poverty:

> The issue of people moving repeatedly between work and unemployment is an endemic problem in the UK and has risen by 60 per cent since 2006, mostly as a result of the recession.

However, 'entering work cannot provide a sustainable route out of poverty if job security, low pay and lack of progression are not also addressed.' Indeed, the whole labour market has suffered from a lack of wage progression since about 2002. As a report by the Resolution Foundation says: '... strong pay growth in the 1990s was followed by a flat-lining in real hourly pay from around 2002.' And since 2009 real wages fell, remaining still £29 a week less overall compared with the 2009 peak.[5]

In summary, then, long-term deterioration of the terms of employment at the lower paid end of the labour market – essentially the bottom 20 per cent – has been a major, possibly *the* major, cause of enduring poverty in the UK.

The drift to part-time work

Even accounting for the setback of the post-2009 recession, between 1975 and 2014, the real hourly wages of the full-time employees found in the middle of the income distribution doubled. Those above the middle increased the most – up to 189 per cent among the best paid among them, despite recent falls. Wages among those below the middle rose by less, typically by about 80 per cent, though the introduction of the minimum wage in 1999 helped to improve the very lowest wages by more.[6] By 2015, the wages of those found at the top 10 percentile of earners (ie, people whose wages were higher than the wages of 90 per cent of others, but less than the remaining 10 per cent), excluding annual bonuses, were nearly four times greater than those found in the bottom 10 percentile.[7]

Among part-time workers, this difference is wider: those in the middle saw increases of 87 per cent over four decades; those below this, less. But part-time workers at the top *tripled* their real hourly wages.[8] As the average hourly wage of part-time workers fell behind that of full-time workers, so part-time work has become more common. Between 1992 (when the Office for National Statistics began its present data series) and 2016, the numbers of part-time workers in the UK labour force – now more than 32 million workers – increased from 6 million to 8.5 million.[9] The proportion of female workers contributing part-time (rather than full-time) hours remained the same (about four in 10), though their numbers grew as more women entered the labour market. Among men, part-time working increased from 7 per cent to 14 per cent. So the UK increased part-time working at wages that grew more slowly than full-time workers' wages. Some of this recent increase is due to the spread of zero-hour contracts, rising in 2016 to 900,000 or 3 per cent of UK workers.[10]

The increase in low-paid self-employment

The proportion of self-employed workers in the UK rose from 9 per cent in 1975 to 15 per cent in 2016, but it is from the turn of this century that the numbers climbed dramatically (Figure 10.2).

Figure 10.2:

Number of self-employed people in UK, 1992 to 2015

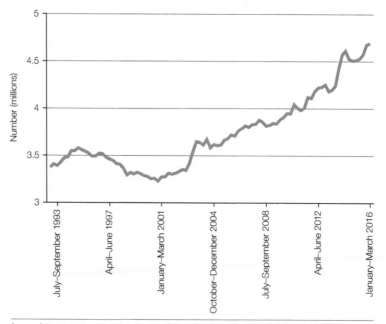

Source: Office for National Statistics, *Trends in Self-employment in the UK: 2001 to 2015*, July 2016

Whereas self-employment was once associated with higher paid occupations, more recently, workers in basic and some skilled occupations, such as taxi driving and the building trades, have become self-employed, often for the convenience of their employers. Median wages among them have fallen significantly between 2006/07 and 2014/15, and the gap between self-employed people's incomes from their work and employed workers' wages has widened since the mid-1990s (Figure 10.3).[11]

In this way, self-employed workers' households have increased their representation among all households below 60 per cent of median income (before housing costs) from 9 per cent to 12 per cent since 1996.

Figure 10.3:

Median weekly earnings of the self-employed and employees, CPI adjusted 2014/15 prices

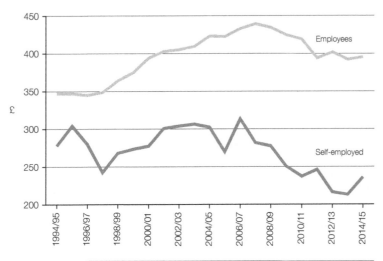

Source: Resolution Foundation, *The RF Earnings Outlook: Quarterly Briefing: Q2 2016*, October 2016, Figure 4[12]

Other pressures on wages

In addition to the spread of part-time working and poorer paid self-employment, the main reasons that wage differentials have increased so much are the following:

- Long-term de-industrialisation displaced many workers into service jobs that, in the private sector, have much lower densities of trade union membership and organisation and so are more likely to be paid at the minimum wage.[13]
- Trade unions' bargaining power has been weakened by legislation, falling membership and the dispersal of workforces away from industrial urban centres.
- Since 2010, public sector wages have been held down by austerity measures.
- The countervailing upward pressure on skilled and knowledge workers' wages, partly through exposure to international markets and the

increasing use of performance bonuses for managers in commerce and finance industries, has increased inequality.

Social security transfers

Is social security sufficient?

Many people define poverty as being 'on benefits'. British newspapers and certain television channels certainly encourage them to do so, but it makes little sense. If the level of means-tested benefits were to be increased, for example, more would qualify for them and so place more people 'in poverty'. That aside, many of those receiving benefits, such as recipients of child benefit, are not poor, because the functions of the benefits and tax credits system are so much broader than simply providing a safety net for those with no other income.[14]

As well as transferring money from the richer to the poorer strata of the population, the social security system does well in transferring resources from times in our lives when we need little assistance to times when we need more: when we are children, parents, or when we are unwell, disabled or simply old, or when we have to live and work in places where decent accommodation is unaffordable to anyone on modest wages. It transfers resources from men to women too. But while the system is well set up to make these essential transfers, and thus reduce tensions and injustice that would otherwise be unmanageable, it must also be judged on how effective the rates of payments are to keep families out of poverty and secure from hardship. In this last dimension, it fails. Following cuts to social security and tax credits during the post-2009 austerity measures, it fails increasingly.

It fails because it gives too little money to people who have no other income. Single people claiming universal credit in 2017/18 are given £73.34 a week to live on, plus all or part of their rent and council tax paid, provided they are over 24 years old; those who are younger get only £58.10. In modern Britain, living on £10 a day or less is an enormous challenge. Sceptical MPs who boasted that it ought to be easy and who accepted the challenge themselves failed, with sometimes comical results.[15] They discovered that as well as feeding themselves (food, and the fuel to cook it), they had somehow to keep warm, keep clean, get around on expensive public transport, perhaps buy clothes or shoes, replace things that break and so on. Charity shops are cheap, but they are not free.

Families with children claiming benefits are in only a slightly better position. On top of their £114.85 a week jobseeker's allowance (assuming one of them is 25 or over), a couple with two children will get £117.52 a week in child tax credit and £34.40 a week in child benefit, £266.77 in all (although they still have to send typically £2 a week to the council to make up the shortfall in their council tax reduction that is now imposed).

All this assumes that the family is not in accommodation that has more bedrooms than the government believes they ought to have. Any more, and their housing benefit will be reduced and they will have to make up the difference in rent or move to smaller accommodation.[16] And it also assumes that they are not receiving more than £384.62 (outside London) a week in total benefits, including all their housing support and some disability benefits too (the 'benefit cap'). Rents in the private sector increased by 15 per cent between 2011 and 2017,[17] which increased housing benefit payments correspondingly. This has made it easier for someone to exceed the benefit cap, solely because her/his rent has been increased. It is now arithmetically impossible for the benefits system to lift them out of poverty. The scale of what they might really need is given by the Joseph Rowntree Foundation's minimum income standard figures: in order to reach an acceptable standard of living in modern Britain, our couple with two children would need to earn £20,400 a year *each*[18] – exactly twice the level of the benefit cap income limit.

Falling benefits and universal credit

The values of the social security benefits shown above were not determined somehow by market forces; they were decided by Parliament.

The effect of changes in the way benefits are uprated, or not

There has been a long-term erosion in the real value of social security benefits. In 1983, annual rises in the value of the main social security benefits were pegged to the retail prices index (RPI). This sounds fair enough, until you realise that people who relied on benefits were no longer allowed any participation in real increases in our national wealth.[19] This is another reason why, by the turn of this century, people receiving benefits had become so much poorer compared with those in well-paid work. Indeed, the large increases in benefit rates introduced in 1999 actually failed to make up all the difference between the improved rates and the amounts claimants would have been getting if benefits had increased at the same rate as wages since 1983. The June 2010 Budget statement changed the uprating index from the RPI to the consumer price index (CPI), which has recently returned lower annual increases compared to the RPI. As wages as a whole usually increase faster than benefits in normal times, so relative income poverty must grow.

New cuts

The 2010 Budget imposed actual reductions in benefits that amounted to £21 billion. Then, in April 2016, benefits were retrenched again, with the rates of many working-age benefits frozen entirely for four years.[20] These new reductions will amount to a further £12 billion taken from families. But there are now further downward pressures on the value of benefits.

By 2022, according to the latest plans, all working-age claimants will have to claim universal credit rather than the six benefits and tax credits it replaces.[21] They will have to claim online – not easy for those without a computer or the skills to use one. When it was first proposed in 2010, universal credit promised to simplify the claiming process, unifying payments into a single amount, bridging the dilemma facing part-time workers by allowing a smoother increase in wages against a progressive withdrawal of benefit, and promising slightly higher net payments than currently available. Since then, weaknesses have appeared:

- It will pay people monthly in arrears, and to one person (not the main carer by default), whereas all research shows that most low-income households budget weekly or, indeed, more frequently. Being paid monthly, including what you need for rent and childcare costs, will be a challenge to manage for many low-income families.
- For new claimants, the child element in universal credit will be paid for the first two children only; nothing will be given for other children. (This cut, together with the withdrawal of the £10 per week family element, also applies to third or subsequent children for child tax credit from April 2017.)

Universal credit also reduces work incentives for lone parents, who are also the biggest cash losers. So the remarkable increase in lone-parent employment since 1997 may go into reverse. Work incentives are also reduced for second earners, which is perverse since this is where any progress to reduce child poverty might come from.

Figure 10.4:

Average annual losses for working-age households from the changes to universal credit and child benefit, for 2020/21 in 2015/16 prices

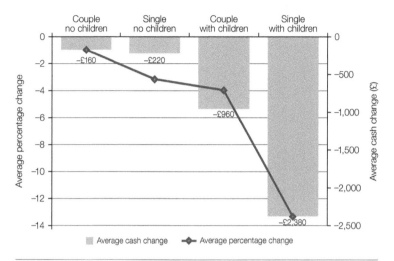

Source: CPAG's analysis of Family Resources Survey 2014/15 using the Institute for Public Policy Research tax-benefit model

Comparing the benefits system incorporating universal credit (and child benefit) as currently legislated with the 2013/14 system, it is apparent that families with children stand to lose out much more severely from the cuts than any other group (Figure 10.4). CPAG's analysis shows that, on average:

- couples with children will be £960 a year worse off;
- lone-parent families will be £2,380 a year worse off;
- families with one child will be £930 a year worse off;
- families with two children will be £1,100 a year worse off;
- families with three children will be £2,540 a year worse off;
- working-age couples without children will be £160 a year worse off;
- single working-age people without children will be £220 a year worse off;
- pensioner couples will be £40 a year worse off;
- single pensioners will be £30 a year worse off.

Figure 10.5:

Average annual losses to households in different equivalised disposable income deciles from the universal credit and child benefit freeze, for 2020/21 in 2015/16 prices

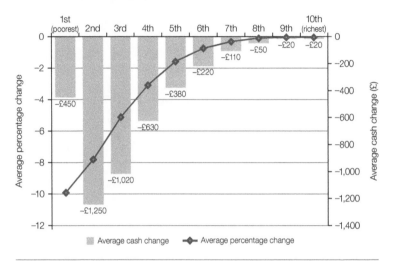

Source: CPAG's analysis of Family Resources Survey 2014/15 using the Institute for Public Policy Research tax-benefit model

The cuts also disproportionately affect lower income deciles (Figure 10.5). These are average losses across the population, including households who do not claim universal credit. This means that, for those claiming universal credit in each group, losses will be higher still. The four-year freeze in the value of most components of universal credit makes a substantial contribution to the losses because prices are expected to rise between now and 2020/21, meaning universal credit will be worth less in real terms each year as long as the freeze is in place.

This last point is especially important: universal credit will impose net reductions in the amount of money going to many claimants compared with the present system of benefits and tax credits, especially to those bringing up children, even when improvements to the minimum wage, income tax and other reforms such as increased allowances for childcare are taken into account. We saw in Chapter 4 that families with children receiving out-of-work benefits still experience unacceptable levels of hardship. Less money will increase their hardship.

Taxation

One of the most difficult problems facing democratic governments every-where – possibly *the* most difficult – is getting their citizens to pay enough taxes.[22] Surveys tend to show that people are broadly in favour of welfare spending, especially for pensions and healthcare, but are reluctant to see tax rises to pay for them. Direct taxes on gross incomes are particularly resented, so governments have moved towards the use of indirect taxes, such as sales taxes (VAT in the UK) and levies on less essential expenditures, such as alcohol and tobacco, which can also be defended on health grounds, for example.

Direct taxes are 'progressive' in the sense that richer people pay more, both in total and as a proportion of their earnings. The poor pay less or none, or they may receive negative income tax in the form of tax credits. Indirect taxes are 'regressive' in that they are paid equally by consumers whatever their income, and so fall unfairly on the poor, who spend a higher proportion of their income out of necessity. It is true that considerable attempts are made to focus indirect taxes on consumption that is more characteristic of better-off households, such as airport transfer taxes (enthusiastically embraced by small poor countries), insurance levies, death duties and property transfers. Council tax is also graduated by the size and value of property, up to a certain limit. Others, though, fall unfairly on the poor, such as VAT on adult clothes, domestic fuel and other everyday consumables.

In the UK, the net effect of this shift to indirect taxation has been that people in the bottom fifth of the income distribution pay the highest fraction of their gross income in taxes, direct and indirect combined. The result is that the bottom fifth end up with 7 per cent of the nation's equivalised income while the top fifth have 42 per cent.[23]

Table 10.1:

Proportion of income paid in taxes, by income quintiles, 2014/15

	Poorest fifth	Second	Third	Fourth	Richest fifth
Direct taxes	11.0	11.5	15.9	19.0	22.8
Indirect taxes	29.7	21.5	19.9	18.5	15.0
Total	40.7	33.0	35.8	37.5	37.8

Source: Office for National Statistics, *The Effects of Taxes and Benefits on Household Income, 2014/15*, 2016, Table 14

As an additional cause of poverty, this is the sting in the tail of the tax and benefits system. Whereas we saw that the UK's social transfers work hard to reduce initial inequalities in income between the poorest and richest, the use of indirect taxes claws back some of the advantages gained.

Why the government's risk factors are not causes

Just as every generation seems to have to discover poverty for itself, so each generation finds its own way to blame 'the poor' for their condition. The contemporary abuse of benefit claimants in the tabloid press and television is familiar enough. More subtle are the recent shifts in government rhetoric and policy pronouncements.

Answering questions in the House of Lords on behalf of the Conservative government, Lord Freud said:[24]

> 'We are trying to move away from the income transfer approaches that we have seen for some time, to try to handle the fundamental causes of poverty.'

Among these 'fundamental causes' were said by Lord Freud to be, '... worklessness, educational attainment and family stability'.

The Conservative party manifesto for the 2015 general election expanded this understanding, stating that these 'root causes' of poverty were 'entrenched worklessness, family breakdown, problem debt, and drug and alcohol dependency'.

Subsequently, the Conservative administration lapsed into a gradual denial of the economic and fiscal causes of poverty in favour of this five-fold behavioural view: people are poor because they lose their jobs, split up their families, get into too much debt, take drugs and drink too much.

The government, of course, had other reasons for discounting the role of cash transfers in relieving poverty: it was reducing them. Its stated ambition to restore fiscal balance in the midst of a severe and prolonged global recession ruled out increased social security transfers and instead introduced the cuts in social security and tax credits detailed above. Having, as a matter of policy, deliberately reduced the incomes of families living in poverty, the government was understandably keen to deny that low incomes were a cause of their poverty.

The new emphasis, apparently, is one that sees the causes of poverty solely as the outcome of degraded life chances. For example, the Social Mobility and Child Poverty Commission was renamed the Social

Mobility Commission[25] and its remit limited to overall social mobility, not poverty. As Ruth Lister comments:[26]

> ... despite the rhetorical emphasis on the 'relentless focus' on the causes of poverty, the notion of child poverty has been expunged legislatively.

Inviting comment on this change of policy, the government:[27]

> ... announced it intends to track child poverty by monitoring educational attainment at 16 and numbers of children living in workless households. It also intends to set out a range of other indicators, including family break-down, debt and addiction in a children's life chances strategy.

Thus, by also shifting the emphasis of *measurement* onto these behavioural factors, the government seeks to redefine popular understanding of poverty away from its immediate and obvious remedy: increased income.

There is no opposition to government efforts and investment to make childhood in the UK as well-supported and as promising as it can be. The acknowledgement that the state has at least some role beyond the love, care and support of parents is welcome. In a recent CPAG publication, leading UK experts set out how government intervention in education and training, health, housing and social policy can contribute to better child outcomes, and how these might be measured.[28] But, as Kitty Stewart makes clear in this work, such effort and investment will mean little unless families with children have an adequate income. She cites extensive evidence that income poverty and poor child outcomes are not somehow joint products of poor parenting, but that the stress, hardship and dismay of endlessly surviving on a low trend income reduces parents' capacity to care for their children patiently and sensitively. The most convincing evidence comes from studies that show the effects of increased income on poor families. She writes:

> ... an increase in income changes the nature of what happens in the household, creating a calmer environment and enabling better engagement from parents.

Put most simply, children brought up in poverty and hardship will find it extremely difficult to respond to interventions intended to improve their 'life chances' if their parents, living in income poverty, are struggling to provide for them and they are going without basics at home. Their degraded outcomes are the effects of living in poverty, not the cause of their persistent low income.

Debt

Another aspect of the government's 'causes' – unmanageable debt – is simply another outcome of the income shortfall caused by low wages and inadequate benefits. A recent expert-led review concluded that it:[29]

> ... did not find any evidence to show that problem debt causes poverty.

But added:

> ... problem debt can deepen people's poverty, even if it is not the direct cause. As a result of repaying problem debts households have less disposable income to live on and have to cut back on other areas of spending. In higher-income households this can mean cutting back on non-essential items; in lower-income households it can mean cutting back on basic necessities such as food, clothes and domestic fuel use. It can also lead to social exclusion (for both adults and children) as households reduce spending on social activities, or become isolated from friends due to feelings of shame and stigma...

Essentially, then, debt deepens hardship. However, while debt is an important outcome of poverty, it is not included among those trends the government says it intends to *measure*.

Addiction: drugs and alcohol

Alcohol

Parental addiction is apparently named as a major cause of child poverty. However, a recent review established that no one actually knows how much alcoholism is concentrated among people living in poverty. Lisa Jones and Harry Sumnall's recent review of the evidence noted that:[30]

> As there are no figures available to determine what proportion of the estimated 13 million adults who live in poverty overlap with the categories of problem drinkers, the extent of the problem is unknown.

> ... According to the 2007 Psychiatric Morbidity Survey, 8.5% of men and 3.0% of women in the lowest income quintile had experienced any symptoms of alcohol dependence in the last 6 months; 2.5% and 0.1%, respec-

tively, had experienced moderate or severe symptoms of dependence that would indicate a need for assisted alcohol withdrawal.

They concluded that:

> There is insufficient evidence to establish that problem alcohol use is a cause of poverty in the UK.

Drugs

The proportion of all UK children living with a problem of parental addiction is not large. Based on estimates from those seeking any help for drug abuse, about 2 per cent of all children in England and Wales and about 4–6 per cent in Scotland have a drug-addicted parent.[31] Of these, only a third of addicted fathers and two-thirds of such mothers are still living with their children and by no means all of these are living in poverty.

Again, helping a small fraction of the lower income population deal with their substance dependence would be welcome, in itself. While not widespread, where they occur the effects of such problems are well documented and have devastating effects on families and their children. Significantly reducing substance dependence will be an important achievement but it will not contribute much to the ending of poverty in the UK. It is also unclear how the government will measure and monitor it, let alone bring it under its 'relentless focus'.

Family breakdown

The risk factor most likely to be mistaken for a cause of poverty is lone parenthood, currently a quarter of UK families with children (which we examined in Chapter 6). Certainly, it is possible to point to aspects of lone parenthood that seem to have nothing to do with economic change. Attitudes changed and the moral stigma once attached to lone parenthood (unless it was also widowhood) diminished. Modern mothers' tolerance for domestic abuse has fallen to a point where marital violence ends far more relationships, irrespective of whether the couple has children.[32]

It is a paradox that women often have to make the choice to be alone with their children at the point when maintaining them is going to be the most difficult. But such family changes are now indelibly part of modern emotional and social life *at all levels of income*. That it is often accompanied by a spell of income poverty is due mainly to the instability of low-waged work for both parents. And doubling your housing costs when you are raising children is always going to stretch modest incomes too far. Much has improved – more than half of lone parents now have their own jobs, similar to women in couples, and many rely on tax credits too, even though short hours, childcare costs (despite recently increased subsidies) and low wages can still leave them below the poverty line. But the reason that the rest remain in relative income poverty – the *cause* of their poverty – is that there is not enough left in the family budget. Governments have never given them enough money to make up all the difference and the present administration is cutting their benefits further.

Troubled families

This false individualistic and behavioural view of the causes of poverty nevertheless led the government to head its list of policy options with the ambition to:[33]

> Help troubled families turn their lives around.

'Poor parenting' and dysfunctional family life was named as a major cause of poverty.[34] This behavioural view of the causes of poverty was also developed by the Centre for Social Justice in its *Breakthrough Britain* report,[35] which heavily influenced the government's view of poverty and its causes, particularly since its chair was also the Secretary of State for Work and Pensions. This view insisted that among those below the poverty line are too many 'troubled families' who between them nationally reinforce a malign cycle of poor educational and career achievement, lone parenthood, drug and alcohol addiction, and wilful failure to participate in the labour market at all.[36] Interestingly, though, the authors agreed with CPAG's view that poverty was costing the public finances a lot of unnecessary expense.

Though persuasive to many, this argument seems unlikely. It might be possible to argue that more resilient families could have responded more resourcefully to the economic shocks that have reduced the relative incomes of people living in poverty in the UK – though this is not likely to be an argument given a sympathetic hearing in de-industrialised communities of the North, Wales and Scotland, for example. And as we discussed earlier, no one could resent attempts to assist families who become troubled in the sense implied. The present administration has charged every local authority with the task of 'turning around' its quota of troubled families, and offered authorities a bonus of £4,000 for each family so helped. (Greater Manchester, for example, was told it had about 2,500 to help.) This effort, though welcome in itself, is unlikely to make serious inroads into the five million children expected to be in relative income poverty by 2020.

Poverty and genes

It is still possible to encounter arguments that poverty is really caused by Darwinian selection – that those better endowed at birth with intelligence, strength and resourcefulness will secure better incomes as adults, and so in turn will their genetically favoured offspring and all this somehow persists down succeeding generations. There is, interestingly, modern medical evidence (called 'epigenetics') that being born poor and remaining a poor child can damage your genes in the same way as smoking, for example, can damage the genetic structure of your body's cells, increasing the risks of later illness.[37] But this is not at all the same thing as being born with inferior, 'poor' genes that will destine you and your children to persisting poverty.

To realise how unhelpful these ideas are, you have only to think about how many of the less able children from rich families end up in poverty. The answer, of course, is very few. To the contrary, recent research by the London School of Economics shows that many do better as adults than bright children from poor backgrounds:[38]

> … children from more advantaged social backgrounds who are assessed at age five as having low cognitive ability are nonetheless significantly more likely to become high earners than their high ability peers in lower income households. Children from high income backgrounds who show signs of low academic ability at age five are 35 per cent more likely to be high earners as adults than children from poorer families who show early signs of high ability.

Conclusions

The increase in relative income poverty in the UK over the past 40 years has been caused by changes in the distribution of market incomes and inadequate amounts of state benefits – amounts that were never adequate and are now falling. Inequalities of income that yawned wide in the 1980s have persisted, despite improvements in benefits and tax credits introduced by the Labour government from 1999 to 2001. Many of these temporary gains have been lost to post-recession austerity measures since 2010, with losses concentrated on working-age families with children. Child poverty rates will return by 2020 to levels thought unacceptable prior to the introduction of the 1999 measures.

The real value of wages has stagnated, especially for unskilled and routine work. This, combined with recurrent waves of unemployment, has established low-pay, no-pay cycles that have affected two generations of UK workers. An increasingly regressive tax system has added to these disadvantages and deepened the risks of hardship.

The basic causes of working poverty are disinvestment, regional disadvantage and deprivation, recurrent unemployment, and suppressed wage progression at one end of the distribution and over-reward at the other. They have remained unchanged over 40 years. But recent shifts in government policy have sought instead to emphasise behavioural shortcomings among families living in poverty, rather than the pressing need to improve family incomes.

Insofar as these growing causes of poverty were avoidable – public policy could instead have redistributed incomes more fairly, public investment could have reduced unemployment, and so on – it seems fair to ask why they were not avoided. There may be many reasons, but there exists one further cause of poverty that receives little public discussion: poor families have less and less capacity to hold accountable those who make policy and those who powerfully influence them. As we said earlier, poverty is something that gets done to people. As Peter Townsend concluded in 1979:[39]

> ... poverty... has to be understood not only as a feature of severe social inequality but also as a particular consequence of actions by the rich to preserve and enhance their wealth and so deny it to others.

The rapid growth of private wealth and corporate control among the elites in the UK is evidence of their capture of the political agenda, removing from that agenda any suggestion of increased priority for a better deal for low-income families.

Notes

1 Part of this 'fall' was the outcome of changes in the way unemployment was counted, excluding people registered as unemployed but not claiming any benefits, moving people onto other benefits, especially benefits for sick and disabled people, placing people on various training schemes, and excluding others by reducing entitlements. Subsequent rises occurred despite these adjustments remaining in place.

2 W Arulampalam, P Gregg and M Gregory, 'Unemployment scarring', *The Economic Journal*, 111(475), 2001, ppF577–84

3 S Thompson, *Poverty in the UK: the low-pay, no-pay cycle,* Joseph Rowntree Foundation, 2015

4 See Joseph Rowntree Foundation, *Cycles of Poverty, Unemployment and Low Pay,* 2010, in which the following four reports are summarised: R McQuaid, V Fuertes and A Richard, *How Can Parents Escape From Recurrent Poverty?,* 2010; H Metcalf and A Dhudwar, *Employers' Role in the Low-pay, No-pay Cycle,* 2010; K Ray and others, *Better off Working? Work, poverty and benefit cycling,* 2010; M Tomlinson and R Walker, *Recurrent Poverty: the impact of family and labour market changes,* 2010

5 A Corlett, D Finch and M Whittaker, *Living Standards 2016: the experiences of low to middle income households in downturn and recovery,* Resolution Foundation, 2016, p12

6 Office for National Statistics, *UK Wages Over the Past Four Decades – 2014,* 2014, Figure 6 – the bottom 1 per cent saw increases of 143 per cent. The enhanced national living wage will have a similar effect.

7 Office for National Statistics, Statistical Bulletin, *Annual Survey of Hours and Earnings: 2015 provisional results,* November 2015, Table 7

8 The Office for National Statistics speculates that the disproportionate rise in top-earner part-time rates is associated with highly skilled non-manual workers using new technology to work fewer hours from home.

9 Office for National Statistics, Labour Force Survey 2016, Table EMP01

10 Office for National Statistics, Statistical Release, *Contracts that Do Not Guarantee a Minimum Number of Hours: September 2016,* 2016

11 Office for National Statistics, *Self-employed Workers in the UK: 2014,* August 2014

12 See also www.resolutionfoundation.org/media/blog/britains-self-employed-workforce-is-growing-but-their-earnings-have-been-heading-in-the-other-direction

13 The Labour Force Survey shows that only 29 per cent of the total workforce is

covered by collective bargaining, dropping to around 16 per cent in the private sector. See M Simms and B Hopkins, *Negotiating Wage (In)equality: UK,* University of Leicester, 2016; and Department for Business, Innovation and Skills, Statistical Bulletin, *Trade Union Membership 2014*, Chart 1.5: only about 4 per cent of workers in the 'accommodation and food services' sector are unionised, compared with 17 per cent in 'manufacturing'.

14 See for example, J Hills, *Good Times, Bad Times: the welfare myth of them and us,* Polity Press, 2017

15 One of the first to try it was Matthew Parris in 1984, who was observed at the time by the novelist Julian Barnes, who wrote: 'with two days to go he was down to his last 61p, and his plan to save £3 out of his £26.80 had collapsed. On his last evening the gas and electricity ran out and he loitered in a working men's club, unable to afford a drink.' See J Henley, 'Iain Duncan Smith is not the first MP to try living on benefits – others have failed before him', the *Guardian,* 2 April 2013

16 This is known to the government as the 'under-occupancy charge' or the 'spare room subsidy', but to everyone else as the 'bedroom tax'.

17 Office for National Statistics, Statistical Bulletin, *Index of Private Housing Rental Prices in Great Britain: July,* 2017

18 A Davis, D Hirsch and M Padley, *A Minimum Income Standard for the UK in 2014,* Joseph Rowntree Foundation, 2014

19 If earnings and other household income increases exceed the rate of inflation, which has been the secular pattern in developed economies until more recent years, then national wealth is said to increase by the difference.

20 The benefits frozen were: jobseeker's allowance, employment and support allowance, income support, housing benefit, universal credit, child tax credit, working tax credit and child benefit. Most benefits for disabled people were not affected.

21 Income-based jobseeker's allowance, income-related employment and support allowance, housing benefit, income support, child tax credit and working tax credit. See *Universal Credit: what you need to know,* Child Poverty Action Group, 2017

22 See for example, Commission on Taxation and Citizenship, *Paying for Progress: a new politics of tax,* Fabian Society, 2000

23 Office for National Statistics, Statistical Bulletin, *The Effects of Taxes and Benefits on Household Income: financial year ending 2015,* May 2016, Table 10

24 Lord Freud, Oral questions on child poverty, House of Lords, 29 June 2016

25 Welfare Reform and Work Act 2016

26 R Lister, 'What do we mean by life chances?' in J Tucker (ed), *Improving Children's Life Chances,* Child Poverty Action Group, 2016, p2

27 Joint statement by the House of Commons Work and Pensions, and Education,

Select Committees, 15 December 2015

28 J Tucker (ed), *Improving Children's Life Chances*, Child Poverty Action Group, 2016

29 Y Hartfree and S Collard, *Poverty, Debt and Credit: an expert-led review. Final report to the Joseph Rowntree Foundation*, University of Bristol Personal Finance Research Centre, March 2014

30 L Jones and H Sumnall, *Understanding the Relationship Between Poverty and Alcohol Misuse*, Centre for Public Health, Liverpool John Moores University, 2016

31 D Lader (ed), *Drug Misuse: findings from the 2014/15 Crime Survey for England and Wales*, Statistical Bulletin 03/15, Home Office, July 2015; and also Advisory Council on the Misuse of Drugs, *Hidden Harm*, 2011

32 The Policy Studies Institute Families and Children Survey found that of those lone parents who had had a partner, four out of 10 had experienced violence during the last year of living together and three-quarters of these, 27 per cent overall, said that they had been injured. See A Marsh and others, *Low-income Families in Britain: work, welfare and social security in 1999,* Department of Social Security Research Report No.138, HM Stationery Office, 2001, p85

33 Department for Education and Department for Work and Pensions, *2010 to 2015 Government Policy: poverty and social justice,* May 2015

34 F Field, *The Foundation Years: preventing poor children becoming poor adults. The report of the Independent Review on Poverty and Life Chances*, HM Government, 2010

35 Centre for Social Justice, *Breakthrough Britain: ending the costs of social breakdown. Policy recommendations to the Conservative Party,* July 2007

36 Announcing new funds for the Troubled Families programme, the then Prime Minister David Cameron said, to underline the importance of strong families in preventing poverty: 'We've got to start talking about parenting and taking action to get it right', press release, 10 January 2016

37 JR Swartz, AR Hariri and DE Williamson, 'An epigenetic mechanism links socioeconomic status to changes in depression-related brain function in high-risk adolescents', *Molecular Psychiatry*, 22(2) 24 May 2016, doi:10.1038/mp.2016.82

38 A McKnight, *Downward Mobility, Opportunity Hoarding and the 'Glass Floor'*, Social Mobility and Child Poverty Commission, 2015

39 P Townsend, *Poverty in the United Kingdom: a survey of household resources and standards of living,* Allen Lane and Penguin Books, 1979

Eleven

The effects of poverty on children

Summary

- In the most deprived areas, boys at birth can expect to live 19 fewer years of their lives in 'good' health, and girls can expect to live 20.2 fewer years of their lives in good health, compared with children in the least deprived areas.

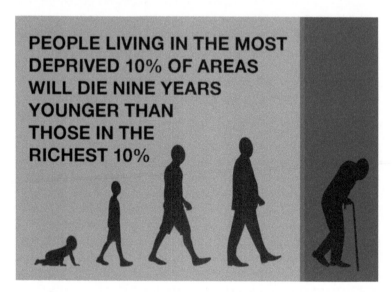

PEOPLE LIVING IN THE MOST DEPRIVED 10% OF AREAS WILL DIE NINE YEARS YOUNGER THAN THOSE IN THE RICHEST 10%

- Children living in overcrowded inadequate housing are more likely to contract meningitis, experience respiratory difficulties and have mental health problems, such as anxiety and depression
- The Millennium Cohort Study shows that poor children are four times more likely to develop a mental health problem by the age of 11.
- Children who have lived persistently in poverty during their first seven years have cognitive development scores that are, on average, 20 per cent below those of children who have never experienced poverty.

- Children living in poverty are affected by a combination of hardship and inequality. They are dismayed and discouraged by their self-evident lack of what other children take for granted.
- The more gifted children from the most deprived families begin school on a par with the more gifted children from the least deprived backgrounds, but their performance falls away by the age of 16.
- In 2015, 33 per cent of children receiving free school meals obtained five or more good GCSEs, compared with 61 per cent of other children.
- Intergenerational mobility is constrained in the UK: fathers' incomes are highly predictive of their sons' at the same age.

Lifetime health

Children born in poverty in the UK will, on average, live shorter and less healthy lives than those in better-off families. Men and women in England living in the most deprived 10 per cent of areas will die nine years younger than those in the richest 10 per cent. Worse, they will spend less time living in good health (Figure 11.1). This lifetime health deficit associated with living in the poorest areas is worst for men's life expectancy and worst for women's lifetime health.

By combining these two numbers, the Office for National Statistics estimates how much 'healthy life expectancy' people can expect.[1] The contrast in fortunes between the most and the least deprived 10 per cent of areas is very clear:

> In the most deprived areas, males at birth could expect to live 19.0 years less of their lives in 'good' health compared with the least deprived areas as measured by the Slope index of inequality (SII). For females, it was 20.2 years less.

At birth, girls living in Richmond upon Thames can look forward to 72 years of living in good health; those born in Manchester, only 54 years. Boys born in Dorset and Wokingham will get 70 years of good health; those in Blackpool, 54 years.[2]

Much of this lifetime health deficit has its origins in childhood poverty and deprivation. Indeed, children from families living in poverty are less likely to make it into the world at all. There is no reliable information directly linking infant mortality in the UK to families' household income at the time of the loss.[3] But there is strong evidence that, despite steady improvements over recent decades,[4] rates of infant mortality remain

Figure 11.1:

Life expectancy at birth and the proportion of their remaining lives that will be spent in good health at age 65

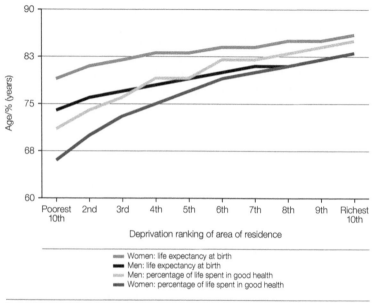

Source: Office for National Statistics, Statistical Bulletin, *Healthy Life Expectancy at Birth and Age 65 by Upper Tier Local Authority and Area Deprivation: England, 2012 to 2014*, March 2016, Figure 2

higher among families in low-paid routine and manual occupations compared with those in professional jobs. Also, infant mortality in the poorest boroughs is significantly higher than in rich ones.[5] This kind of risk persists throughout childhood; children in poor boroughs are significantly more likely to die in accidents and of other causes.[6]

Across Europe, child mortality is closely aligned with each country's rate of child poverty:[7]

> In children under five, the UK mortality rate is the highest in western Europe, double that of Sweden.

About one in nine child deaths in the UK are due to accidents, and these are strongly linked to differences in social status and income:[8]

Figures from 2001 to 2003 show that the risk of accidental death for all children aged between 28 days and 15 years was 4.5 times higher in the routine class (NS-SEC class seven), and 5.3 times higher in the non-occupied class (never worked, long-term unemployed, full-time students or unclassified) than for a child with at least one parent in a higher managerial or professional occupation.

Housing and child health

Chapter 4 made clear the extent to which children living in income poverty experience the worst housing conditions in terms of damp, cold and overcrowding.

The National Centre for Social Research estimated in 2013 that:[9]

Over 975,000 children living in social rented housing are living in bad housing. Approximately 845,000 children living in private rented housing are living in bad housing. And over 1.7 million children living in owner occupied housing are living in bad housing.

And its analysis of the 2012 Health Survey for England found that:

Children living in bad housing are disproportionately more likely to suffer from poorer general health, poorer respiratory health and asthma – with children from private rented housing more likely to have poorer general health and wheezing problems.

The 2013 British Medical Association report also linked poverty and poor housing conditions to child health:[10]

As well as being associated with debilitating, and even fatal, accidents, children living in overcrowded, inadequate housing are also more likely to contract meningitis, experience respiratory difficulties, and have mental health problems, such as anxiety and depression. Physical and mental health conditions related to poor housing can also have associated impacts on a child's education: the Shelter report found that children in unfit and overcrowded homes miss school more frequently due to illnesses and infections and may experience delayed cognitive development.

Income, hardship and child health

There is surprisingly little data in the UK directly linking *income* poverty in childhood with health outcomes. However, a recent analysis linked together all the 78,500 observation points made on the children included in the eight waves of the Families and Children Study between 2001 and 2008. It is probably the only such study where both exact income and comprehensive hardship measures are available to compare with child health outcomes.

Whereas much earlier research focused on health deficits among very young children, this study found that health problems emerged disproportionately among the children of low-income families from the age of two, and that this deficit remained consistently up to adulthood at 17. The researchers say:[11]

> ... our results indicate that the gradient in general health reflects a greater prevalence of chronic conditions among low-income children and a greater severity of these conditions. Taken together, these findings suggest that income does matter for child health in the UK and may play a role in the intergenerational transmission of socioeconomic status.

This study was able to show the strong association between income poverty and poor child health independently of confounding factors such as parents' health and even mothers' smoking habits. Moreover, it was able to show direct links between hardship and health. For example:

> ... there is a positive and significant impact of weatherproof coat and all-weather shoes ownership on child health.

Importantly, though, low family income, especially consistently low incomes over the eight-year period, reduced children's health even independently of reports of child-related hardship. Money matters to child health, whatever other circumstances are linked to income.

These results were found in low-income families between 2001 and 2008, before the period of fiscal austerity beginning in 2010, when the real value of cash benefits for children began to be reduced. An All-Party Parliamentary Group examined the likely effects of the Welfare Reform Bill on increasing child poverty and child health and noted the extent of cuts in family benefits imposed and expected in the following years. The All-Party Parliamentary Group opposed many of these cuts and called for their reversal, citing a submission from the University of Liverpool's Institute of

Psychology, Health and Society, whose evidence stressed that:[12]

> Eliminating UK child poverty would save the lives of 1,400 children under 15 annually.

The review by Wickham and others leaves no remaining doubt that income poverty damages child health:[13]

> The poor health associated with child poverty limits children's potential and development, leading to poor health and life chances in adulthood.

And Cooper and Stewart's equally authoritative worldwide review found 51 studies of the highest evidential quality that:[14]

> ... provide strong evidence that income has causal effects on a wide range of children's outcomes, especially in households on low incomes to begin with. We conclude that reducing income poverty can be expected to have a significant impact on children's environment and on their development.

It must be obvious that poverty affects the health of both parents and their children. Chapter 4 showed clearly that poor children are less well nourished and more socially isolated, often unable to entertain friends or join them on trips. Poor mothers are less well nourished during pregnancy, have more recourse to anxiety-reducing habits such as smoking, and have less access to better antenatal care:

> The health of children born to mothers in/experiencing poverty is more likely to be compromised due to their mothers' poor nutrition, exposure to stress, and poor working conditions, as well as limited access to poorer quality public services.

More than anything, it seems, income poverty undermines mothers' mental health,[15] which in turn can affect children's mental health. These impacts are not trivial. For example, in the UK's Millennium Cohort Study, poor children were four times more likely to develop a mental health problem by the age of 11:[16]

> Seventeen per cent of 11-year-olds in 2012 from families in the bottom fifth of [the] income distribution were identified as having severe mental health problems compared to 4 per cent in the top fifth.

Seventeen per cent is a very high proportion and goes a long way towards explaining why, at every level of early ability measured, children in families living in poverty tend to do much less well than expected. Among children and their parents living in the greatest poverty, 'aspirations' – so valued by current theorists as the antidote to underachievement – are better expressed as hopes, much less as expectations. They are hopes that the effects of poverty will dash for so many, as we shall see below.

Before school

Following 25 years of relative decline, the proportion of the UK's GDP spent on education rose from 4.3 per cent in 1999 to 5.9 per cent in 2010. As well as employing more teachers and refurbishing schools, the policy was aligned with the Sure Start programme (later children's centres) and the National Childcare Strategy, offering a wide range of parenting and childcare support, especially for parents in deprived areas.

There is good evidence for the UK that high-quality early childhood education and care improves child outcomes and the effects can be the most long lasting for the most disadvantaged children.[17] It is widely understood that the chief marker for quality is graduate qualified staff and leadership. Only high-quality provision delivers improved child outcomes; anything less does not deliver improvement. Evidence shows that provision of childcare in the maintained sector and in children's centres is, on average, of higher quality, and thus better for young children and their development, than that provided through the market.[18] However, it remains the case that four-fifths of provision in the UK is in the private, voluntary and independent sectors. Provision in the private sector includes some of the best and worst. Therefore, quality is still a work in progress in the UK childcare sector, as is cost (see Chapter 5).

The first childcare strategy in the UK did not start until 1998, and the first ever Childcare Act was in 2006. It included the free early educational entitlement and the ambition to create comprehensive before- and after-school activities and care from 8am to 6pm and throughout school holidays. Significant investment was made to improve qualifications in the sector, including through new Early Childhood Professional qualifications and through the Graduate Leader Fund – since abolished. An approach based on child development principles incorporating both education and care was introduced through the early years foundation stage. Although the free entitlement has been expanded from 12.5 to 15 and now 30 hours a week, comprehensive extended school provision has not yet been delivered.

Evidence has accumulated over many years showing that poor children from income-poor families *arrive* at school less well equipped to learn. For this reason, part of the reinvestment in education concentrated on early childhood education and care in nursery schools, including the Sure Start scheme in deprived areas. English children aged two to three who are eligible for free school meals[19] already showed a substantial developmental deficit: 36 per cent achieved expected levels in the 17 developmental assessments applied, compared with 52 per cent of children from better-off families.[20] Again, this represented an improvement on earlier results, or perhaps it showed that pupils were trained to be better at taking tests. But the effects of poverty measured by entitlement to free school meals persisted (Figure 11.2).

Most recently in the UK, evidence from the Millennium Cohort Study – the latest in our series of birth cohort studies, following nearly 19,000 children born in the same week in 2000 – has produced startling results:[21]

- From birth to the age of seven, about a fifth of Millennium Cohort children were in poverty at some point – living in households with below 60 per cent of median income. This fifth were not always in the same families, so more children experienced poverty at some point.
- At the age of three, children born in poverty were already behind in their cognitive development scores – essentially showing them to be relatively less responsive to the earliest life-learning.
- At the age of five and again at seven, the gap between those born poor and other children widened.
- More importantly, children who were persistently in poverty during their first seven years recorded combined cognitive development scores fully 20 per cent below children who had not experienced poverty at all.

On one crucial test of 'school readiness',[22] children in persistent poverty scored an unadjusted average of 33 points, while all other children scored an average of 62.[23] And this was the first cohort swept up in the early years programme, which should have benefited most from the new pre-school interventions. The children were also growing up in years recording lower and falling child poverty rates. This deficit persisted even though, by the age of seven, most of them had had three years in school.

Figure 11.2:

Percentage of children achieving a 'good level' of development on the early years foundation stage profile, by eligibility for free school meals, 2007 to 2012

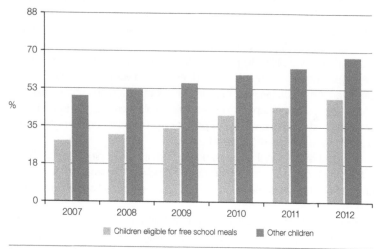

Source: Department for Education, Statistical First Release, *Early Years Foundation Stage Profile Attainment by Pupil Characteristics: England 2013*, 2013

The deficit also persisted despite the analysts accounting for '… a wide range of background characteristics and parental investment'. This means that, on average, children living in persistent poverty entered school with a significant learning deficit, irrespective of their families' structure, their ethnic group, their type of housing, and so on. This also happened independently of how much their parents helped them at home by reading to them, taking them to libraries, and similar investments of time and effort. Low income was the cause of this cognitive deficit – both directly by lowering the children's wellbeing and indirectly through their parents, whose ability to help and encourage their very young children was depressed by the stresses and strains of coping with poverty.

Others who have looked at older birth cohort data stress the complexity of the interaction between income, family characteristics and parents' behaviour. But in most reliable studies, the role of income poverty itself, particularly the effects of persistent poverty, emerges as the core problem. One study shows that, once income and related factors are accounted for, the cognitive deficit of persistently poor children by the age of five has no relation to the factor most often blamed in popular views – lone parenthood. The children of poor married couples do just as poorly, it seems.[24]

Earlier birth cohorts have produced similar results. For example, Feinstein showed for the 1970 cohort that:[25]

> The children of educated or wealthy parents who scored poorly in the early tests had a tendency to catch up, whereas children of worse-off parents who scored poorly were extremely unlikely to catch up and are shown to be an at-risk group. There is no evidence that entry into schooling reverses this pattern.

The Department for Education's own data for the English cohort born in 1991/92 shows that this pattern has persisted over 30 years. The more gifted children from the most deprived families begin school on a par with more gifted children from the least deprived backgrounds, but their performance falls away by the age of 16. The least gifted children from the least deprived backgrounds move the other way and begin to converge with their most deprived, but brighter, classmates (Figure 11.3).[26]

Gregg and Macmillan reviewed all the major UK longitudinal and cohort studies, the children from the second of which (the 1958 National Child Development Study) are now approaching retirement, and noted just how consistently birth into a poor family confers a lifelong disadvantage.[27]

Similar findings of a direct link between family income and child development, independently of all the other factors like lone parenthood, poor housing and so on, have been found elsewhere. Researchers in the United States have been able to give it a multiplying value:[28]

> ... a $1,000 increase in income raises combined math and reading test scores by 6 per cent of a standard deviation in the short run. Test gains are larger for children from disadvantaged families and robust to a variety of alternative specifications.

Education, education...

There is a great deal of evidence showing wide differences in educational attainment between poor children and their better-off classmates. Perhaps the simplest measure of school attainment is the proportion of pupils reaching key stage 4 and getting five or more GCSE results (including maths and English) with a 'C' grade or better. In 2015, 57 per cent of all key stage 4 pupils in England achieved this benchmark exam result, much better than the 44 per cent who did so in 2005, despite changes to marking that lowered scores in 2013. But only 33 per cent of children receiving free school meals[29] reached this level in 2015, compared with 61 per cent of the rest. This 28 per cent 'free school meals gap' has proved stubbornly resistant to rising school quality, being the same in 2015 as 10 years earlier (Figure 11.3).[30] A recent Parliamentary inquiry noted that:[31]

> Twice the proportion of poor children attending an outstanding school will leave with five good GCSEs when compared with the lowest rated schools, whereas the proportion of non-FSM [free school meal] children achieving this benchmark in outstanding schools is only 1.5 times greater than in those rated as inadequate.

However, this does not fully acknowledge that 'inadequate' schools are more often found in deprived areas:[32]

Figure 11.3:

Progress in school attainment up to age 16

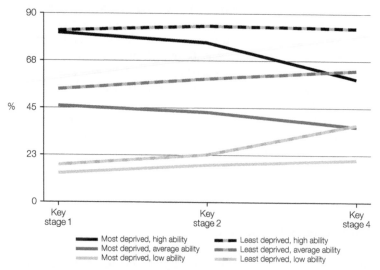

Source: S Iniesta-Martinez and H Evans, Research Report DFE235, *Pupils Not Claiming Free School Meals*, Department for Education, 2012

Even if every school in the country was outstanding there would still be a substantial difference in performance between rich and poor children. Ofsted data confirms that the FSM [free school meal] 'gap' exists in outstanding schools as well as inadequate schools.

Nevertheless, the apparently clear role of educational attainment in leading at least some children living in poverty into well-provided adulthood led to a concentration of policy and greater investment in education, especially by the Labour governments between 1997 and 2010. Almost every state school in the land was refurbished or rebuilt, and teachers became better rewarded and more numerous. As Figure 11.4 shows, there are steady improvements in the proportion of all pupils leaving school with acceptable qualifications and the attainment gap closed.

But the persistence of the 'free school meals gap' is puzzling. And it is not just a UK problem; the OECD reports that across 35 countries, children from the bottom quarter of the income distribution of each coun-

Figure 11.4:

Percentage of pupils at the end of key stage 4 attaining five GCSEs at grades A* to C, including English and maths, by free school meals eligibility

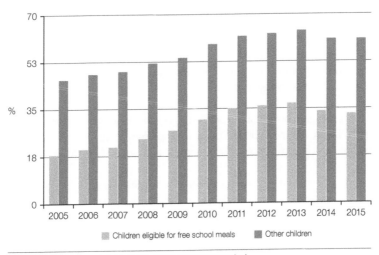

Note: After 2013 there was a change in the way the exams were marked.

Source: Department of Education, *Revised GCSE and equivalent results in England, 2014 to 2015*, SFR 01/2016, 21 January 2016

try are, on average, lagging behind those from the top quarter by more than *two years* of educational progress.[33] The effects of the recession have made improvements in this learning gap less likely, with '... some 1.6 million more children... living in severe material deprivation in 2012 (11.1 million) than in 2008 (9.5 million) in 30 European countries.'[34]

There is a paradox in that the education system offers a route out of poverty for some children, but has built into it some structural barriers opposing their progress. The many extra costs of state schooling – trips, equipment, and so on – can be unaffordable for poor families.[35] The 'post-code lottery', recently lamented by Prime Minister Theresa May, restricts access to the best-rated schools to those who can afford the premium on accommodation in their catchment areas.[36]

During their progress through education, children living in poverty can be disadvantaged in many small and subtle ways. Poor families, especially among some minority ethnic groups, may not share all of the coded middle-class values schools and their staff promote and celebrate, or all the 'fundamental British values'[37] schools are now instructed to instill in their pupils. So they and their children can be marked down as lacking the right ambition and aspiration, less likely to respond to the top-grade and more demanding teaching.

Goodman and Gregg's comprehensive study of the relationship between achievement and aspiration noted wide gaps between high- and low-income families:[38]

> ... parental aspirations and attitudes to education varied strongly by socio-economic position, with 81 per cent of the richest mothers saying they hoped their nine-year-old would go to university, compared with only 37 per cent of the poorest mothers.

It is important to note that the problem is not that low-income parents have no ambitions for their children or fail to help them at all; it is that better-off parents can actually *do* so much more. Goodman and Gregg also noted:

> ... at both primary and secondary school aspirations and expectations for HE [higher education] among parents and children were generally high even among young people from the poorest backgrounds. For example, at age 14, far more parents and children reported that they were likely to go on to HE than eventually would go, from all income backgrounds including the poorest.

It is not having aspirations that is so important, it is the belief that such aspirations can be achieved.[39]

Research by Tess Ridge and others has shown just how much children living in poverty are aware of their families' disadvantage and lack of money. It makes them anxious, imposes a self-image they feel is glum and scruffy, excludes them from many of the things their classmates have and do, and sets them aside in an unpromising corner of their social world. Ridge's review of qualitative research gives direct voice to children's concerns about their lives in poverty:[40]

- They are anxious about the lack of money coming into their homes.
- They are keenly aware of material deprivation, both of basic essentials for their families and toys, cycles and games for themselves.
- They are restricted by a lack of access to social activities or being able to invite friends home.
- They are excluded from important school activities, unable to pay for school trips, buy materials for projects, or even compulsory uniforms.
- They feel vulnerable to bullying because of their inferior clothes and social exclusion.
- They feel fearful for their parents and the pressures their needs as children place on them.
- They are sometimes at odds with their parents, who often work long hours.
- They are badly affected when placed in temporary accommodation or during periods of homelessness.
- They feel insecure in deprived and sometimes dangerous neighbourhoods.

Inferior and unfashionable clothing alone can mark out poor children. Ridge quotes a seven-year-old girl:[41]

> 'If you don't have the same clothes as other people, they say that you've got rags. If the whole school has got the same clothes except for you, they will tease you until you have the right clothes... when you don't have any clothes and you don't have any shoes people bully and people laugh at you when you go somewhere.'

Young though they are, children living in poverty know exactly what Ruth Lister means by the 'othering' of people living in poverty. Ridge says:

> ... poverty penetrates deep into the heart of childhood, permeating every facet of children's lives from economic and material disadvantage, through the structuring and limiting of social relationships and social participation to

the most personal often hidden aspects of disadvantage associated with shame, sadness and the fear of social difference and marginalisation.

Although children living in poverty can be resilient, this resilience can be of a kind that does little to help a child's own development. As Ridge says:

> ... they were not passive 'victims' of poverty: many employed coping strategies such as taking jobs so they could contribute financially to their families, taking on caring duties so parents could work, and restricting financial demands (for example, not telling parents about school trips) to ease financial pressures within the home.

'Poor but happy' childhoods are an offensive myth. Again, parents, even those living in poverty, do not lack aspiration and hope for their children. Far from it. But there is a world of difference between aspiration and expectation. Parents and their children are aware of the barriers that confront them and can share a gloomy view of their future which, in itself, is quite enough to depress children's school performance.

The combined effects of poverty and inequality

We emphasised in Chapter 2 the importance of seeing the difference between poverty and inequality. Poverty is experiencing the consequences of being on a low income for a long time, leaving families short of necessities and isolated from the social life of the community, while inequality is the extent to which some people have more money and resources – often much more money and many more resources – than others have. But they are linked: when inequality increases, the contrast in incomes, lifestyles and wellbeing between the poorest and the better-off households becomes so much greater. This both conditions public debate about poverty in ways that further estranges and demonises those left in poverty and vastly discourages them, as they look up at so long and steep a journey to self-sufficiency of incomes.

Being brought up in poverty in a very unequal country seriously reduces your chances of upward social and economic mobility. So much is stacked against you. Your initial poverty imposes a poor diet, damp and overcrowded housing, social isolation, humiliation and discouragement, which all combine to reduce the chances of your being able to succeed well in exams and take a place among better rewarded people when you leave school and seek work. But Tess Ridge's work shows that the dismay expressed by children arriving at school from families living in poverty arose more from their perceived *inequality* than from the direct effects of poverty upon them. Not merely were they living in poverty, which was uncomfortable enough in itself, they saw that other children were not poor, and, painfully, it showed.

Restrictions on upward social mobility in the UK are about more than income alone. Working-class families whose incomes never dip below the poverty line are still far less likely to see their children rise into the higher reaches of society's professional elites than are middle-class families, especially middle-class families who buy their children's social and educational advantages for them. Only 7 per cent of children go to fee-paying schools, yet 71 per cent of senior judges, 62 per cent of senior members of the armed forces, and 55 per cent of civil service departmental heads are chosen from these alone.[42] So those born below the poverty line are already looking up at a social structure whose inequalities of opportunity and barriers to progress are long established.

Solely in terms of income, the UK has, compared to other countries, a relatively inflexible relationship between the incomes of fathers and sons in middle age. The lack of independent income data for mid- to late-twentieth century women, and their more complex life course varying between work and childcare, makes a similar calculation for mothers and their children too difficult, for the present at least. There is, however, a wealth of evidence that mothers, especially mothers' own educational level, have strong effects on their sons' and their daughters' prospects for social mobility.[43]

Figure 11.5 is based on estimates of the extent to which a father's income in middle age predicts his son's at a similar age. A national score of zero predicts that there is no relation at all between a father's income when his son is young and his son's income when he is an adult – that rich fathers are as likely to see their infant sons become poor adults as they are to become rich, while poor fathers are equally as likely to see their sons become rich as they are to see them poor. This never happens, of course. Nor does the reverse, where a score of '1' would show that every son grows up exactly as rich or poor as his father. But there is a connection – called the 'intergenerational income elasticity' – and its strength is measured by how closely the estimate approaches '1'.

In the UK, the estimate is almost exactly 0.5, which, given the amount of random error that exists in this kind of intergenerational data, is a high score. It is far higher in the UK than, for example, in Scandinavian countries, though similar to the United States and Italy. Among those

Figure 11.5:

Intergenerational income mobility

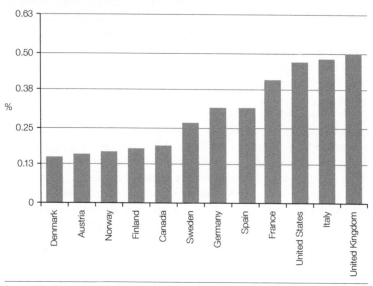

Source: P Serafino and R Tonkin, *Intergenerational Transmission of Disadvantage in the UK and EU*, Office for National Statistics, 2017

shown, the UK, United States and Italy are the three most unequal countries in terms of their present income distribution: they have the highest Gini coefficients, as we saw in Chapter 3, while Denmark, Austria and Norway have the lowest. So, the more unequal your country is, the harder it is to do better – or, for that matter, to do worse – than your father.[44]

There is some evidence that this inflexibility in the UK is getting worse. Such intergenerational income mobility was found to be lower among the 1970 birth cohort compared with the 1958 birth cohort (Table 11.1).[45] Thirty per cent of sons in the 1958 cohort whose fathers were in the bottom quarter of the income distribution were themselves in the bottom quarter. This rose to 37 per cent among the 1970 cohort. The sociologist John Goldthorpe challenged these findings with more extensive evidence of continuities in status and occupation in post-war Britain that indicated that nothing much had changed – that old class-based inequalities are being reproduced at the same rate.[46] The large expansion of non-manual work in the 1960s and 1970s caused an illusion of upward mobility that did little to change people's relative positions in terms of sta-

tus and resources, while real status mobility has now '...subsided to earlier levels...'. All the evidence, though, agrees that the UK has not become
a substantially fairer society.

Table 11.1:

**Birth cohort evidence of decreasing income mobility between
fathers and sons**

		Father's income	
Son's earnings at age 33/34		Bottom 25%	Top 25%
Bottom 25%	Born in 1958	30	18
	Born in 1970	37	13
Top 25%	Born in 1958	18	35
	Born in 1970	13	45

Source: J Blanden and S Machin, *Recent Changes in Intergenerational Mobility in Britain*, Sutton Trust, 2007

Conclusions

This brief review of a vast literature confirms that family incomes below the
poverty line affect children's health, wellbeing and development. Poor diet,
bad housing, restricted social lives and an impoverished environment
damage both their physical and mental health. The poverty of their parents
isolates them from the activities of children in better-off families and
reduces their social learning. Their experience of inequality discourages
them, and they are strongly aware of their disadvantage. This imposes a
corresponding deficit in their capacity to learn and flourish at school. It
burdens poor children's progress throughout their schooling and lowers
their attainment in exams compared with the average attainment of children
from better-off families. Persistent poverty has persistent and severe effects.

The greater investment in schools and early years support over the
past 20 years has improved the school attainment of children from low-
income families, who now return significantly better test scores than in earlier decades – a measure both of just how badly they fared in the past and
of how much, and how effectively, public investment can help. But this
investment has improved the performance of better-off children too, and
by a similar margin, so disadvantage remains.

Policy efforts in the UK have shown child poverty and its consequences to be policy responsive. However, the foot has been taken off the

pedal in this period of austerity and retrenchment since 2010. Nevertheless, it is clear what should be done. There is clear evidence that the policy response that would additionally and most reliably challenge the disadvantage imposed on children in low-income families is an increase in their present resources. The best strategy that will both improve the health and development of children living in poverty and reduce their social and educational disadvantage is that they should not be poor.

Notes

1   Office for National Statistics, Statistical Bulletin, *Healthy Life Expectancy at Birth and Age 65 by Upper Tier Local Authority and Area Deprivation: England, 2012 to 2014*, March 2016, Figure 2

2   This does not entirely take into account the extent of a 'fit worker effect' whereby more successful people will move away to 'better' areas to live.

3   Better data is available in the US – see J Brooks-Gunn and GJ Duncan, 'The Effects of Poverty on Children', *The Future of Children*, 7(2), 1997, pp55–71

4   The overall rate of infant mortality in England and Wales fell from 9.5 per 1,000 births in 1984 to 3.7 per 1,000 in 2015. Office for National Statistics, Statistical Bulletin, *Childhood Mortality in England and Wales: 2015: stillbirths, infant and childhood deaths occurring annually in England and Wales, and associated risk factors*, April 2017, Figure 1

5   'The 2014 birth cohort tables for infant deaths show that for singleton births, the highest infant mortality rate was for the NS-SEC groups describing routine and manual occupations (Groups 5 to 7) with 5.1 deaths per 1,000 live births (the three-class version of NS-SEC has been used, background note 9 has more detail). In contrast there were 2.1 deaths per 1,000 live births for higher managerial, administrative and professional occupations (Groups 1.1, 1.2 and 2) and 3.0 deaths per 1,000 live births for intermediate occupations (Groups 3 and 4).' Office for National Statistics, Statistical Bulletin, *Childhood Mortality in England and Wales: 2014: stillbirths, infant and childhood deaths occurring annually in England and Wales, and associated risk factors*, April 2016, Table 1

6   S Wickham and others, Poverty and child health in the UK: using evidence for action', *Archives of Disease in Childhood*, 101(8), 2016, pp759–66

7   A Zylbersztejn, R Gilbert, P Hardelid and A Hjern, 'Why do more infants die in the UK than in Sweden? An intercountry comparison of birthweight-specific infant mortality', *The Lancet*, Vol. 386, 13 November 2015

8   E Rough and others, 'Inequalities in child health', in G Foyle and V Nathanson (eds), *Growing Up in the UK: ensuring a healthy future for our children*, BMA Board of Science, 2013

9   M Barnes and others, *People Living in Bad Housing: numbers and health*

impacts, National Centre for Social Research for Shelter, 2013

10 E Rough and others, 'Inequalities in child health', in G Foyle and V Nathanson (eds), *Growing Up in the UK: ensuring a healthy future for our children,* BMA Board of Science, 2013

11 B Apouey and PY Geoffard, 'Family income and child health in the UK', *Journal of Health Economics,* 32(4), July 2013, pp715–27

12 All Party Parliamentary Group on Health in All Policies, *Child Poverty and Health: the impact of the Welfare Reform and Work Bill 2015–16,* February 2016. Around 6,000 children and young people die each year in the UK – about 0.75 per cent of all under-16-year-olds. Over two-thirds of these are aged under five, and the majority are under the age of one.

13 S Wickham and others, 'Poverty and child health in the UK: using evidence for action', *Archives of Disease in Childhood,* 101(8), 2016, pp759–60

14 K Cooper and K Stewart, *Does Money Affect Children's Outcomes? An update,* Centre for Analysis of Social Exclusion London School of Economics and Joseph Rowntree Foundation, 2017

15 See I Elliott, *Poverty and Mental Health: a review to inform the Joseph Rowntree Foundation's anti-poverty strategy,* Mental Health Foundation, 2016

16 See I Elliott, *Poverty and Mental Health: a review to inform the Joseph Rowntree Foundation's anti-poverty strategy,* Mental Health Foundation, *2016.* Overall, the prevalence of severe mental health problems among 11-year-olds participating in the Millennium Cohort Study using the 'strengths and difficulties' scale was 10 per cent: 13 per cent of boys and 8 per cent of girls.

17 K Sylva and others, *The Effective Provision of Pre-School Education (EPPE) Project: final report, a longitudinal study funded by the DfES 1997–2004,* The Institute of Education, 2004

18 E Lloyd and S Potter, *Early Childcare Education and Care and Poverty,* University of East London, 2014; K Sylva and others, *The Effective Provision of Pre-School Education (EPPE) Project: final report, a longitudinal study funded by the DfES 1997–2004,* The Institute of Education, 2004

19 Now, all nursery-age pupils can get free school meals, which ended this trend analysis. Around 19,600 under-fours were recorded as claiming free school meals at January 2012. This equates to 6 per cent of the under-four school population.

20 Department for Education, Statistical First Release, *Early Years Foundation Stage Profile Attainment by Pupil Characteristics: England 2013,* 2013

21 A Dickerson and GK Popli, 'Persistent poverty and children's cognitive development: evidence from the UK Millennium Cohort Study', *Journal of the Royal Statistical Society A: Statistics in Society,* 179(2), 2016, pp535–58

22 See JE Panter and BA Bracken, 'Validity of the Bracken School Readiness Assessment for predicting first grade readiness', *Psychology in the Schools,*

46(5), 2009, pp397–409. The Bracken test contains six sub-tests the child is tested on: colours: the child needs to identify common colours by name (ie, red, blue); letters: the child needs to know lower-case and upper-case letters; numbers and counting: the child must identify single- and double-digit numerals, and must be able to count items from 1 to 99; sizes: the child must demonstrate knowledge of words used to depict size during the Bracken test (eg, short, long); comparisons: the child needs to differentiate or match objects based on a specific characteristic; and shapes: the child needs knowledge of basic shapes by name.

23 A Dickerson and GK Popli, 'Persistent poverty and children's cognitive development: evidence from the UK Millennium Cohort Study', *Journal of the Royal Statistical Society A: Statistics in Society,* 179(2), 2016, pp535–58

24 I Schoon and others, 'Family hardship, family instability, and cognitive development', *Journal of Epidemiology and Community Health*, 66(8), 2012, pp716–22

25 L Feinstein, 'Inequality in the early cognitive development of British children in the 1970 cohort, *Economica*, 70(277), 2003, pp73–97. He means the children who scored poorly, not the parents.

26 C Crawford, L Macmillan and A Vignoles, *Progress Made by High-attaining Children from Disadvantaged Backgrounds*, Social Mobility and Child Poverty Commission, 2014

27 P Gregg and L Macmillan, 'Family income, education and cognitive ability in the next generation: exploring income gradients in education and test scores for current cohorts of youth', *Longitudinal and Life Course Studies*, 1(3), 2010, pp259–80

28 GB Dahl and L Lochner, 'The impact of family income on child achievement: evidence from the earned income tax credit', *American Economic Review*, 102(5), 2012, pp1927–56

29 Eighteen per cent of primary school and 15 per cent of secondary school pupils in England and Wales got free school meals in 2013, mainly because their parents received benefits or, up to a certain level, some tax credits; 60 per cent of them were estimated to be living in families below the poverty line. See *Free School Meal Entitlement and Child Poverty in England,* Department for Work and Pensions, 2013

30 To be fair, the significance of 28 per cent has changed in the sense that, in 2005, it meant that children entitled to free schools meals scored just 39 per cent of others' scores and in 2013 they scored 58 per cent of others' scores. An improvement from 18 to 33 per cent may impress more than an improvement from 48 per cent to 64 per cent. On the other hand, not all pupils entitled to free schools meals have parents who claim them. Fourteen per cent of eligible pupils aged four to 16 fail to claim (200,000 of them), so appear in the non-free school meals side of the comparison. Thus, the real free school meals gap is almost

certainly larger. See S Iniesta-Martinez and H Evans, Research Report DFE235, *Pupils Not Claiming Free School Meals*, Department for Education, 2012

31 Ofsted, *Unseen Children: educational access and achievement 20 years on,* Figure 19 (based on open secondary schools with a published section 5 inspection report at 31 December 2012)

32 J Clifton and W Cook, *A Long Division: closing the gap in England's secondary schools*, Institute for Public Policy Research, 2012, p22

33 Organisation for Economic Co-operation and Development, *PISA 2012 Results: excellence through equity. Giving every student the chance to succeed (Volume II)*, OECD Publishing, 2013

34 G Fanjul, *Children of the Recession: the impact of the economic crisis on child well-being in rich countries*, Innocenti Report Card 12, UNICEF, 2014

35 See also S Spencer, *The Cost of the School Day*, CPAG in Scotland, 2015

36 Which of course ignores the question of why schools are not all equally 'outstanding', abolishing the need for postcode premiums.

37 Department for Education, *Promoting Fundamental British Values as Part of SMSC in Schools: departmental advice for maintained schools,* 2014

38 A Goodman and P Gregg, *Poorer Children's Educational Attainment: how important are attitudes and behaviour?* Joseph Rowntree Foundation, 2010

39 See also L Menzies, *Educational Aspirations: how English schools can work with parents to keep them on track*, Joseph Rowntree Foundation, 2013

40 T Ridge, *Living with Poverty: a review of the literature on children's and families' experiences of poverty,* Department for Work and Pensions Research Report No. 594, 2009

41 T Ridge, 'The everyday costs of poverty in childhood: a review of qualitative research exploring the lives and experiences of low-income children in the UK', *Children & Society*, 25, 2011, pp73–84

42 See Social Mobility and Child Poverty Commission, *Elitist Britain?*, 2015

43 See for example, the review by J Erola, S Jalonen and H Lehti, 'Parental education, class and income over early life course and children's achievement', *Research in Social Stratification and Mobility*, Vol. 44, June 2016, pp33–43

44 See AC d'Addio, *Intergenerational Transmission of Disadvantage: mobility or immobility across generations? A review of the evidence for OECD countries,* OECD, 2007, p46, Figure 3

45 J Blanden and S Machin, *Recent Changes in Intergenerational Mobility in Britain*, Sutton Trust, 2007

46 See J Goldthorpe, *Understanding – and Misunderstanding – Social Mobility in Britain: the entry of the economists, the confusion of politicians and the limits of educational policy,* Barnett Papers in Social Research, University of Oxford, 2012

Twelve

What is it like to experience poverty?

Summary

- People living on a low income want to work, but face barriers to employment, the most prominent of which is childcare and, perhaps, other caring responsibilities such as someone in the family having a disability.
- Parents worry about the impact poverty has on their children, particularly that they may be bullied: children living in poverty frequently report being bullied, citing it as a 'key source of unhappiness'.
- People living in poverty are more likely to live in disadvantaged neighbourhoods and have a lower quality home that may be overcrowded or unsuitable for their needs.

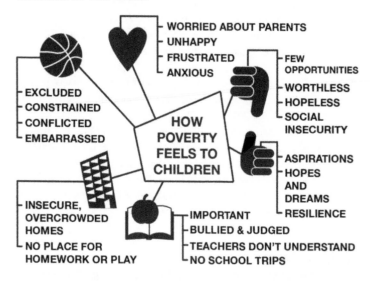

WORRIED ABOUT PARENTS
UNHAPPY
FRUSTRATED
ANXIOUS

FEW OPPORTUNITIES
WORTHLESS
HOPELESS
SOCIAL INSECURITY

EXCLUDED
CONSTRAINED
CONFLICTED
EMBARRASSED

HOW POVERTY FEELS TO CHILDREN

ASPIRATIONS
HOPES AND DREAMS
RESILIENCE

INSECURE, OVERCROWDED HOMES
NO PLACE FOR HOMEWORK OR PLAY

IMPORTANT
BULLIED & JUDGED
TEACHERS DON'T UNDERSTAND
NO SCHOOL TRIPS

- Poor parents are less likely to go out and socialise, primarily because they cannot afford it, but sometimes because they cannot face it. They forego weddings, birthday celebrations and other family gatherings because they cannot afford to participate.

- All areas of a child's life are adversely affected by poverty: home, school, friendships and more. The most visible aspect is that they do not have what their friends have.
- Children living in low-income families have high hopes and aspirations, but are not quite sure how to realise them.
- Children often find it difficult to make and sustain friendships because these require access to economic resources.
- Poverty is an impediment to development and personal progress, yet children display extraordinary strength and resilience in continuing to try pushing forwards.

This chapter takes you on a journey of how poverty is experienced and what it feels like for both parents and children. This can only ever be a partial journey: it is not possible to describe in a few thousand words the entirety of a parent's or child's life as lived in poverty. But we hope to reveal the types of situations you would encounter and how they might make you feel.

The experience for parents

Poverty is an 'overwhelmingly negative experience' that adversely affects all areas of your life 'psychologically, physically, relationally and practically' and has particularly damaging personal and social effects.[1]

As a parent living in poverty, you may be working in low-paid, insecure employment, not working at all or cycling between these two states.[2] The repercussions are painful and the systems in place to help you financially are slow, overly complex, subject to delays and errors, and hugely stigmatising. You budget carefully, trying to balance insufficient funds to make a little money go a long way, but often there is just not enough to manage. As Sarah, a lone parent of a 12-year-old boy says:[3]

> 'I live on a fiscal knife-edge and as soon as there's anything out of kilter it all just falls apart.'

As a result of your insecure, unpredictable income, you are likely to have few savings or assets. This makes you extremely susceptible to destabilising internal and external shocks, like Fiona, the lone parent of two boys who, for once, found a silver lining in a harsh winter:[4]

> 'Robert came in, just at the winter, just after Christmas it was, and it was

snowing, and he came in with his school shoes with no sole on them… and I was like, "How am I going to manage to get his school shoes?" You can't out of one weekly money, there's no way you can go and buy something extravagant. So it was quite good, because the week after he lost the sole off his shoes, it was snowing, so he went to school in his wellies. So it worked out in my favour, it gave me a couple of weeks to put a wee bit of money back to then buy him school shoes… You can't plan for unforeseen circumstances.'

Liam, a lone parent of a 10-year-old boy, like many parents living in poverty, often has to make the most difficult of decisions:[5]

'It's hard when you have to make choices. Do you cut down on the electricity you're using or do you cut down on the food? And when you're cutting right down to the bare minimum, it's hard to cut back any more.'

Paying for food and fuel are two of the most pressing issues for you. While having a pre-payment meter allows you to pay for your gas and electricity weekly, running out of money means no heat and light. Despite the severity of the situation, however, you are keen to protect the children and you go to imaginative lengths to do so. Like Jennifer, the lone parent of three boys who says to her children:[6]

'… "see tonight, we'll light candles, and we'll get our books in bed." And it's because I've no electricity. And when I've run out of gas, and there's no hot water, we'll be boiling kettles for the bath… and you don't want to tell [her son], because you don't want him thinking, "Oh my god, my mum hasn't got any money"… so I'll say, "I can't get that pilot light to light, I'm going to have to phone [the housing association] in the morning".'

Sometimes you make the decision to take money out of the food budget to pay for gas and electricity,[7] although you always ensure that your children eat and you may sacrifice your own chance of eating to do so:[8]

'I watch every single penny that I have… I mean, I've seen times where I haven't had enough to buy food for me and the kids… I would give my kids before I would give myself or I would take maybe a slice of toast and give them 'uns the proper meal… I mean they need nutrition before I do.'

Families are increasingly turning to food banks for help, the idea of which fills you with horror. Janice, a disabled woman with a partner and daughter also has mixed feelings about using a food bank:[9]

'I was grateful for it… but I was so ashamed, I'll tell you.'

If you are working, you are likely to be earning such a low wage that you will be relying on in-work benefits such as working tax credit. This can be paid weekly and is often the lifeline that allows working families living in poverty to just about manage. It is an unwieldy system though, full of errors and delays, leading to overpayments and debt. You think that it is no wonder that only two-thirds of those eligible actually make a claim.[10]

If you are unemployed, you face barriers to employment, the most prominent of which is childcare and, perhaps, other caring responsibilities if there is someone with a disability in the family. You very much want to work. You have a work ethic and you want to set a good example to your children. You want so much more for your children and understand when others say, 'I would be disgusted if my children ended up living on benefits when they are older.'[11] You feel the stigma and shame of receiving benefits acutely. Shame and stigma have serious negative consequences for people living in poverty. Robert Walker explains that:[12]

> Institutional stigma, variously manifest in the framing, structure, and delivery of policy is often deliberately imposed as a punishment or deterrent to influence behaviour but is sometimes an unintended consequence of poor policymaking.

The negative effects of stigma and shame lead to 'social exclusion, limited social capital, low self-worth, and a lack of agency that could all serve to prolong poverty', all of which are likely to be counteractive to initiatives to mitigate poverty.

You have a strong motivation to escape a life on benefits, like Jennifer:[13]

> 'I want to move on… I don't want to be on benefits. I don't want that stigma. I want to work, and I'm not looking for an all-singing, all-dancing job with a massive pay, I just want enough money to provide for myself and my sons without having to rely on anybody, or get handouts… and you're just constantly penalised for that. There's all the barriers, the stigma, everything that goes with that.'

Despite desperately wanting to work, you experience a strong sense of hopelessness that you will never find suitable employment:[14]

> 'All I want to do in five years is have a job somewhere… I would want a job, but where do I get one? I don't know.'

You are more likely to experience poor mental health:[15]

> 'The stress is horrific. And at the same time, you're trying to put your happy face on and be [there] for your kids. It's hard, really hard.'

> 'My anxiety is making me really, really ill. My anxiety has gone through the roof. I can sleep, but the minute I wake up, all I'm thinking about is money, money, money. What have I to pay tomorrow? How am I going to get the electricity to do another two days? It's quite scary.'

> 'I'm really tired: physically, mentally and emotionally. I'm done in.'

> 'I just ended up in this place of being really really ill and not being able to cope. If it weren't for the fact I have [my son] I wouldn't be getting out of bed in the mornings.'

Despite your own sense of despair and hopelessness, it is vital to you that you protect your children as much as you can. You make great efforts to ensure they do not feel ashamed, as does Sarah:[16]

> 'I put a lot of energy into him not feeling poor. Even though we are. I really try to not make him feel poor, because that's not a good psychological place to be in.'

You worry about the impact of poverty on your children; you are worried that they will get bullied. And with good reason: children living in poverty frequently report being bullied, citing it as a 'key source of unhappiness'.[17] For Fiona, the lone parent of two boys, this is her son's reality:[18]

> 'I had to go and pick him up from the school one day because he had been sick. Just before lunchtime. He never had any dinner money left. And I said to him, "What's happening? What's going on?" and he said, "I'm getting bullied because I'm poor and I've not got any money for a bacon roll".'

Although you worry about the current impacts on your children's lives and wellbeing, you have hopes and aspirations for them,[19] although you may not know how to develop and support these.[20] Liam, the lone parent of one son, is succinct:[21]

> '[I want him] to become a better man than I ever could be. That's my aspiration for him.'

For many parents, the main aspirations for their children are for a good education and a good job,[22] but for Mary, it is for the facilitation of choice:[23]

> 'There's nothing here for them. I think there are a lot of towns the same. I think there are a lot of towns worse off. There's a lot of poverty and that here, but I want him to go out and live his life and just experience things in life. I'm always saying to him, "I want you to make the best of your life. If you can get a good job with good money…" I want him to have freedom. I've never had freedom. I've never been able to just say, "Right. I'm going to do this, I'm going to do that." I want him to be able to have that. I want him to have a life. To live it how he wants to live it.'

Due to your insecure, unpredictable income, you are likely to have incurred debt. This debt is often cyclical: as one lot is paid off another lot is taken on, resulting in a permanent reduction in income. You also experience particular seasonal difficulties – for example, increased costs during the school summer holidays for lunches and school uniforms. Christmas becomes a permanent event, as you borrow money to buy your children presents one year and take until the following Christmas to repay the debt, before restarting the cycle.[24] Families often borrow from doorstep lenders, as cash is offered there and then, usually by local agents known to them. This can have detrimental and embarrassing implications, as Mary discovered:[25]

> 'It was horrendous what I had to do, and I can imagine that other people are the same. You close the blinds, you stand behind the curtains waiting on them going away and everything, they know that you're there. She actually said to me one day, "I was at your door on Tuesday, I seen you moving about".'

Although taking on debt may offer short-term relief, the longer term ramifications can be severe. When Pauline thinks about the debt she was in, she says:[26]

> 'I get a picture of myself being underwater. That's what it felt like… Not functioning properly… You go completely numb and you bury your head in the sand… You ignore it, you ignore the phone, you ignore dealing with stuff and you just pretend that it's not there. But there's an underlying anxiety all of the time, but you sort of muffle it with this numbness.'

They say an Englishman's home is his castle, but for you, just having your own home, fit for purpose, is difficult to imagine. You are likely to live in a disadvantaged neighbourhood and have a lower quality home that may be overcrowded or unsuitable for your needs.[27] As more and more council homes are sold off, with a low replacement rate, the prospect of finding secure, good-quality housing becomes ever more remote. Sarah has a private rented home and has recently found out that her landlord plans to sell it. She is worried about where she and her son will go, as she has previously been unsuccessful in trying to secure a council house:[28]

> 'I was offered one when I was pregnant with him down in [local area] and I stood there, and I was just like, "Oh my word"... There was just this tower block and it was like a circle with a line where the broken glass started, you know, and the whole area was just covered in broken glass and again it was the junkies. And the whole building was just totally derelict, and I thought, "Are they serious? Who comes up with this?" Knock it down and start again. You just can't put people in these places.'

With secure affordable housing becoming more difficult to access, you are more likely to have to move, often to places where you have few social connections. This can reinforce your sense of isolation, particularly if you are a lone parent. As a poor parent, you are less likely to go out and socialise, primarily because you cannot afford it, but sometimes because you cannot face it.[29] You are likely to forego weddings, birthday celebrations and other family gatherings because you cannot afford to participate. Although damaging to social and family relations, and to your own wellbeing, this may also have a detrimental impact on the support and goodwill available to you as your unexplained absence can be badly received. Mary could not attend a family weekend away and so her sister stopped speaking to her. She is becoming increasingly isolated:[30]

> 'I've not gone out for months. I've got three weddings this year that I'm not going to. I've got my best friend's 40th that I'm not going to.'

It is common for parents living in poverty to be frightened of the future, scared that their situation may get worse.[31] Like other families, you feel this intensely:[32]

> 'You're scared to look to the future. That's what scares me more than anything'.

> 'You just can't look forward to anything. It's just so hard. I just think, all this time I've been trying to make it better for [my sons] and I've not made it better for them. We're still struggling along.'

'I feel like there's no light at the end of the tunnel. I don't know what way to go. I don't know where to turn.'

The experience for children

As a child living in poverty, all areas of your life are adversely affected: home, school, friendships and more. The most visible aspect for you is that you do not have what your friends have. This makes you feel conflicted, because on the one hand you wish that you did, but on the other hand you understand your parents' financial situation.[33] You find yourself 'negotiating complex family terrains' where family needs are in tension with your 'own social and material needs and desires' and so you 'moderate and constrain' your demands.[34] Your feelings towards your family situation are complex, however, as you also have great empathy and understanding towards the financial pressures your parents experience.[35] Jelani, aged 14, sums this up well:[36]

'… [my mum] can't cope. We're always asking for too much… she's asking for loans and debts… she's putting her own life at risk… sometimes I need something, yeah, but I see what she's going through and I keep quiet.'

In fact, you have a highly attuned awareness of, and sensitivity to, your parents' situation.[37] So much so, that you exercise control and agency by withholding letters from school for costly trips and activities and, if you are able to do so, for example, by having a part-time job, you give your parents money to ease the pressure.[38]

When Jelani was asked how he had spent his 14th birthday, he said he stayed at home and they had a party, just for the family. Asked if he got presents, he said yes, from his friend, but not from his mother. Jelani gave the £10 he received from his friend to his mother, to help towards the cost of school uniforms.

Although you understand your family's lack of income, it can still be embarrassing for you at times. To avoid situations you find shameful, you have tricks up your sleeve. For example, you save up weekly instalments for a school trip until you have the full amount of money to present at once. This way, no one knows that your parents cannot afford a one-off payment.[39]

> [Ralph, a widowed father of five] saved £45 for a three-day school trip for [his daughter] Louise and gave her the money on a weekly basis to hand in to the school. Later he discovered that she had carried it for weeks in her bag until she had the full amount. She did not want the school to know that he could not pay in one instalment.

Poverty constrains you from the outset and you feel the frustration and injustice of living with such constraints. You have high hopes and aspirations for yourself; no way do you want to be in the same situation as your parents when you grow up, but you are not quite sure how to realise your aspirations.[40] Like all poor children, your hopes and dreams can be further away: 'it is much harder for them to realise these hopes because they have fewer chances or opportunities'.[41]

> In the future Jelani hopes to study and get a job in business or engineering. In order to afford to go to university, Jelani says he will try and save up when he gets to age 16.[42]

Although you have high hopes and aspirations, you are still constrained. You have no money for school costs, no place to do homework, no computer, no internet and maybe no pencil case or stationery.[43] You are entitled to free school meals, but you do not want to take them because your friends will find out you do not have money:[44]

> 'People don't claim free school meals out of embarrassment. I would let people with money go ahead of me in the queue so they wouldn't see.'

School is important to you and sometimes you are happy there.[45] For some children, especially those growing up with adverse situations, as well as living in poverty, school is very much valued.[46] However, sometimes you get into trouble because some teachers do not understand the extent and implications of your educational resource deprivation or the huge efforts you make just to participate in school.[47] In fact, you get the distinct feeling that some teachers think you and your family are a bit inept and the other children in the class always seem to know what to do and always seem to have the right equipment. So you can feel judged and anxious in school.[48] Sometimes this discomfiture manifests itself as sullen or rebellious behaviour, even though, paradoxically, you value school.[49] So, once again, poverty makes your situation conflicted because, although your 'experiences of school are diverse' and sometimes you have 'good experiences at school', for 'the great majority' of children like you, poverty has a corrosive and damaging impact' on 'school careers'.[50]

> 'Teachers don't understand that we have problems at home – we're passed round to different teachers and end up walking around school. Getting kicked out of school is down to stress at home for poor families and teachers not prepared to listen and help out with problems.'[51]

> 'You're stressed, you kick off, you're kicked out of school. You get no education so you can't get a decent job and you're stuck in poverty.'[52]

For you, there are other social and financial costs outside school. The cost of participation in social, peer and leisure activities can mean that you cannot take part. You are excluded and you are forced to self-exclude.[53]

This can have a detrimental impact on your social relationships with your peers and friends because although you long to 'take part in events and shared activities and belong to social groups', these 'essential and formative social interactions are severely tested and often undermined' by the restrictive and constraining effects of poverty.[54] This can make you experience 'considerable anxiety, unhappiness and social insecurity' in relation to your friendships.[55] This will mean that you do not have the same level of social assets that could otherwise be a valuable resilience factor, because friendships are important to you, as they are to all children. 'Secure social networks and good friendships confer a high degree of social security and social connection' and foster a 'sense of wellbeing and belonging'. However, 'making and sustaining friendships requires access to economic resources', which is something you do not have.[56]

Living in poverty for you means living in a 'poor quality, inadequate, unfit' and insecure home.[57] This is having a negative impact on your health, wellbeing, social and school life.[58] There is little communal or safe space for you to play, nowhere for you to do your homework and a lack of privacy for you and your parents.[59]

> 'I like the house because I at least have somewhere to stay... It would be better if only we had a house with stairs in it and then there would be more space to play around... and I'd like to get my own bedroom... but... I'd share it with my little sister so only two people... but like not three or four people crowded in one bedroom.'[60]

> Jelani complains about the state of their flat every day to their mother. He frequently tells her that he does not want to stay in their flat because 'there's damp, I feel sick all the time. When can I get a new house?' Jelani thinks the

damp has an effect on him. He says, 'I have asthma and at night I can't breathe properly.'[61]

As well as your physical health and diet, poverty is having a detrimental effect on your psychological wellbeing too.[62] Like other children living in poverty, you sometimes have 'feelings of worthlessness' and a lack of belief in yourself, which for some 'could lead to depression and sometimes suicidal feelings'.[63]

Living in poverty can make you feel sad, anxious, frightened, frustrated and/or angry.[64] As well as your own anxiety, you are aware of the stress your parents are under and you worry about their wellbeing too:[65]

'[When mum is stressed it] makes me like feel unhappy inside 'cos, 'cos if she's stressed then there's nowt that I can do about it.'

You are more likely to face other challenges such as 'the ill-health of a parent or sibling, unemployment, family breakdown and separation, domestic violence, poor housing and homelessness'.[66] On top of all that, you face stigma because of your poverty and you sometimes get bullied because of it too:[67]

'It was in school and they said, one of my friends says, "I've got more money than you 'cos you're really, really poor, your family will always be poor" and it really upset me.'[68]

Despite the avalanche of negative associations and experiences you face because you are growing up in poverty, you can still see the positive side of life and there are things in your life that you value. Family is the most important thing for children living in poverty,[69] which is why your family's wellbeing is so intrinsically tied up with your own. Having strong family relationships is highly protective and can create stability and resilience in the midst of the many problems poverty brings. Relationships with grandparents are often highly valuable[70] and positive relations with non-resident parents, usually fathers, can also be a good source of support.[71] However, there are many cases in which non-resident fathers are not helpful or supportive, which can be particularly detrimental to children.[72]

Like other parents and children, you experience poverty as a catch-22 situation where you really do not know what possibilities are out there and, if you do become aware of them, you have not got the first idea of how to make them available to you. It is not knowing what opportunities exist, not knowing the people who do know what opportunities exist and not understanding how other people have this knowledge. It is feeling hopeless and wondering if anyone can help. It is – confidence and self-esteem allowing – knowing that you have potential but not knowing how to use it, or who to show it to, or how. Poverty is an impediment to development and personal progress. And yet you, like other children and families, display extraordinary strength and resilience in continuing to try pushing forwards when there is so much pushing you backwards.

Notes

1   T Ridge, *Living with Poverty: a review of the literature on children and families*, Department for Work and Pensions Research Report No.594, 2009, p62

2   T Shildrick and others, *Poverty and Insecurity: life in low-pay, no-pay Britain*, Policy Press, 2012

3   Ongoing qualitative research being undertaken on behalf of CPAG in Scotland on the cumulative impact on welfare reform on low-income families. All the respondents' names have been changed. See http://www.cpag.org.uk/content/case-studies-meet-families for more details.

4   See note 3

5   S Spencer, *The Cost of the School Day*, CPAG in Scotland, 2015

6   See note 3

7   J Harris and others, *Below the Breadline: a year in the life of families in poverty*, Barnardo's, 2009; C-A Hooper and others, *Living with Hardship 24/7: the diverse experiences of families in poverty in England*, The Frank Buttle Trust, 2007

8   J Harris and others, *Below the Breadline: a year in the life of families in poverty*, Barnardo's, 2009, p41

9   See note 3

10 65 per cent take-up across the board; 91 per cent take-up for families with children: HM Revenue and Customs, *Child Benefit, Child Tax Credit and Working Tax Credit Take-up Rates 2014–15*, 2016, www.gov.uk/government/uploads/system/uploads/attachment_data/file/577510/Child_Benefit_Child_Tax_Credit_and_Working_Tax_Credit_Take-up_rates_2014_to_2015.pdf.

11 J Harris and others, *Below the Breadline: a year in the life of families in poverty*, Barnardo's, 2009, p12

12 R Walker, *The Shame of Poverty*, Oxford University Press, 2014, p49

13 See note 3

14 J Harris and others, *Below the Breadline: a year in the life of families in poverty*, Barnardo's, 2009, p23

15 Jennifer 2013, and Mary and Sarah 2016: see note 3

16 S Spencer, *The Cost of the School Day*, CPAG in Scotland, 2015

17 C-A Hooper and others, *Living with Hardship 24/7: the diverse experiences of*

families in poverty in England, The Frank Buttle Trust, 2007, p56

18 See note 3

19 J Harris and others, *Below the Breadline: a year in the life of families in poverty*, Barnardo's, 2009

20 R St Clair, K Kintrea and M Houston, 'Silver bullet or red herring? New evidence on the place of aspirations in education', *Oxford Review of Education*, 39(6), 2013, pp719–38; K Kintrea, R St Clair and M Houston, *The Influence of Parents, Places and Poverty on Educational Attitudes and Aspirations*, Joseph Rowntree Foundation, 2011

21 See note 3

22 J Harris and others, *Below the Breadline: a year in the life of families in poverty*, Barnardo's, 2009

23 See note 3

24 J Harris and others, *Below the Breadline: a year in the life of families in poverty*, Barnardo's, 2009

25 S Spencer, *The Cost of the School Day*, CPAG in Scotland, 2015

26 S Spencer, *The Cost of the School Day*, CPAG in Scotland, 2015

27 J Harris and others, *Below the Breadline: a year in the life of families in poverty*, Barnardo's, 2009; C-A Hooper and others, *Living with Hardship 24/7: the diverse experiences of families in poverty in England*, The Frank Buttle Trust, 2007

28 S Spencer, *The Cost of the School Day*, CPAG in Scotland, 2015

29 J Harris and others, *Below the Breadline: a year in the life of families in poverty*, Barnardo's, 2009; C-A Hooper and others, *Living with Hardship 24/7: the diverse experiences of families in poverty in England*, The Frank Buttle Trust, 2007

30 See note 3

31 C-A Hooper and others, *Living with Hardship 24/7: the diverse experiences of families in poverty in England*, The Frank Buttle Trust, 2007

32 Janice 2014, and Fiona and Mary 2016: see note 3

33 G Whitham, *Child Poverty in 2012: it shouldn't happen here,* Save the Children, 2012

34 K Bullock and others, 'Educational relationships in out-of-school-time activities: are children in poverty missing out again?', *Education, Citizenship and Social Justice*, 5(2), 2010, pp103–16

35 A Crowley and C Vulliamy, *Listen Up! Children and young people talk about poverty,* Save the Children, 2007

36 J Harris and others, *Below the Breadline: a year in the life of families in poverty*, Barnardo's, 2009, p8

37 G Whitham, *Child Poverty in 2012: it shouldn't happen here,* Save the Children, 2012

38 J Harris and others, *Below the Breadline: a year in the life of families in poverty*, Barnardo's, 2009, p8

39 J Harris and others, *Below the Breadline: a year in the life of families in poverty*, Barnardo's, 2009, p22

40 R St Clair, K Kintrea and M Houston, 'Silver bullet or red herring? New evidence on the place of aspirations in education', *Oxford Review of Education*, 39(6), 2013, pp719–38; K Kintrea, R St Clair and M Houston, *The Influence of Parents, Places and Poverty on Educational Attitudes and Aspirations*, Joseph Rowntree Foundation, 2011

41 A Crowley and C Vulliamy, *Listen Up! Children and young people talk about poverty,* Save the Children, 2007, p28

42 J Harris and others, *Below the Breadline: a year in the life of families in poverty*, Barnardo's, 2009, p8

43 J Harris and others, *Below the Breadline: a year in the life of families in poverty*, Barnardo's, 2009

44 A Crowley and C Vulliamy, *Listen Up! Children and young people talk about poverty,* Save the Children, 2007, p15

45 K Bullock and others, 'Educational relationships in out-of-school-time activities: are children in poverty missing out again?', *Education, Citizenship and Social Justice*, 5(2), 2010, pp103–16

46 C-A Hooper and others, *Living with Hardship 24/7: the diverse experiences of families in poverty in England*, The Frank Buttle Trust, 2007

47 S Spencer, *The Cost of the School Day*, CPAG in Scotland, 2015

48 K Bullock and others, 'Educational relationships in out-of-school-time activities: are children in poverty missing out again?', *Education, Citizenship and Social Justice*, 5(2), 2010, pp103–16

49 A Crowley and C Vulliamy, *Listen Up! Children and young people talk about poverty,* Save the Children, 2007

50 K Bullock and others, 'Educational relationships in out-of-school-time activities: are children in poverty missing out again?', *Education, Citizenship and Social Justice*, 5(2), 2010, pp103–16

51 A Crowley and C Vulliamy, *Listen Up! Children and young people talk about poverty,* Save the Children, 2007, p17

52 A Crowley and C Vulliamy, *Listen Up! Children and young people talk about poverty,* Save the Children, 2007, p17

53 See T Ridge, '"We are All in This Together"? The hidden costs of poverty, recession and austerity policies on Britain's poorest children', *Children & Society* 27(5), 2013, pp406–17; T Ridge, 'The Everyday Costs of Poverty in Childhood: a review of qualitative research exploring the lives and experiences of low-income children in the UK', *Children & Society* 25(1), 2011, pp73–84

54 K Bullock and others, 'Educational relationships in out-of-school-time activities: are children in poverty missing out again?', *Education, Citizenship and Social Justice*, 5(2), 2010, pp103–16

55 K Bullock and others, 'Educational relationships in out-of-school-time activities: are children in poverty missing out again?', *Education, Citizenship and Social Justice*, 5(2), 2010, pp103–16

56 K Bullock and others, 'Educational relationships in out-of-school-time activities: are children in poverty missing out again?', *Education, Citizenship and Social Justice*, 5(2), 2010, pp103–16

57 K Bullock and others, 'Educational relationships in out-of-school-time activities: are children in poverty missing out again?', *Education, Citizenship and Social Justice*, 5(2), 2010, pp103–16 p77

58 K Bullock and others, 'Educational relationships in out-of-school-time activities: are children in poverty missing out again?', *Education, Citizenship and Social Justice*, 5(2), 2010, pp103–16; J Harris and others, *Below the Breadline: a year in the life of families in poverty*, Barnardo's, 2009

59 J Harris and others, *Below the Breadline: a year in the life of families in poverty*, Barnardo's, 2009, p66

60 J Harris and others, *Below the Breadline: a year in the life of families in poverty*, Barnardo's, 2009, p53

61 J Harris and others, *Below the Breadline: a year in the life of families in poverty*, Barnardo's, 2009, p53

62 G Whitham, *Child Poverty in 2012: it shouldn't happen here,* Save the Children, 2012

63 A Crowley and C Vulliamy, *Listen Up! Children and young people talk about poverty,* Save the Children, 2007, p18

64 C-A Hooper and others, *Living with Hardship 24/7: the diverse experiences of families in poverty in England*, The Frank Buttle Trust, 2007, p59

65 C-A Hooper, *Living with Hardship 24/7: the diverse experiences of families in poverty in England*, The Frank Buttle Trust, 2007, p59

66 T Ridge, *Living with Poverty: a review of the literature on children's and families' experience of poverty*, Department for Work and Pensions Research Report No.594, 2009, p29

67 J Harris and others, *Below the Breadline: a year in the life of families in poverty*, Barnardo's, 2009; T Ridge, *Living with Poverty: a review of the literature on children and families*, Department for Work and Pensions Research Report No.594, 2009; C-A Hooper and others, *Living with Hardship 24/7: the diverse experiences of families in poverty in England*, The Frank Buttle Trust, 2007

68 Eight-year-old girl in C-A Hooper and others, *Living with Hardship 24/7: the diverse experiences of families in poverty in England*, The Frank Buttle Trust, 2007, p68

69 J Harris and others, *Below the Breadline: a year in the life of families in poverty*, Barnardo's, 2009; T Ridge, *Living with Poverty: a review of the literature on children and families*, Department for Work and Pensions Research Report No.594,

2009; A Crowley and C Vulliamy, *Listen Up! Children and young people talk about poverty,* Save the Children, 2007; C-A Hooper and others, *Living with Hardship 24/7: the diverse experiences of families in poverty in England*, The Frank Buttle Trust, 2007

70 C-A Hooper and others, *Living with Hardship 24/7: the diverse experiences of families in poverty in England*, The Frank Buttle Trust, 2007

71 C-A Hooper and others, *Living with Hardship 24/7: the diverse experiences of families in poverty in England*, The Frank Buttle Trust, 2007

72 J Harris and others, *Below the Breadline: a year in the life of families in poverty*, Barnardo's, 2009; C-A Hooper and others, *Living with Hardship 24/7: the diverse experiences of families in poverty in England*, The Frank Buttle Trust, 2007

Thirteen
Conclusions: the new poverty

Summary

The evidence in this book shows that poverty in the UK remains widespread and damages the lives and the opportunities of many families. Having fallen during the first years of this century, poverty has begun to increase once more. Unless prompt action is taken by the government and other public agencies, or there is an unexpected upturn in national wealth that is also shared more widely, poverty is set to grow rapidly worse, especially for families with children. One in six households in the UK live in relative income poverty, but this rises to three out of 10 among families with children. Far more share the risks of poverty as their fortunes fluctuate over months and years. But the overall trend is unfavourable. By 2022, we will have more than *five million children in relative income poverty*, after housing costs are paid: a third of our children.

% CHILDREN LIVING IN POVERTY

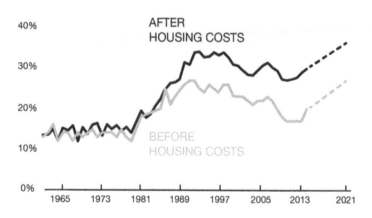

Equally though, we show clearly that poverty is not an inevitable outcome of unregulated economic forces. While it has origins in failures of the labour market to provide access to decently paid work for everyone, poverty rates are also determined by political choices and they respond to government policy. Other countries really no richer than the UK do better in keeping their citizens out of poverty. These are some of the main points:

- **The definition of poverty holds.** The basic definition of poverty – of persistent low incomes and lack of resources, leading to material hardship and social isolation – remains as valid and important now as it was when Peter Townsend first formulated it in 1979. In many ways, it has become a more important and urgent problem because people living in poverty now face a far greater degree of inequality too. As better-off people have become so *much* better off, so the painful discouragement of life in persistent income poverty has grown more acute. The contrast in lifestyles and opportunity between those in the bottom fifth of the income range and those in the top fifth – or even with those simply in the top half – is now so vivid that it is sometimes hard to believe they are citizens of the same country. People in poverty are sometimes accused of a lack of aspiration. But what they are now expected to aspire to contrasts so painfully with what they have, real progress out of a life in poverty must seem unrealistic to many of them. To be poor in a rich country is to go without a great deal.

- **The effects of poverty are serious.** People living in poverty experience more illness and die sooner. Family incomes below the poverty line, perhaps through the stress and anxiety this creates, reduce parent's capacity to care well for their children and affect children's wellbeing, damaging their physical and mental health. This reduces their capacity to learn and flourish at school. It burdens the progress of children from families living in poverty throughout their schooling. It discourages them and lowers their attainment in exams compared with the average attainment of children from better-off families. Persistent poverty has persistent and severe effects. The greater investment in schools over the past 20 years improved the school attainment of poor children, who now return significantly better test scores – a measure in part of just how badly they fared in the past. But investment has improved the performance of better-off children too, and by a similar margin, so disadvantage remains.

• **We know what went wrong.** The post-war consensus that rising productivity, better technology and (more or less) full employment would abolish poverty collapsed in the 1970s. Since then, enduring weaknesses in the UK labour market, especially those associated with industrial disinvestment and regional disadvantage, resulted in the growth of insecure low-wage jobs that offer few prospects, accompanied by recurrent waves of unemployment. Real wages in the lower half of earnings have stagnated since the mid-1990s and fallen since the 2008 financial crash. At the same time, inadequate social security transfers, and the increasingly unequal distribution of incomes, power and resources, left many disadvantaged people without access to enough regular income to maintain an acceptable standard of living. Now, the official mantra that 'work is the best way out of poverty' no longer holds for many: two-thirds of children in poverty have a parent in low-paid work. Their additional income from child benefit and tax credits, frozen for four years from April 2016, fails to lift them beyond the poverty line, above 60 per cent of the national equivalised median income.

• **We know what works.** The actions taken during the first years of this century reduced poverty and hardship in the UK. The benefit rates for the youngest children of unemployed parents rose 83 per cent, for example. Child poverty began to fall at an annual rate in line with a 20-year plan to abolish it. We saw convincing evidence that, far from feeding some kind of 'dependency culture' among unambitious parents, the new money was spent directly on family welfare, easing petty debt, providing better diets and clothing for children and so on. Overall rates of severe material hardship among out-of-work families halved in two years and almost vanished among the lowest paid working families. Alongside this direct help, welfare-to-work programmes increased flows into work, even among long-term unemployed people. There was substantial reinvestment in education, health and other social programmes such as Sure Start and the national childcare strategy which led to the first ever Childcare Act in 2006. This decade of improvement, however, was also marked by growing inequality in wages, as those in the top half of the income range surged ahead, and by widening inequalities in wealth, led by the increased scarcity of good housing for those on lower incomes. Since 2010, these earlier gains have been steadily lost to policies of austerity and fiscal retrenchment. The greatest impact of these policies will be felt by 2020, the year child poverty was to end.

What should be done

Income: meeting a new crisis of child poverty

People living in relative income poverty in the UK, especially those bringing up children, do receive help; it just is not enough. And the present direction of policy will *reduce* the help they receive. The real value of cash transfers from the government and local authorities has fallen and will continue to fall. It will fall most for those least able to replace their lost benefits and tax credits with earned income. Lone parents will lose nearly £50 a week, on average, from cuts to universal credit and child benefit.

Unemployed families will suffer most, but working families face increasing difficulty. Even two-parent families, with both working full time on the present minimum wage, already fall £50 a week short of the income they need to meet the real costs of raising a child. The introduction of a national living wage (presently targeted to reach about £9 an hour) will do little to improve the final incomes of low-paid families, because their income from universal credit will dwindle as their wages rise.

Benefits must once more reflect the real needs of families receiving them, which has always been the fundamental principle of the UK's welfare state. There is, therefore, a list of actions to be taken urgently to reduce the threat of a calamitous fall in family wellbeing in the UK over the next five years.

Increase payments

- Rather than freezing their value until 2021, annual benefit and tax credit rates should rise in the same way that UK pensioners' benefits have risen in line with earnings, price inflation or 2.5 per cent, whichever is the greater.
- Child benefit must be restored to its 2010 value, rising by at least £5 per week for each child. Without this simple remedy, child benefit alone will have lost 23 per cent of its real value by 2020.
- The new restriction of the child element in tax credits and universal credit to just two children, with its invasive rules, will plunge a further 200,000 children into income poverty. The two-child limit must be abolished and payments restored for all children irrespective of how many brothers and sisters they may have. Disabled children should receive more.

- A further 200,000 children would be safeguarded from income poverty simply by lowering the withdrawal rate of universal credit from 63 per cent to 55 per cent, as was the lowest rate when working families' tax credit was first introduced.
- Even more children, about 400,000, would be protected by restoring the tax credit work allowances and then extending them to second earners, improving their incentives. This is probably the weakest aspect of the 'reformed' version of universal credit and will unfairly restrict income advancement among many low-income families.
- Abolish the £20,000 a year limit on total benefit incomes (the so-called 'benefit cap') which denies the needs of large families. Families *earning* £20,000 are anyway given a lot of extra help in benefits and tax credits, acknowledging that £20,000 is not enough to keep many families in a decent standard of housing and daily life.

Improve delivery

Though a rich nation, we have somehow become used to people queuing at food banks. Each year, more than a million boxes of emergency food supplies are passed out by The Trussell Trust alone. Research by CPAG and others has shown that the main cause of such referrals (and you cannot just turn up – you have to be officially referred) lies in the administration of the benefit system. Delays in payments, over-zealous application of sanctions and outright errors leave increasing numbers of claimants destitute and unable to feed themselves and their families. Since new rules were introduced in 2012, more than two million claimants of jobseeker's allowance alone have been sanctioned, even after appeals.[1]

> '[I was] sanctioned for writing down the wrong number in a code for a job I applied for on the job centre system. They said the numbers didn't match the job name that came up when they put it in. All the job adverts have eight digit codes I explained I must have accidentally written the wrong number. They said that was enough for "reasonable doubt".'
> Sanctioned claimant, the *Guardian*, 23 October 2016

The most urgent reforms needed are as follows.

- Reduce the present waiting period for a first payment from six weeks to two.

- Restore rapid access to hardship payments, benefit advances and other local welfare assistance.
- Restore the assumption that claimants behave honestly, issuing fair warnings – a 'yellow card' – rather than imposing sanctions for minor departures from work requirements and application errors.
- Restore staffing levels that will allow more advice and help to be given when claimants struggle to understand or meet requirements and fund independent advice agencies now lacking financial support at both national and local level.
- Set up listening facilities to detect and act upon the early warnings evident in the roll-out of universal credit, which has so far been the most problematic and error-prone project in recent government experience, its completion date slipping from 2017 to 2022.

Free parents to work, if they can

Since the introduction of the National Childcare Strategy in May 1998, a great deal of progress has been made in freeing the parents of young children to work and to work more hours. It helped many more lone parents, in particular, to enter work sooner than they might otherwise have done. But childcare remains the single most expensive item in the budgets of working families with small children, its cost rising 42 per cent since 2008, twice the rate of inflation. The government will need to restore a new national childcare strategy, including the following measures.

- Fully fund a high-quality model of the 30-hour free entitlement to childcare.
- Abolish the work rule for the extra 15 hours so more disadvantaged children can benefit from the policy.
- Make two-year-old places universal.
- Increase support for children's centres.
- Develop comprehensive, 8am to 6pm out-of-school and holiday childcare though extended schools.

More broadly, we must end the growing impermanence of paid work. Part-time and 'zero-hour' contracts, temporary jobs and spurious forms of self-employment evade employment protection laws. We will need to do a lot more to help those who leave the out-of-work benefit system to stay in work and advance their earnings over time. Many of these developments affect women more than men and a gender pay gap of about 18 per cent (10 per cent among full-time workers) persists despite decades of equal pay legislation. If work is really to be the best way out of poverty, it simply has to pay better and pay consistently. The UK has relatively high employment rates but has an unstable labour market, causing us to have average poverty rates among OECD countries but much higher rates of entry and exit in and out of poverty. Thus, UK households have much greater risks of poverty. Reducing these risks, slowing the flow into unemployment and back into impermanent low-wage work, grounding workers in better-paid permanent jobs instead, would have a dramatic effect on reducing the numbers in poverty at any one time.

Restore a national commitment to end child poverty

More than anything, as a nation we need to recommit to ending poverty, as a national priority. A commitment to end poverty is also a commitment to measure it properly. This is to be done in Scotland, which requires a proper explanation of why it should be different in England and Wales.

The official target to abolish relative income poverty among UK families with children by 2020 was abandoned by the Welfare Reform and Work Act in 2016. No better reason for this abandonment was given, other than that we should no longer give increasing amounts of money to families living in poverty but instead improve their 'life chances' and so advance 'social justice'. CPAG has long urged and supported every effort to improve children's life chances. Social policy in advanced countries has always striven to improve life chances, through education, healthcare, support for decent housing standards, and all the things governments do to encourage national growth and improvement. The commitment in 1999 to end child poverty by 2020 put none of these essential efforts aside. Spending on education, health and welfare-to-work programmes greatly increased at the same time as cash transfers were increased, all to good effect. After all, if there were no one in relative income poverty, would any government somehow stop doing its best to improve everyone's life chances?

An integrated approach to ending poverty, involving all national and local government agencies, is entirely supportable. But it bears repeating that none of these efforts at social improvement (many of them immensely more costly than simply raising family benefits) will be very effective while three out of 10 of our children continue to be brought up in households that have not enough money, or other material resources, to maintain a decent standard of living: good nutrition, warmth, presentable clothing, an acceptable home and a full social life in the mainstream of their communities. In the here and now, only improved cash incomes can do that.

By strange contrast, the successful effort to reduce poverty rates among pensioners in the UK concentrated single-mindedly on money. As a priority of policy, pensioners' incomes were increased significantly. As a result, their poverty rates halved to a point that is now below the average among younger working people, much lower than those among families with children. Hardship among pensioners greatly reduced. And when additional care has been needed, those without savings or other resources to pay for them, or who have no family willing or able to help, are looked after at the public expense.

This policy has gone virtually unchallenged until recently, now that the accelerating cost of care requires refinancing. Little of this new debate on social care has become mired in concerns that giving old people in poverty more money is somehow bad for them, that it has disincentivised an ageing population from striving to provide properly for themselves. They are thought to be survivors of a productive life during which they participated in a welfare state and contributed to national insurance. The system now recognises their needs and provides the money required to relieve those needs. What was intended for pensioners was intended for everybody.

We especially need to end the narrative that has demonised working age people in poverty and instead see more clearly that we all have the same positive interest in bringing people out of persistent poverty and into full participation in society and the economy. Public attitude research indicates that a majority, though not a large one, believes that poverty remains a problem in the UK, that its causes are more likely to be structural rather than individual, and that the government is responsible for addressing the problem. More than a third say they are prepared to pay more taxes to increase spending on social welfare.[2] By 2016, the proportion agreeing that benefit recipients 'don't deserve any help' fell from typically more than a third in past years to one-fifth.[3] No one will doubt or deny that an end to poverty will require large long-term investment. Our investment will be rewarded by greater productivity, higher tax receipts and lower social costs, enriching everyone financially, socially and morally.

Notes

1   The Department for Work and Pensions reports: 'There have been 2 million decisions to apply a sanction under the new rules. The trends illustrate the impact of the introduction of Mandatory Reconsiderations. Not all decisions with an outcome to apply a sanction will result in a claimant's benefit being reduced.

Where a claimant's benefit is reduced the claimant may be eligible for Hardship payments.' Department for Work and Pensions, *Quarterly Benefits Summary: Great Britain Statistics to May 2016*, November 2016

2   A Park, C Bryson and J Curtice (eds), *British Social Attitudes: the 31st report*, NatCen Social Research, 2014, available online at www.bsa-31.natcen.ac.uk.

3   B Baumberg Geiger, A Reeves and R de Vries, 'Tax avoidance and benefit manipulation', in *British Social Attitudes: the 34th report*, NatCen Social Research, 2017